A History of Ireland

A History of Ireland

Mike Cronin

palgrave

First published 2001 by
PALGRAVE
Houndmills, Basingstoke, Hampshire RG21 6XS and
175 Fifth Avenue, New York, N.Y. 10010
Companies and representatives throughout the world

PALGRAVE is the new global academic imprint of
St. Martin's Press LLC Scholarly and Reference Division and
Palgrave Publishers Ltd (formerly Macmillan Press Ltd).

ISBN 0–333–65432–3 hardback
ISBN 0–333–65433–1 paperback

This book is printed on paper suitable for recycling and
made from fully managed and sustained forest sources.

A catalogue record for this book is available
from the British Library.

Library of Congress Cataloging-in-Publication Data
Cronin, Mike.
    A history of Ireland / Mike Cronin.
        p. cm. – (Essential histories)
    Includes bibliographical references (p.) and index.
    ISBN 0-333–65432–3 (cloth)
        1. Ireland–History. I. Title. II. Series.

DA911 .C76 2000
941.5–dc21   00-042057

10 9 8 7 6 5 4 3 2 1
10 09 08 07 06 05 04 03 02 01

Printed in China

Contents

Preface

The aim of this book is to introduce newcomers to, or refresh the minds of those who are already familiar with, the long, often complicated, but ultimately fascinating history of Ireland. A wealth of work has been written which covers the history of Ireland; much of it general in scope, but the majority, usually emerging from doctoral research or other forms of academic endeavour, has concentrated on the minutiae of Ireland's past. It would be an impossible task to include the many treasures that have emerged from such work, as the scope of such an undertaking would contravene the very nature of the books in this series. As such, this book has taken the long political story of Ireland's history as its main focus. At times it touches on the wider social and economic features of Irish life that have impacted on Ireland's passage through the centuries. However, for a fuller interpretation of themes such as these, the reader should refer to the Further Reading section as a way of fulfilling any interests that are sparked here.

The book takes a broadly chronological and narrative approach in its attempt to explain the nature of Irish history. There are some themes that reappear at regular intervals throughout the text, but ultimately the story of Ireland's history that is offered here should prevent the reader facing the kind of confusion that has been ascribed to the nineteenth-century British Prime Minister William Ewart Gladstone, who

> spent his declining years trying to guess the answer to the Irish Question; unfortunately, whenever he was getting warm, the Irish secretly changed the Question.[1]

What the history of Ireland demonstrates is that the series of questions relating to the past of that island have constantly

---

1. W. C. Sellar and R. J. Yeatman, *1066 and All That* (London, 1998; first published 1930)

shifted. Some of those difficult questions have been resolved. Others, perhaps sadly, still create problems for all the peoples of Ireland, as any common and lasting resolution to the list of contemporary questions and issues cannot be found.

To write a book like this is ultimately a solitary pastime, but I have to acknowledge the assistance, help and guidance of friends and colleagues in the world of Irish history who have directly and indirectly shaped this work and my very understanding of Ireland. The series editor, Jeremy Black, deserves special praise for applying his creative mind to the manuscript, and for spending many of his precious hours on improving the text immeasurably. On a personal note I take the opportunity to acknowledge the friendship of the Terrill family. To them this book is dedicated.

Introduction

For such a small landmass on the western edge of Europe, Ireland has had a huge impact on the wider world. In the last two centuries alone Ireland has witnessed a major famine which decimated its population and produced one of the largest emigrant waves ever to leave Europe. The Irish diaspora is now integrated into countless nations across the globe. Their impact on their new homes has been immense, yet any effects that they have had are always tempered by the links with 'home'. Ireland has given the world some of the most important literature of the modern era, such as the works of Joyce and Yeats, and, in these days of globalisation and mass culture, the impact of its popular music has been equally profound. Finally, in the last thirty years, the island of Ireland has been the location of a struggle between the forces of nationalism and unionism which has cost countless lives, a conflict which has been played out in front of the world's media, and yet is one which has been difficult to end.

IRELAND AND HISTORY

Ireland. How do we understand the history of such a significant, yet such a geographically and demographically small nation? To write the history of a nation is problematic at the best of times. For some of the other books in this series the task is made slightly easier as the established reality of the nation has been long standing, as borders and sovereignty, once founded, have rarely been successfully challenged. However, an instant problem for anyone writing a history of Ireland is to deal with the question of what is meant by the term 'Ireland'. As a geographical concept, Ireland is straightforward. The island of Ireland is a clearly definable landmass located in the eastern Atlantic. Since the twelfth century, however, Ireland has been a contested area in political, religious and military terms. There has been a continuous battle for control of the island. At times this has been an internal battle, while, more usually, the fortunes of Ireland have been linked to its proximity to, and problematic relationship with England or a British state dominated by England.

In many parts of the world, in recent years, people have been fighting for their national cause. Super-powers have broken up and new nation-states have come into existence. In the struggle for the formation of many of these new nations, such as those in the former Yugoslavia, the death rate has been far higher than in Ireland, but the Irish situation remains one of the longest running and seemingly most intractable. Some people view the modern situation in the north of Ireland as a product of hundreds of years of history, while others see its roots in the economic and social dislocation of the 1960s. While the past and the future of the nation are still so contested, the task of writing a history is difficult. Whereas in Britain or the United States, for example, the historian could point to certain long-standing and agreed beliefs, such as a commonly shared set of religions or system of government, there is no agreed single view of Irish history.

While contemporary Britain is a country where it is possible to celebrate and acknowledge multiculturalism and religious tolerance, the actual history of state, crown and religion turned on Henry VIII's need to remarry. We can therefore locate the link between the state, the crown and Anglicanism as the nation's main religion in the sixteenth century, and understand the succeeding history of Britain within this context, as the dominant place of that religion is subsequently little challenged. The same is true of the United States. With its emergence from colonial rule in 1776, the Americans set about drawing up their Constitution, which still underpins that society today. Without suggesting for one minute that history ever arrives at the point where it ends, a country's history does, however, arrive at the point where there are substantial norms, which underpin society. British and American society may have transformed themselves hugely over the last four hundred, and two hundred, years respectively, but the religion or the constitution of each has provided one constant (among many others) through which history can be judged. In Ireland those constants do not exist so clearly. We may talk of Ireland's close relationship to England, the importance of the land, the impact of sustained emigration, and so on, but we are unable to speak of one common denominator which unites the history of the island of Ireland. There is no historical continuum with which we can chart our way through the past few hundred years. Ireland in this sense is an anomaly, a difficult history to write as there is no historical plateau – which, for most other countries in Western Europe, was signalled by the establishment of a democratic and singularly agreed nation-state. Ireland was invaded by the Normans, ruled over by the English crown, brought under the Union of a greater Britain, and finally partitioned so that one part views itself as Irish and sovereign, the other as British and loyal. Throughout this history there has been a process of coercion, acceptance, assimilation, rebellion, positive choice, and a welter of other attempts to make the different groups within and outside the island of Ireland agree on any one vision of the future.

For the historian writing at the end of the twentieth century, Ireland presents itself as a commonly agreed idea of what it encompasses geographically (the thirty-two counties of north and south), but fails to present itself as a single nation-state, and its story becomes instead a history of the eventual evolution and ultimate experiences of an Irish Republic, existing alongside the evolution and experiences of Northern Ireland, which is part of the United Kingdom.

Joseph O'Connor summed up the insecurities present in this search for a rationale of Ireland's history when he wrote

Ireland is an idea with many histories. Even the phrase Irish history is fraught with deconstructionist possibilities. What do we mean by the words Ireland and Irish? And what do we mean by history? The retrospectively linear narrative that leads neatly to national independence or the more accurate if unwieldy chaos of revisionism suggests we still do not know quite what we are? Irish history. What inclusions and, more importantly, what exclusions, does the phrase imply? Historically, geographically, socially, what *is* Ireland?[1]

What we can say about Ireland with certainty is that it is an island of some 32,595 square miles. At present, it is made up of

1. J. O'Connor, *The Secret World of the Irish Male* (London, 1995), p. 144.

four provinces: Munster, Leinster, Connacht and Ulster. These are subdivided into thirty-two counties. Six of the counties, much but not all of the historic province of Ulster, form Northern Ireland, which is part of Britain and ruled from the Palace of Westminster in London, while the other twenty-six counties form the Irish Republic, which is governed from Dáil Éireann in Dublin. The population of the island of Ireland is just over 5 million, 1.5 million of whom reside in Northern Ireland. All of these certainties, apart from its geographical size, are products of the lived history of Ireland. A history which is rich in detail, is long and complex. Centrally it is a history which is still alive.

In Ireland, north and south, and for the Irish across the world, history is vitally important. For the politically active, the history of previous generations provides martyrs, victories and a sense of being on the winning (or losing) side which they can transpose on their current situation. For the millions around the world who claim Irish descent, the history of famine, poverty, struggle and emigration provides a sense of belonging, idealistic notions of 'home', and the reassurance that they have successfully survived and prospered in a new land, while never forgetting where they came from. History is a ghost to be conjured up and used to justify many different ideas of Ireland, and what it is to be Irish. In this there is no one Irish history.

In June 1996, Northern Ireland's political parties attended Stormont to begin the all-party talks which everyone hoped would bring a peaceful and negotiated resolution to the Province's problems. With any major political process there is always a sense of expectation, but for these talks expectation was heavily overlaid with history. On the morning of the talks, the journalist David Sharrock wrote,

> there is so much history pressing down upon Ireland, it seems almost surprising at times like this that the island manages not to sink below the Atlantic. Today, however, genuinely deserves the epithet 'historic', for at two o'clock this afternoon the British and Irish governments will open the widest ranging negotiations on Northern Ireland's future ever to be held.
>
> (*Guardian*, 10 June 1996)

The 'historic' moment was used by the Prime Ministers of Britain and Ireland to distance themselves from history. John Major stated that 'for too long the history of Northern Ireland has poisoned the present and threatened the future', while John Bruton added 'the challenge is nothing less than to overcome the legacy of history' (*Guardian,* 11 June 1996).

When writing a history of Ireland, where one is forced to think through the years since the late twelfth century, it seems incredible that the leaders of Britain and Ireland want to distance themselves so readily from Irish history. The situation in the north of Ireland over the last thirty years is a tragedy, but unless we are prepared to embrace and understand the history of Ireland, both north and south, loyalist and nationalist, then we cannot understand the context within which the current conflict is fought out. This is not to suggest that there is a long narrative history of Ireland which began with the Norman invasions and which, at some future date, should end with British withdrawal and reunification. The history, the present and future of the island of Ireland are far more complex than that, and its story should be inclusive of all traditions in Ireland, as should any peace process in the modern north.

In accepting that there can be no one history of Ireland, this book sets out to deal with the events of a geographical place, an island in the eastern Atlantic, which is west of the British 'mainland'. The status, identity and relationships formed by the people of that island have changed with the passing of history. As far as such a short book, with such a wide chronological time span, can ever achieve much beyond the charting of the historical background, it is hoped that the different histories of the peoples of Ireland are explained here. As J. C. Beckett wrote in 1951, in the introduction to his *Short History of Ireland,* 'I have traced the historical background of the two states of contemporary Ireland. I have no theory to vindicate, no policy to defend. I am concerned only to disentangle a confused stream of events and make the present situation intelligible by showing how it arose.'[2] Although events in Ireland have moved on rapidly since Beckett wrote his book, the aims he set out with remain a worthwhile guide for anyone writing such a text on the history of Ireland.

---

2. J. C. Beckett, *A Short History of Ireland* (London, 1951), p. 8.

Map 1   Ireland before 1700

Map 2 Ireland before 1900

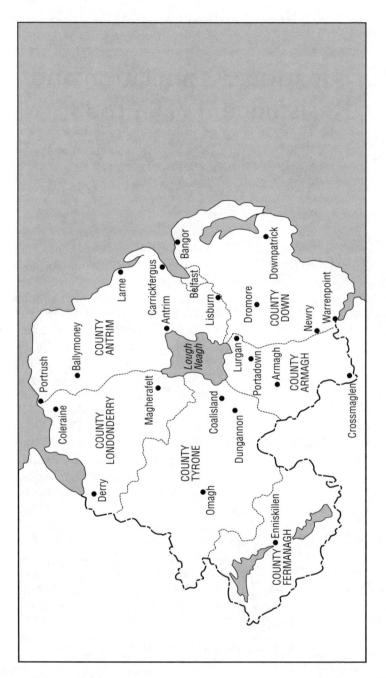

Map 3 Northern Ireland

1

Occupation, Assimilation and Resistance, 1170–1533

The history of Ireland stretches back into the depths of time. The first settled inhabitants of Ireland were groups of hunters and fishers who travelled the short distance across the water from Scotland into north-eastern Ireland during the Mesolithic (Middle Stone Age) era. Remaining artefacts from these people are few and far between, but archaeologists are certain they inhabited the areas around modern-day Antrim, Down, Louth and Dublin in the years after 6000 BC. They were followed, a mere two and a half thousand years later, by the Neolithic (New Stone Age) settlers. Although the exact origins of these travellers are uncertain, the huge array of megalithic remains which they left behind have similarities with megaliths in England such as Stonehenge, and those in France at Carnac. The Neolithic settlers brought such diverse skills as agriculture, pottery and weaving to Ireland. Their lasting testaments, however, are the megalithic remains. These can be found today at Knowth and Newgrange in County Meath. Essentially the remains are great passage tombs. These tombs demonstrate that the Neolithic Irish had great artistic and construction skills, and the tombs at Newgrange are clearly linked with knowledge and understanding of planetary activity, and especially of the movements of the sun at solstice time. Apart from the megalithic passage tombs and other stone constructions, little remains and little is known of the Neolithic settlers. Their civilisation, judging by the dating of the built remains, certainly appears to have survived across several thousand years, but beyond such basic facts, it is the legends which persist.

GAELIC IRELAND

In approximately 700 BC the Gaels began arriving in Ireland, having spread across the rest of western Europe. It is perhaps unsurprising that such an enterprising people would eventually arrive at the continent's westernmost outpost, but it is possibly in Ireland that their legacy has been most profound. The Gaels, as with most invaders who would follow, brought their own distinctive culture with them, but also adapted much that was specific to Ireland. This resulted in a composite system of religious beliefs and power structures drawn from both the indigenous and settler traditions. The old Neolithic gods (tuatha) who had underpinned the Irish belief system prior to the arrival of the Gaels were adopted, and over time became identifiable as Gaelic gods. In appropriating the old Irish gods, the Gaels also adapted and continued to use the important sites, such as Newgrange, as part of their own religious system. The Gaels did not destroy those groups that existed on the island; indeed it appears that they only ever formed a powerful minority within the total population. They held the best land, wielded the most power, and made the native population pay tribute to them, but they were a minority of the population. This minority position was diluted over time, as would be the case with later invaders such as the Normans, as the Gaels intermarried, forged local alliances and slowly assimilated native customs into their own way of life.

The Gaels based their power structure around a monarchical system. At first the whole system ran on very localised lines. In time there developed a network of local ring forts, remains of which can still be found. Each of these forts served as the centre of a local area of influence for a single king or chieftain who was elected by those regarded as freemen. There was no system of direct succession for those who would be king. The elections drew candidates from anywhere within the ruling family, not necessarily the eldest son. This arrangement, although appearing simplistically as highly democratic, would cause problems as it did little to ensure continuity of rule.

In total the island of Ireland contained around a hundred small kingdoms. The small kingdoms were arranged into five bigger groupings, which form the basis of Ireland's modern provinces: Ulaid (Ulster), Midhe (Meath), Laigin (Leinster), Muma

(Munster) and Connacht. At the head of this system was a single High King (Ard Rí), who would rule a province of his own, but would also exert his supremacy over the other provinces. At times there were legendary High Kings who did manage to rule over the five provinces, but more usually the High King had to rule with the support of others. It appears that the first genuine High Kings, who could claim supremacy over the other provinces, did not come into existence until the fifth century AD. Ultimately the provincial and monarchical system made for an unstable, and at times highly violent, society as coalitions were made and broken and as different local kings sought to propel themselves to the highest power. This meant that Ireland never developed a system of central power, and, as a result, there was little unity across the land. Any unity which did exist was a product of cultural forces, such as a common language and a shared religion. Even the brehon laws, which are accepted by many scholars as having been an important sign of Gaelic sophistication, advancement and unity, were weakly implemented. The brehon laws were overseen by the brehons themselves, who can be considered akin to a group of professional lawyers. Recorded precedents underpinned the whole system. Although national, and therefore an important signifier of a semblance of Gaelic uniformity, the system too often relied on arbitration, rather on enforced judgement. This meant that what could have been a vehicle for the sustained development of a national system, which might have resulted in a more integrated political unity, was ineffective. Despite the problems which accompanied the power structure in Gaelic Ireland, it became, by the end of the first century AD, a centrally important focus for Gaelic culture. The Irish Gaels traded by sea with other Celts around northern Europe, bringing a degree of prosperity, both material and cultural.

Despite the prosperity afforded by the Celtic trading alliances, Ireland, it could be argued, missed out on a more fundamental advance in the first centuries following the birth of Christ. Unlike the bulk of southern and central Europe, Ireland was not invaded by the Romans. It is impossible to argue that this was a bad thing for Ireland historically, as the continuation of an unmolested Gaelic system free of Roman control certainly had its benefits. Roman invasion, however, did have a remarkable effect on other lands across Europe and brought about quite revolutionary advances in the technological, architectural, military and governmental fields, among others, all of which Ireland missed out on. Put simply, while mainland Britain (south of Hadrian's Wall) witnessed the development of a road system, the introduction of a judicial system, and other trends which, in the context of the time, can be considered as 'civilising', Ireland continued with a society that remained based around the norms of the bronze age.

THE ADVENT OF CHRISTIANITY

Although missing out on the possibly positive effects of Roman civilisation, Ireland was the location for a golden age of Christianity and monasticism. The Christian mission to Ireland began during the third century AD. In a relatively short space of time, the old Gaelic religion, although still practised and retaining a function within society, was replaced by Christianity. In the wake of the collapse of the Roman Empire, Ireland, which had avoided any major contact with Rome, perversely became the centre of European Christianity. As the Roman Empire disintegrated and a state of near anarchy, resulting from the success of the Barbarians, spread across western Europe, Ireland became a safe haven for those who followed Christ. In this, Ireland's comparative isolation from the rest of Europe worked to its advantage rather than its detriment. Different religious orders settled across Ireland, and, once established, these orders flourished. In the wild and untamed landscape, made more isolated by its lack of communication, the orders existed in splendid solitude. The monasteries were centres of learning, the most notable and important being those at St Edna's on the Aran Islands, Clonmacnoise in Offaly and Clonard in Meath. In Clonard alone, it is believed that as many as 3000 monks were working and studying.

One of the leading figures in the Christian mission in Ireland was St Patrick. Patrick had first been brought to Ireland as a slave. After escaping, he had travelled to Gaul where he was consecrated as a bishop. In the thirty years following his return to Ireland in 432, until his death in 465, Patrick travelled the length and breadth of Ireland preaching the Gospel. He established churches in those places he visited and introduced others to the religious order. St Patrick's importance lies in his role as a catalyst for transforming what was essentially a system of religious orders, churches and monasteries, all of which were functioning as separate and discrete entities. Patrick changed that by bringing about a semblance of central ecclesiastical authority. After his ministry, the Irish Church was firmly established.

The structure of the Church in Ireland duplicated the power system that was already in place. St Patrick and others accepted the Celtic system that was based around local kingdoms which, in turn, was underpinned by powerful families and loose alliances, and adapted the Church's system of internal government around such. The bishops of the Irish Church were located around the families who ran the small kingdoms, and were not based around a geographical unit of governance, such as the diocese, as would have been the case elsewhere in Europe. As previously mentioned, the number of local kingships were many, and hence the number of bishops across Ireland was equally plentiful. St Patrick alone is credited as having created some 300 bishops. As the Church structure was essentially a mirror of the Celtic power system, bishops did not develop personal power bases, as was the case in Europe. As a result of this lack of personal power, and the nature of the Church's governing structure, the monastery became all-important in Ireland.

The introduction of Christianity to Ireland at this time was accompanied by the advent of the written word. Irish society under the Celtic system, although developing a written script, which can be seen on standing stones, did not use the written form as central to its way of life. For them the oral tradition had been far more valuable. The monasteries as centres of learning spread throughout Europe the written word and the Latin language. Within the monasteries, religious instruction and learning flourished, and reached new heights of skill and technical ability. The illuminated manuscripts which emerged at the time, such as the *Book of Kells* (written in approximately AD 700 and currently housed in Trinity College, Dublin), are considered some of the finest examples of such work anywhere in the world. Despite having missed out on the civilising mission of the Romans, Ireland, by performing its role as a safe haven for

Christianity, was a bright light through the so-called dark ages. While the rest of Europe slipped into the post-Roman chaos of terror and destruction, Ireland was thriving. Trade continued along the Atlantic seaboard, as it had done under the pre-Christian Celts. Ireland internally was relatively peaceful and ordered, while learning, Christianity and Gaelic scholarship flourished. The strength of the Irish monastic system was demonstrated in the middle years of the first millennium. Whereas Ireland had originally served a function as a safe haven for Christians and scholars fleeing Europe, it later became the launching pad for the re-emergence of Christianity across the continent. The religion had taken refuge in Ireland and had flourished there. In time, this solace was used as a source of strength and later, when the time was right, Christianity was delivered back to those lands from where it had first come. Leading Irish figures in the deliverance of Christianity back to Europe included St Columba, who founded a monastery in Iona in 563, and is credited with having undertaken the evangelisation of southern Scotland and northern Ireland in the years following. There was also St Columbanus, who travelled to Germany and Italy where he eventually founded a monastery at Bobbio, while other Irish bishops were responsible for the Christian recolonisation of Brittany.

VIKING INCURSIONS

Peace and tranquillity could not last forever. Under the golden age of monasticism Ireland had been relatively quiet, although internal warfare and division had continued. Christianity, for all the benefits that it brought to Ireland, could not bring about any kind of central political system which would break the cycle of violence and inter-monarch competition. In the past, this lack of internal coherence had not been problematic for the actual survival of Ireland, as the land had not been under threat. As such, its relative weakness had not been uncovered. This situation changed radically, and Ireland with it, in the eighth century with the advent of the Viking invasions. At first these incursions had been localised and had been more concerned with plunder and quick reward than with settlement. A response to this type of raid, which was a common feature of eighth-century life, was the construction of defensive Round Towers within the monasteries. The towers were used to watch over the surrounding land, and, at a time of attack, were places of sanctuary. An excellent example of this type of structure can still be seen at Glendalough, Co. Wicklow. The monasteries were obvious targets for such attacks of plunder because of the immense wealth which some of them possessed.

Ultimately, plunder was not enough and in 795 Ireland suffered a full-scale Viking invasion. The Viking presence had an important impact on Irish life. At one level the Viking legacy continues today. Whereas Irish settlement had previously been based around forts or monasteries, the Vikings brought with them to Ireland the idea of the walled city. Obviously the central reason for such a city was defensive, and many of those cities remain today. The modern towns and cities of Dublin, Wexford, Waterford, Youghal, Cork, Bantry and Limerick all originate from the time of the Viking invasions. The Vikings were great traders and their operations brought wealth to their cities and the surrounding districts. The cities were centres of trade, manufacture and commerce. All this, conducted as it was behind the city walls, was carried out in relative peace. From ports such as Dublin the Vikings traded with a large number of different areas and brought a variety of goods back into Ireland. As with the Celts when they arrived, the Vikings adopted certain native ways. They intermarried, converted to Christianity, and, when not battling with them, accepted the power structures of the Irish kingships.

In the context of Irish power structures, the Viking presence in Ireland brought about a realignment of the different kings. If this had been sustained it might have radically altered the future history of Ireland. The comparative weakness of the High King system meant that there was no central focus for opposition against the Vikings once their incursions had begun. If a more centralised political system had emerged over the preceding years, then the Viking forces might have been rebuffed. As it was, it took until the first years of the second millennium before Irish forces rallied around a single High King who engendered enough of the support necessary to take on the Vikings. In 1014, the High King, Brian Boru, defeated the Vikings at an infamous battle at Clontarf. It had taken the Irish two hundred years, but with Boru's victory they finally saw off the threat of being permanently transformed into a Viking colony.

The victory at Clontarf should have been the precursor to the emergence of some kind of centralised Irish power structure, based around the person of Brian Boru. The emergence of a strong centralised rule would have avoided the type of infighting and division that would form the preamble to the English invasion. In a similar vein, it has been argued that the Viking destruction of certain parts of England, such as Northumbria and Mercia, weakened inter-regional rivalries to the point where one region, in the English case, Wessex, was able to become all-powerful. Once Wessex was in the position of primacy over its weakened neighbours it was able to bring about the essential unity of England. Boru's own career demonstrates quite clearly that he was trying to bring about unity in Ireland, albeit a unity engendered by the use of force. He had attacked his main rival, the then High King, Malachy II, and encouraged the Vikings to take Malachy's lands in Connacht and Meath. In 1002, Malachy accepted that Boru should take the High Kingship, as he was the more powerful. Despite taking the High Kingship, Boru depended on the south for the bulk of his support and not all the Irish rallied around him. At Clontarf, the Leinster Irish sided with the Vikings in an attempt to preserve their independence in the face of an all-powerful High King. Unfortunately for any sense of Irish unity, and the possible emergence of a more dynamic centralised rule, Boru was murdered shortly after his famous victory.

Those Vikings who remained in Ireland following their defeat, continued to live in the cities which they had established. The general process of assimilation with the native population continued unabated. Following the death of Boru, however, the Viking communities in the cities were not destroyed or taken over as they might have been had Boru, and the unity he brought to the Irish, survived. In the years following Boru's death, the High Kingship became a battle between different families, most importantly O'Conner of Connacht, O'Brien of Munster and MacLochlainn of Ulster. At various times the heads of these families claimed the High Kingship, but all of them ruled with opposition, and none of them was ever as strong as Boru, or even his predecessor Malachy, had ever been. In the wake of Boru's death, essential unity was more distant than ever, and Ireland was becoming weaker and increasingly open to destructive forces from outside.

THE PRE-NORMAN CRISIS

During the battles between the Irish and the Vikings, and as one of the main parties to suffer at the hands of the Vikings during their plundering raids, the Irish Church was in a greatly weakened position in comparison with its strength during the golden age of Irish monasticism. Some of the monasteries had been broken up, the process of learning had been disrupted and the success of the missions to the rest of Europe had weakened the place of the Irish Church in the grand scheme of things. Distanced as it was from Europe, Ireland was playing no part in the twelfth-century renaissance that was taking place elsewhere. It also seemed clear to Irish bishops that the Irish Church, because of its isolation, had developed an individual system which was out of step with the rest of the wider European Church. By comparison the Irish Church was outmoded and inefficient.

During the twelfth century the Irish Church attempted to bring itself into line with other European systems. Geographically determined dioceses were introduced, under the Archbishops of Armagh, Dublin, Cashel and Tuam. This replaced the old arrangement, which had relied too heavily on the Gaelic kingship system. The new Archbishops were formally recognised by the Pope, thereby inextricably linking the Irish Church to the Vatican. A major driving force behind the reform was St Malachy, who had visited Rome on behalf of the Irish Church in 1139. Malachy had been frank in his discussions with the Rome authorities, and in doing so had presented a less than favourable report on the state of the Church in Ireland.

The role of Rome and the Irish bishops in transforming the Church is instructive when we seek to understand the advance of the Normans into Ireland. With the establishment of Norman rule in Britain in the eleventh century, the Normans had become the controllers of large parts of Europe. They were also closely linked with Rome, and through diplomacy and intermarriage, with most of the major courts in Europe. In the context of the eleventh and twelfth centuries Europe was becoming a smaller place. Ireland, however, having avoided contacts with continental Europe to its possible detriment in the past, was once more on the outside. In other European regions the development of a strong central system of government, which was the by-product of foreign wars or invasion, had hastened Church reform. In Ireland, the lack of a strong central authority in the country meant that reform of the Church had been, at best, patchy and incomplete. The Church was not cajoled into reform by a strong secular authority, nor could it overcome the divided, destructive and self-interested forces which perpetuated the fragmented kingship system. Neither the Irish bishops nor the Church authorities in Rome wanted that situation to continue. Any further delay in reform would be detrimental to the Church. For them, the arrival of a strong outside force in the shape of the Normans might be welcome, as it would galvanise the whole situation in Ireland.

Whatever the wishes of the wider Church might have been, the post-Boru power vacuum was itself bringing matters to a head. In 1166, Rory O'Conner of Connacht seized power and with it took the title of High King. He was not without his opponents: most notably one Dermot MacMurrough. MacMurrough had been a supporter of the previous High King, MacLochlainn of Ulster. MacMurrough, who ruled over Leinster, was not a popular king amongst his fellows. He had carried off the wife of the King of Breffni in 1151, and had later blinded MacLochlainn of Ulster as a way of taking control for himself. MacMurrough's basic problem was that, in allying himself with MacLochlainn and then usurping him, he had backed the wrong horse. In 1166, it was MacMurrough who paid the price for his previous misdemeanours. With O'Conner as High King, and without the patronage of MacLochlainn, MacMurrough was attacked by O'Rourke of Breffni. O'Rourke was supported by the old Viking community of Dublin (the Ostmen) and various Leinster chiefs, and driven by a need to revenge the theft of his wife fifteen years earlier. MacMurrough was defeated and had to flee Ireland.

For a king to be beaten in battle, and to be forced from his native land, is not unusual in the annals. Dermot MacMurrough ensured his place in Irish history as a result of his actions once defeated by O'Rourke. Rather than accepting defeat, or attempting to struggle back to prominence from a position of weakness by making local coalitions, MacMurrough travelled to England, and then on to France. There he sought the help of the king of England, Henry II, in restoring his crown. In seeking such help, MacMurrough would fundamentally and permanently change Ireland. He would open Ireland to her powerful neighbour across the Irish Sea, and in doing so would form relationships which, although not completed and formalised until later centuries, would radically alter the nature of the traditional Gaelic power structures.

THE ENGLISH INVASION

In the first instance, MacMurrough was not seeking the direct intervention of Henry II, nor did he want to see the English annexation of Ireland. The help that he wanted from Henry was to be allowed to raise troops from among Henry's subjects. Such a request was granted and MacMurrough enlisted the help of the Marcher Lords of Wales in an attempt to regain his kingdom. The Marcher Lords were a mixture of Normans, Flemings and native Welsh. They were experienced fighters who had all the tools of contemporary warfare at their disposal. In return for their help, MacMurrough had made promises of lands and bounty. Foremost amongst his new allies was one Richard de Clare, the Earl of Pembroke, and known by most as Strongbow. MacMurrough cemented the offer of help by giving his daughter Aoife to Strongbow as a wife, thereby beginning a long and popular process of English–Irish intermarriage.

MacMurrough returned to Ireland in the autumn of 1167 and waited for his newly formed band of mercenaries to arrive. In May 1169, the first of the Marcher Lords, Robert Fitzstephen arrived with knights and archers, quickly followed by Maurice de Perendergast and his band of Flemish mercenaries. Joining with MacMurrough, this group laid siege to Wexford, which capitulated in a day. As a result of the quick victory, the opposing forces, which had fought against him years earlier, ceased hostilities. Thus with the support of the Ostmen and the disaffected Leinster clans, MacMurrough reclaimed his Leinster throne, and settled his differences with the High King. MacMurrough, however, as can be gauged from his wife-stealing, the blinding escapade and the excursion to see Henry II, was not the kind of man to settle quietly for what he had.

After regaining Leinster, MacMurrough set his sights on the High Kingship. In 1170 he once again contacted Strongbow and requested his help in taking control of wider areas across Ireland. In May of that year, Strongbow sent ahead a Geraldine (descendants of the eleventh-century Welsh princess Nesta), Raymond Le Gros, with a small force. They landed in the south of Wexford and soon came under attack from a combined force made up of Ostmen from neighbouring Waterford and the native Irish of Munster. With their military expertise and their greater technological advancement, Strongbow's representatives easily defeated a much larger army.

As the summer of 1170 progressed, Strongbow gathered together an impressive force and prepared to embark for Ireland. As he stood ready, with two hundred knights and a thousand archers, all of whom were the contemporary epitomes of modern warfare, he was sent messages by Henry II, forbidding the attack. Henry was concerned that with such a strong army, Strongbow would not only easily take control of Ireland, but once established, would turn that force against his English king. Strongbow ignored Henry's orders and set sail. He landed in Waterford on 23 August 1170. Strongbow quickly took control of the town, and once established there, was visited by MacMurrough who, as previously agreed, handed over his daughter for marriage.

The combined English–Irish forces of Strongbow and MacMurrough then set out to conquer as much of Ireland as was possible. They took Dublin from the Ostmen who were holding the city, a feat accomplished under the nose of the High King O'Conner, who was camped south of the city waiting to repel the invaders. Once it had been lost, O'Conner gave up the city and retreated. Strongbow took control of Dublin and cemented his control over it and the surrounding area, while MacMurrough set out for Breffni to settle old scores.

The Strongbow–MacMurrough alliance could possibly have brought about the national unity Ireland needed to repel a full-scale English invasion. By linking Strongbow to his daughter, MacMurrough had essentially Gaelicised Strongbow, while Strongbow's close links to the English Crown sheltered Ireland from an all-out assault. The combination of MacMurrough's local knowledge and Strongbow's military strength would undoubtedly have been strong enough to suppress the other local kings across Ireland. The Gaelic–English balance which the partnership afforded would have contented those looking across the Irish Sea that Ireland would not become a troublesome outpost that could threaten the Crown. All such plans were destroyed in May 1171 when MacMurrough died.

It appears that in promising his daughter to Strongbow, MacMurrough had also decreed that when he died his powers would pass to his English ally. The problem for this cosy arrangement was that no such precedent existed in Irish law. The wider royal family elected new kings. Despite any loyalty that the family may have had towards MacMurrough, there was no likelihood that they would accept the cuckoo in the nest. The delicate power balance which might have emerged under a Strongbow–MacMurrough coalition, imploded completely. In the process, the Irish were, in part, suppressed and many traditional power structures were challenged. Put simply, too many external and internal power groups became fascinated by the prospect of controlling Ireland.

In the face of the Strongbow claim for the MacMurrough crown, a nephew, Muirchertach, emerged as the family champion. His family group supported him, along with the men of Leinster and the other kingdoms who were fearful of Strongbow. Their fear was not of a new king; after all, power struggles after the death of the monarch were not unusual. The fear was of an Englishman, an outsider, taking control of Ireland. The opposition from the native Irish to Strongbow's presence was aided by the Vikings of the West of Scotland and the Isle of Man, who were outraged at the treatment of the Ostmen at the hands of the English invader.

The remainder of 1171 witnessed a battle for the control of Ireland. This was focused on Dublin, but it would settle the future power dynamics of Ireland for years to come. The Vikings freely attacked Dublin from the coast and were a constant threat to the resident English forces. More serious, however, were the combined Irish forces ranged outside the city walls. As High King, Rory O'Conner had brought together a force of some 30,000 men from across the land. After a two-month siege, the Irish were caught off guard by a Norman breakout from the city, and, despite a numerical supremacy of fifteen to one, the Irish were routed. It had been a difficult year for Strongbow, but his position, in Ireland at least, was secure because of his military might.

The rise of Strongbow, and his emergence as the most powerful entity in Ireland, brought Henry II's attention back to his western neighbour. His concerns, which he had stressed in 1170 when trying to prevent Strongbow from embarking for Ireland, had come to fruition. Despite Strongbow's protestations that he had won Ireland for the Crown, Henry decided to act. In 1172, Henry gathered together a huge force and set sail.

Once in Ireland Henry did not have to fight to win subservience from either the resident English or the native Irish. Strongbow had no choice but to accept Henry as his ruler. His best lands on the eastern seaboard were transferred to royal ownership, and he was only granted control of Leinster as a tenant. The former Viking towns still in the hands of Ostmen were taken directly into royal ownership. Many of the native Irish kings paid tribute to Henry and agreed to accept him as overlord. For them it seemed more comforting to accept the rule of a fair-minded foreign king, than to have to fight self-interested aggressors such as Strongbow for control of the land. It was equally reassuring to know that Henry was intent on keeping Strongbow in check.

It is difficult to know exactly why Henry decided to embark for Ireland. The control of an itinerant and possibly problematic knight was undoubtedly an important motivating factor, but it also seems that religion, once again, played an important role in affecting the course of Irish history. Churches in Ireland had been placed under the control of Canterbury as early as the time of St Augustine. This control had been depleted when the Vikings had converted to Christianity. They had placed their faith in the Synod of Kells, thereby cutting the Irish Church off from Canterbury's control, and distancing it from Rome. Effectively it had become an independent Church. The archbishops at Canterbury had always wanted to regain control of

Ireland. Theobald, Archbishop of Canterbury, first suggested it as a definite plan to Henry in 1155. A year later, the idea was given Papal sanction by Adrian IV, who granted control of Ireland to Henry with the understanding that the Irish Church would be returned to Rome. Despite all the pressure that was being applied to Henry, he was seemingly in no hurry to actually make a move and claim Ireland either for himself or in the name of the Church. Events elsewhere forced action. In 1171, Thomas à Beckett was murdered in Canterbury Cathedral. Henry was roundly condemned and held responsible for the murder. He was duly banished from the Church until such time as his guilt had been discharged. In searching for a suitable deed that would return him to favour, Henry's eyes were drawn to Ireland and the memory of Papal pleadings of years earlier to intervene. The potentially threatening activities of Strongbow added to the justification for action, if anymore were needed, and enabled Henry to kill two birds with one stone.

Following the favourable reaction from the Irish kings, Henry called an Irish synod together at Cashel. The synod brought the Irish Church back into line with the greater Church and enacted reforms which addressed Papal concerns. Through his actions, Henry brought a level of peace to Ireland which had been absent for years, reformed the Church and won the approval of the majority of the different native kings.

THE LORDSHIP OF IRELAND

Unfortunately for Henry, his stay in Ireland was curtailed by the actions of his son, also named Henry, who was planning a rebellion in his absence. Quickly leaving Ireland to deal with problems at home, Henry left Hugh de Lacy as chief officer (justiciar) to assert the royal power in Ireland and, more immediately, to continue keeping Strongbow in check.

De Lacy, like Strongbow, was Welsh–Norman. His presence alongside Normans, Flemish, English, Ostmen and native Irish was symbolic of the wide mix of races that were living, and assimilating into, Irish life. It was the assimilation of the different groups, especially the Normans, into Gaelic culture, combined with the lack of a clear Irish policy from the various

English monarchs, which would prevent Ireland from becoming a peaceful colony, as seemed possible at the time of Henry's visit. The lordship of Ireland, despite its promising and peaceful beginning, signalled four hundred years of power struggles, warfare, and a reassertion of an Irish way of life distinct from the English, which would not be combated until Henry VIII took direct control of the country in the sixteenth century.

The doubts left by Henry II's rapid departure from Ireland before his work was complete led to Church intervention in an attempt to secure a lasting peace. The major problem was the High King, Rory O'Conner. Although he had travelled to meet Henry's envoys, he did not meet the King himself and did not submit to Henry's overlordship. The lack of an agreement between Henry and O'Conner could have caused problems in the future if O'Conner had ever chosen to rise against the new English ruler of Ireland. It is doubtful that O'Conner would have been successful in the face of English military technology, but he could have made the country ungovernable and required the commitment of a disproportionate amount of Henry's resources to keeping Ireland quiet. The Archbishop of Dublin, Laurence O'Toole, recognised this and brokered an agreement between Henry and O'Conner in 1175, the Treaty of Windsor. In agreeing to the treaty, O'Conner recognised Henry as his overlord, while Henry accepted that O'Conner was the ruler of Connacht and the Irish High King. In his role as High King, O'Conner would have to collect tribute from other kings, which would be forwarded to Henry.

As with the potential Strongbow–MacMurrough alliance that might have brought a degree of stability to Ireland, the same is true of the Treaty of Windsor. In forging an alliance between the Norman and Irish kings, O'Toole had brokered a reciprocal agreement that should have secured the peace of Ireland. The difficulty was that there were too many loose cannons in Ireland at the time. Whereas Henry could genuinely claim to rule over his kingdom and have a level of undisputed power (his rebellious sons notwithstanding!), O'Conner could not make the same claim. MacMurrough and others had challenged O'Conner as High King. Following the English invasions he was in an even weaker position. How could he, in these circumstances, ever successfully claim tribute from other Irish kings on behalf of a foreign ruler, when they did not even wholeheartedly support (or acquiesce) to his High Kingship? An additional problem was posed by the English representatives who remained in Ireland after Henry's departure, men such as Strongbow and other adventurers, who although professing loyalty to Henry, had no respect for the Irish kings, and coveted the land and wealth which were available in Ireland.

Soon after his departure, the two men that Henry had left in Ireland with sizeable grants of land, Strongbow in Leinster and Hugh de Lacy in Meath, both sought to enlarge their territories. The expansion was not merely concerned with the gaining and holding of lands, but was also driven by a desire to transform Ireland into a society run along English lines. In Leinster and Meath the way of life, especially administration of the land, was changed so that it duplicated the norms of life in England. The territories of Strongbow and de Lacy were placed under the control of a manor house. Alongside the establishment of the manor evolved a system of basic land management involving the use of sub-tenants. Charters were granted to towns, so that their existence became formalised and recognised; many abbeys were founded and defensive fortifications were built around important areas of settlement. In the years following Strongbow's initial invasion, and Henry's reconsolidating of the English presence in Ireland, the cultural and economic colonisation began. The aim was to make Ireland part of the English world.

It quickly became apparent to others watching from foreign shores that the success of Strongbow and de Lacy could be duplicated. Ireland appeared a nation rich in resources, full of opportunities and one that no longer needed to be conquered before it could be exploited. The seemingly free hand which Strongbow and de Lacy had in Ireland, despite any controls that Henry had attempted to put into place, only served to encourage other speculators. As the twelfth century ended and the thirteenth began, English adventurers began arriving in Ireland in increasing numbers looking to make a name, and wealth, for themselves.

Some of the adventurers to Ireland were of sufficient prestige that their arrival there and their claims on Irish lands, despite the Treaty of Windsor, had to be recognised by Henry. Others, ignoring the Treaty and the sensibilities of Irish–English relations, took the land which they desired. Many of the maverick adventurers to Ireland who were operating without Royal backing depended on their military superiority to defeat the Irish, yet others were also helped to pursue their claims for land by the Irish themselves. In the post-MacMurrough uncertainty, and with the inability of O'Conner to establish himself clearly as the High King, remained countless disputes relating to land and title amongst the Irish kings. The different disputes could be settled far more quickly if one of the kings in question was prepared to utilise the services of an English invader and his forces. The problem for the Irish was that once they had invited the English in to assist them, the English often proved untrustworthy and used the request for help as a springboard to domination of the local area. Effectively, the process witnessed years earlier with MacMurrough and Strongbow, where the English came out on top, possessing all the land and the title, was being repeated across the country. The nature of this second wave of English conquest directly challenged the scheme of politics that Henry and O'Conner had attempted to put into place to secure the long-term peace in Ireland. Through the Treaty of Windsor, Henry had recognised the rights of the different Irish kings and had secured for them the future ownership of their lands. In granting land titles to those English adventurers he supported, and lacking the will or the force to control the mavericks, Henry had undermined the treaty which was supposed to bring stability. By the middle of the thirteenth century, English influence, with the exception of specific pockets of resistance (such as Ulster), stretched across three-quarters of Ireland.

The gradual annexation of Ireland created a series of problems which would make the long-term tenure of control in that country difficult, if not impossible. Ireland had no central scheme of control before the English arrived. As the conquest of Ireland was carried out by a series of different adventurers – most of them motivated by their own greed – rather than by a campaign under the control of a single authority, conquest, once achieved, would itself be piecemeal. Without any form of central control over, rationale for, or driving force behind the conquest, it would be difficult for the English to control Ireland and make it a model in their own image. It is true that they brought the feudal system of land ownership and administration to Ireland, but, though imposing it in places, they failed to destroy or replace the Irish system of kingships and law. In total, the nation was neither Irish nor Norman, but perpetually weak and unstable as neither group had an authority that stretched across Ireland.

The lack of leadership from Henry served only to increase these difficulties. He was too involved in political intrigue elsewhere to devote much attention to Ireland. He hoped instead to rule it through a justiciar. However, without a central administrative and legal system which was commonly understood and acted on by both invader and native alike, then the power of the justiciar would always be minimal.

In an attempt to force his authority, Henry put forward his son John for the lordship of Ireland. This was done in 1177, when John was nine, and thus by virtue of his age, despite any authority he may have had, was as good as useless in maintaining control. Indeed, it took eight years, until he was seventeen, before John travelled to Ireland. The trip of 1185 was designed so that the English and Irish nobles and kings could pay their dues to, and recognise, their new lord. As with many seventeen-year-olds, royal or otherwise, John was full of his own self-importance and exerted his father's power over Ireland in a dreadful manner. He offended the Irish kings by insulting them and their traditions, and distanced the nobles by choosing to ignore the advice they offered on the state of Ireland. To add the final insult to injury, John began granting land titles to his young friends and followers, most notably in Tipperary and Limerick, thereby taking titles from older settlers and placing the Irish under the control of new, less experienced and more boisterous overlords. After a few months, even the seemingly uninterested Henry realised that John was doing more harm than good and recalled him home.

After John's return to England the justiciar, Hugh de Lacy, was replaced by John de Courcy; de Lacy's loyalty to the crown was called into question, like Stronghow's years earlier, as he had taken the daughter of an Irish king for his wife. De Courcy remained in office until 1192, when he was replaced by Peter Pipard and William le Pettit. The reason for his fall from grace was that he backed the claims of John's elder brother Richard in the battle for succession following Henry's death. In 1199, John took the crown for himself, and in 1205 granted de Courcy's lands to the rival de Lacy family (who had to take them by force). In doing so he settled an old score, and Ireland had once more been used as a place to resolve intrigues and power struggles which emerged from the English court.

Once in power John's attitude to Ireland was in marked contrast to the immaturity of the seventeen-year-old who had first made the trip across the Irish Sea. On his succession he merged the lordship of Ireland with the monarchy, thus making the king directly responsible for his western land. John's greatest aim was to bring Ireland under the control of the English system of law. He was well aware that the conquest of Ireland had been a makeshift affair, and that royal power over Ireland was not complete. One of the great weaknesses of the legal system was that the settlers, individuals as they were, did not follow the law or any central administration. The Irish kings, after the failure of the Treaty of Windsor, were equally immune to any central authority. John introduced a system of sheriff's courts, assizes, travelling judges and trial by jury which brought Ireland into line with the English system. The construction of Dublin Castle was begun. This building was envisaged as the centre of English rule over Ireland. John also tamed and utilised the geography of Ireland: county boundaries were made clearer and the coastline was used in an attempt to create a more sustained system of sea trading. In addition to all the legislation, which he put in place from afar, John made his second visit to Ireland in 1210.

The reason behind John's visit was the same that had driven his father across the Irish Sea years earlier: the power of the monarch's subjects in Ireland was becoming a cause for concern. As the struggle for succession had taken up so much of John's time, Ireland had not only been ignored, but had also avoided such struggles and had been left untouched by division. In place of the factions that had ravaged England, the settlers in Ireland had set about consolidating their power in a way that ignored the authority of the throne. To put down his increasingly powerful barons, John brought a large army to Ireland. He stayed in the county for a mere two months, but, in that time, marched from coast to coast. He reinforced the power of the monarchy across all the English-controlled parts of Ireland. In reasserting his power in such an overt fashion, he underpinned his strength of commitment to the English system of law within Ireland. Put simply, those barons who did not submit to it would face military attack at a future date.

John's problem, however, was that Ireland was not comprised solely of disloyal barons. The settlers may well have agreed to obey the letter of the English law and to operate within the English system which John had introduced. What though of the Irish? In legal terms the Irish were to be considered as serfs (betaghs) by the English. This would have been fine, and could have worked quite simply, if Ireland had been like other settled lands where the native populations were subservient and recognised the laws and customs of their overlords. This was not however the case. The Irish had never been settled in the true sense, and their way of life was never supplanted by the English system. As a result, the settlers in Ireland were colonisers surrounded by a hostile population. In not being able to enforce English law beyond his own settlers, John's system of rule became ineffective. What was needed was a complete conquest of Ireland – not just of the land, but also of its people – at which point genuine central government and control could follow. Another difficulty was that Ireland was not simply a nation that had not been fully conquered; it was a land where the colonisers were adapting to the habits and the systems of the native through inter-marriage. With the emergence of an Irish–Norman elite (shown by the marriages of men such as Strongbow and de Lacy), the law, and its central strength in underpinning the system of government, was further weakened.

THE FAILURE OF THE LORDSHIP

Despite the concerted efforts made by John to bring effective and unified rule to Ireland, his mission was to fail in the long term. The nature of the conquest of Ireland, which had been partial and had been driven by individuals who were not under the central control of the monarch or his agents, weakened English rule from the start. The continued presence of the Irish kings as a powerful group further added to the difficulties, and the rate of assimilation between English and Irish reduced the links between coloniser and home. All of this was compounded by the lack of interest which the different English monarchs had in Ireland. After John's visit in 1210, it was not until 1394 that an English king, Richard II, visited Ireland again.

With the actual monarch having so little interest, it is hardly surprising that the justiciars were in such a weak position and were so ineffective in attempting to control events in Ireland. While English law functioned so ineffectively, baron and Irish king alike sought to settle their differences through war. The barons would form alliances between themselves, and with Irish kings, in an attempt to build power bases and to take land. In all this the justiciar was weak, and the chances of English law being effective became less and less likely. The nature of localised wars and shifting power relationships meant that, by the beginning of the fourteenth century, two-thirds of the island of Ireland was under English control. The total number of English at this time was probably no more than 2500. It is clear that their power far outstretched their comparative numerical strength. The hope amongst these English had always been that the attractions of land and wealth that were available in Ireland would bring other migrants. In reality this never happened. Although many came over in the years following the establishment of Strongbow in Leinster, the passage of the years and the continuing instability of Ireland made it an unattractive trip to make for the English. Under Henry III, they were too preoccupied with wars elsewhere to go and struggle in Ireland. As a result, the total number of settlers was always to remain low. While they remained a small group, the Normans' hold on power would always be tenuous, and their need to intermarry greater, despite the English military strength, which had taken them into positions of power across the country. The Irish were still strong and controlled most of Ulster, and parts of Connacht, Leinster and Munster. In other areas where they did not have direct power, the Irish kings were enough of a threat to the settlers that they could not be driven off the land, and had to be brought into power alongside the invader.

For the settlers, their small numbers were a cause of concern. Families were dying out, and the numbers for expansion were not present. By contrast, the Irish were plentiful in number. The multitude of kingdoms meant that the different combinations of alliances, which could create difficulties for the English, were huge. Significant victories were won by the Irish in the second half of the thirteenth century in Sligo, at Kenmare, Carrick on

Shannon and at Loch Neagh. The English tenure of Ireland, in the second half of the thirteenth century, was reaching a point of crisis.

Despite the impending difficulties, some aspects of the lordship did develop during the thirteenth century in the way envisaged by John. The system of counties and their borders was completed, and each county was given its own sheriff and shire court. Under this system all lawmaking and decisions were driven by the English system. The justiciar used his power to summon Irish parliaments, whose membership was drawn from all the knights of the different counties. The only people who could attend the parliament were those who were either settlers or their descendants. Any legislation which emerged from the parliament could only be applied to areas controlled by the English, and the Irish-controlled regions were beyond the law.

Any chance of success for John's system of government, which seemed, by Irish standards at least, to be flourishing under the rule of Edward I (reigned 1272–1307), was destroyed by the Scottish invasion of 1315. Despite any consolidation in the field of administrative government that may have occurred under Edward's reign, his problems elsewhere in his kingdom cost him dear in Ireland. Edward embarked on, and fought, a long and costly campaign against the Scots at the end of the thirteenth century. The cost of his campaign was spread across all territories which he controlled. Ireland was duly called on to provide men and wealth for the campaign. In total nearly 8000 men were sent from Ireland to fight in Scotland, all at the cost of the Irish purse. The effects of such demands were hugely damaging to Ireland. The Irish treasury could barely cope with the cost of a domestic campaign, and while this money was being spent in Scotland, very little was being used to preserve the peace in Ireland.

This regression of the situation in Ireland was not lost on Edward II. He promised that all money in the Irish treasury would be spent on Ireland in order to try and prevent the slide into anarchy and lawlessness which seemed to be taking place. The barons could not be controlled as they were now beyond the reach of English law and only serving their self-interested needs. Alongside this collapse in the strength of the relationships between the settlers and their king, was a resurgent Irish race.

Since the middle of the thirteenth century, the Irish kings had been using the services of the gallowglasses, a group of mercenary troops from north-west Scotland. They fought with huge axes, wore body armour and were experienced in the ways of contemporary warfare. They brought to the Irish everything they had lacked in modern warfare technology since the arrival of Strongbow. The gallowglasses had been instrumental in the small victories claimed by the Irish in places such as Sligo, mentioned earlier. Their role in the Scottish invasion would be crucial.

The English–Scottish war ended in 1328 with Robert the Bruce's victory over the English at Bannockburn. As a result of this success, and bearing in mind the close proximity of Scotland to Ulster, with regular contacts between the two nations, and the victories inspired by the gallowglasses, Donal O'Neill, the King of Ulster, approached Edward the Bruce (Robert's brother) to become High King. To extend the title of the High Kingship to a foreigner did have a precedent as in 1263, Haakon, King of Norway, had been made a similar offer. Edward accepted the offer made to him with the backing of his more famous brother.

The adventures of Edward in Ireland make for fascinating reading. Looking at the position in 1315, the date of Edward's arrival in Ireland, it appears that the combined strength of a rebellion against English dominance in Scotland and in Ireland, led by the two Bruces, could seriously, if not irrecoverably, damage the settler community in Ireland. In contrast with these hopeful beginnings for a combined Gaelic onslaught against English power, the actual story of Edward ended in failure, and eventual rejection by the Irish.

Edward landed in Ireland in May 1315 at Larne. His force was one of the largest that had ever gathered in Ireland, and numbered in excess of 6000 soldiers, supported by the gallowglasses who were already in Ireland, and by the native Irish. Unlike the invasions which had been ongoing since the first of the Viking incursions, the aim of Edward's expedition was to place the Irish back in a position of primacy and to drive out the English. The justiciar demanded that all allies of the English and the barons rise to resist the invasion. Nevertheless, the forces under Edward's control seemingly could not be halted. They won immediate victories in Ulster, took and burned Dundalk, before moving to Meath. They swept through Meath and had arrived in Leinster by the start of 1316.

In the face of Edward's force, the rulers of Ireland were seemingly powerless. All the failures to invest in and impose a central control over the whole of Ireland and her people, became apparent, and all the problems came home to roost. Without central control and an ability to conduct a sustained and co-ordinated defence of the country, the official government was as good as powerless to do anything. It could not coerce the different barons into defending the country against Edward as they were weak, divided and self-interested. They would rather come to an accommodation with Edward, thereby preserving their lands and titles, than risk a humiliating defeat. The Irish were as belligerent as the English were weak; after years of English interference, they finally had the opportunity, and more importantly the means, to rise up.

Edward did not press home his obvious advantage of 1316 and returned to Ulster to be crowned. He established his court at Carrickfergus in September 1316 and consolidated his position by establishing a rule of law. In 1317, he journeyed back to Scotland and persuaded his brother Robert to join him for a tour round Ireland, during which they would establish their position over the kings of Ireland so that Edward could emerge as the undisputed High King. The tour, rather than being a triumphal procession, was in fact a desperate rout. Ireland, as with much of Europe, suffered from dreadful famine during 1317 and the Scots, rather than winning over the Irish, abused their power and took animals, crops and money from them. While this may have shown the strength of their authority, such actions, at a time of famine, distanced the cause of Edward and the dream of a Gaelic alliance.

In the early summer of 1317, Robert the Bruce and many of his followers returned to Scotland, while Edward and his supporters went back to Ulster. The combined weight of the Scots invasion and the famine had destroyed Ireland financially. The government in Dublin could no longer afford to run the campaign against Edward, and could raise no further money from those barons who remained, to start a campaign afresh. England finally stepped in, and dispatched a new justiciar, Roger Mortimer, to take control. Mortimer was successful in returning Meath, Leinster and Munster to Crown control and in 1318,

English forces under John de Bermingham defeated Edward the Bruce in a battle at Faughart in Ulster.

Edward's time was not favourably remembered by the Irish. Their supposed saviour had in fact overseen a period of war and famine which was to the detriment, not the benefit, of the Irish. More profoundly than Irish disappointment at the failure of their saviour, the Scottish invasion fully revealed the inadequate nature of English rule over Ireland. Although Mortimer had been successful in restoring Crown rule over most of the country, this was as tenuous as it had been before 1315. Mortimer had ensured that those Irish kings who had fought for Edward made their peace and those few Irish-English who had sided with the Scots returned, albeit chastised, to the fold. The greatest difficulty was that, despite any wavering loyalties to the Crown amongst the different residents of Ireland, there was simply no infrastructure through which the English could confidently see Ireland defended or administered. The lack of control had been exacerbated by the effects of the famine, and the financial insecurities of the country had prior roots, dating back to the Anglo-Scottish wars of two decades earlier. Revenue from Ireland collapsed after the Scottish invasions; land values fell to a fraction of their previous worth and customs duties became almost non-existent. Because of the lack of revenue, government officials took to supplementing their income with bribes and fraudulent activity, which only served to make a bad situation worse. Put simply, Ireland in 1317 was a mess.

Despite Mortimer retaking those areas lost to the Scottish invaders, the number of settlers was now so depleted that the native Irish were steadily regaining the initiative. The English were spread too thinly and were too weak to continue to occupy unchallenged the parts of Ireland which they held. The Black Death of 1350 further depleted their number, while the growing fragility of the Irish situation convinced others that they were better off back in England. The case for the weakened position of the settlers is shown by the events of 1316. It is widely accepted that the de Burgh victory over the O'Conners of Connacht that year was the final victory by the English leading to the holding of new land. Although Mortimer was successful in defeating combined Scots–Irish forces after this date, his campaign produced only a re-annexing of lands previously held.

For the Irish, the problem of the settlers holding their lands was exacerbated by the effects of absenteeism. Absentee landlords had begun establishing land holdings soon after the first incursions into Ireland, and this problem, in various forms, would haunt the Irish landscape and affect politics into the early twentieth century. The major English figures that involved themselves with Ireland were also likely to have land interests in England and France. The prestige of their other holdings was far greater than those in Ireland and it became common practice to leave the Irish properties and run them from afar. This created problems locally as the infrastructure which supported the land was allowed to decay: garrisons were not kept in a good condition, and, without this support, the baron's tenants were left to fend for themselves. Once alone, the tenants were likely to come under threat from the local Irish, or else had to come to accommodations with them. This process fundamentally undermined the whole English annexation of Ireland. Without strong central landowners who were prepared to stay in residence to run their estates, thereby providing support for their tenants, English rule, and the application of its laws and customs, would always be weak. Those tenants left behind, poorly served and defended, would have little time for their overlords and little affinity with central administration.

The powers in England attempted to halt the process of absenteeism through legislation, such as that enacted in 1297 which made it an offence for absentees to continue neglecting the defence of their lands. This legislation, as with all subsequent laws which were applied to the absentees, was difficult to enforce and certainly did little to effect a change in the situation. Similar laws in 1380, which demanded that all absentees return to their land in Ireland, merely encouraged many landowners to jettison their interests altogether. They sold their lands to local Irish kings. The laws had forced them into a position where crown control, rather than being reinforced by the return of absentees, was weakened.

The difficulties which absenteeism caused were added to by the actions of those English who actually remained in the country. Following the Scottish invasions the power situation in Ireland was highly fluid. Boundaries between the holdings of different barons were challenged as families sought to gain more lands and influence. In the 1330s, the de Burgh family who controlled Connacht and Ulster slipped into an acrimonious row over who should control the destiny of the family lands. Cousin locked into battle with cousin, until one of their number, William, the Brown Earl, was murdered. His lack of a male heir meant that the de Burgh lands were split between different sections of the now divided family. The effects of the breakup of so dominant a family were disastrous for the Crown, which should have been looking to families such as the de Burgh's to ensure a continuity of power in Ireland that afforded a degree of strength and stability; such fracturing brought only division and weakness.

The paucity of the situation of the English colonisers was exacerbated by the Black Death, which ravaged Europe during the fourteenth century. All Ireland suffered, but it was the settlers, living as they did at close quarters with each other in towns, who lost most. Nearly 40 per cent of the colonising population is reputed to have died. By contrast, the Irish, living in the open in less densely populated groups, were less affected. The colonisers were losing the numbers game badly.

Another ongoing problem for the English trying to control their colonisers in Ireland was the increasingly common process of Gaelicisation. This began, as has been explained, with Strongbow's marriage into the MacMurrough family, but by the fourteenth century, the process was not only taking place more often, but was becoming irreversible. A classic example of the Gaelicisation process is again the de Burgh family. Defying the English law that stated that all lands and titles should pass to the eldest son, two brothers opted instead to divide the family lands between them. They also changed their name to a Gaelic form, spoke the Irish language and intermarried with local Irish royalty. Their houses were open to poets, harpists and other forms of Irish cultural expression that distanced them further from their own heritage. In effect the de Burgh's of Connacht, who should have been bastions of the English order in Ireland, became Irish. Once transformed, their allegiances would be to the Irish way of life, Irish customs and their Irish allies, rather than to the authority of the justiciar in Ireland and the English Crown. Such transformations were completely undermining any remaining vestiges of Crown authority in Ireland. The situation in the first half of the fourteenth century was bad enough as it was, but for some of those remaining settlers to Gaelicise themselves in this way was the last straw. Royal intervention was needed to save Crown authority in Ireland. It was accepted that, for various historic reasons, the whole of Ireland could not be conquered as that opportunity had been missed centuries earlier, but the Crown had to try and maintain what was still held there.

It fell to Edward III (reigned 1327–77) to rescue some semblance of Crown authority in Ireland. He accepted that Ireland could not be conquered, and that the Lordship of Ireland could only be maintained by constant military intervention. This recognition of the true state of affairs also implicitly recognised that the loyalty of many of the original settlers could no longer be relied on. Rather than the Irish assimilating into and accepting English norms and the letter of the English law, many of the settlers were assimilating in the opposite direction. This offered succour to the Irish and strengthened their resolve to oppose the English. By the time of Edward III, the area of Crown influence in Ireland was reduced to approximately one-third of the country, surrounding Dublin. To protect the influence of the Crown and to save the remaining parts of English Ireland, the reign of Henry III witnessed the passage of the infamous statutes of Kilkenny.

In 1361, Henry III had sent his son Lionel, duke of Clarence, to Ireland to act as justiciar. Clarence's role was to act as a strong English leader in Ireland, something which had been lacking for years. He was given the task of retaking lands that had been lost to the Irish, preventing warfare between the loyal settlers, improving and regulating the balance of trade in Ireland, and ensuring that the long-term defence of the Crown's authority in Ireland was secured. Clarence took his forces to Ulster, Leinster and Munster in an attempt to regain lost lands and to stem the advance of the Irish. He found it incredibly difficult to gain the support of the English settlers in his wars against the Irish. As a result, any lands he did win back were only held in the short term, and he could not make his victories permanent. Militarily Clarence was a failure. He could not carry out the king's wishes. The parts of Ireland which had been lost to the Irish could not be recovered, and the defence of those areas still held by the English could not be ensured. Despite the intervention of Clarence, the Crown control of Ireland was contracting daily.

In a major attempt to restore order, the statutes of Kilkenny were passed at a parliament held in Kilkenny, called by Clarence. The idea underpinning the statutes was simple: if Ireland could not be held militarily, then the two parts of Ireland (Irish and English-settler) had to be kept separate. In ensuring a level of purity, the advance of the Irish into Crown-held lands by the process of assimilation could be halted. The statutes recognised that the ideal process of assimilation (from the point of view of the English) would have resulted in the Irish copying English forms of behaviour and obeying English law. This would have created an Ireland that was governed by the English crown. The process had been supplanted however, and reversed so that the Norman colonisers were now integrating into Irish customs and adopting Irish ways. This current practice of reverse assimilation was challenging the future stability of Crown control in Ireland. The statutes introduced a whole swathe of legislation designed to reverse this process. The English in Ireland would have to return fully to the control of English law. They were no longer allowed to settle disputes through recourse to the Irish brehon laws. They were forbidden to marry the Irish, they could not adopt their own children born to the Irish, and they were prohibited from sponsoring Irish children at baptism. They must retain the English version of their names and not convert to the Gaelicised form. Likewise all Irish in their service must adopt English forms. The common language would have to be English in future. This was seen as a vitally important statute in the context of retaining a common identity between the colonisers and their home across the water. It has many fascinating allusions to the notions of common identity and nationhood, as would be advanced by the Gaelic League and others in their battle to preserve the Irish language and culture in the nineteenth century. In the aim of practical defence of the Crown areas, the English were forbidden from selling horses and armour to the Irish; they could not employ poets and other Irish artists, as these were allegedly often spies, and they were to practise archery regularly so as to be ready for war. Anyone who broke the statutes would not only suffer the full force of law, but would also be excommunicated.

With the statutes in place, Clarence left Ireland to seek greater victories in England and France. What effect would the legislation he left in place have? Could it possibly secure the future safety of the lordship of Ireland as his military campaigns had been unable to do? Despite the threatened weight of legal and spiritual sanction against those who defied the statutes, they were, even from the day of their inception, unenforceable. In parts of Connacht and Ulster the levels of assimilation between the Normans and Irish were so far advanced that the application of the laws, even if the people involved had wished to be compliant, would have been impossible. Across Ireland, even in those areas which could still be considered to be under Crown authority, the development of close relationships between settler and settled had proved in the long term to be mutually beneficial. To destroy those links by obeying the statutes would only have caused the colonisers to suffer. Admittedly they would have been in step with the wishes of their monarch, but their monarch and the semblance of his power were distant and abstract ideas that had little or no impact on their daily lives. The reality was that they had to live with their Irish neighbours, and seek accommodation accordingly. They did not have to live with the power of their monarch and so this could be easily ignored.

The less than positive reaction of the colonisers to the laws was reinforced by the historical problem of central authority in Ireland. As the actual ability of the justiciar to enforce English law in Ireland was profoundly weak, and as a strong central administration, commonly respected, had never developed, so the ability to enforce the statutes was missing. From the inception of the statutes in 1366 and into the next century, the level of English control and the presence of English laws and customs in Ireland diminished. By 1500, English control could only be exerted in a small area surrounding Dublin, known as the Pale. As the fifteenth century progressed, the statutes, although remaining part of the law, became a total irrelevance. The ways of the Irish, their language, their laws and their customs came to dominate. The statutes of Kilkenny were as ineffective in saving Ireland for the Crown as Clarence's attempt at military intervention had been.

THE SHRINKING PALE

The continuing loss of influence in Ireland prompted Edward III's successor, Richard II (reigned 1377–99), to travel to Ireland in 1394. Richard's stated aim for his visit was to reassure the colonisers, as well as the Irish, that Ireland was of importance to him, and not merely a neglected outpost of the Crown. Richard travelled to Ireland with over six thousand troops and forced many of Ireland's absentee landlords to accompany him. While in residence in Dublin Castle, Richard was visited by some eighty Irish kings, who all paid him tribute and accepted his power in Ireland. In return for their tribute, Richard agreed to honour and recognise all land titles held by the Irish, with the exception of those lands between Dundalk to the north of Dublin, and Waterford to the south. This strip of land, the English land, was known as the Pale. Richard's vision was that the Pale would be a specific English area, where the power of the Crown, conducted through the justiciar and English law, was recognised and undisputed. The Pale, once functioning in this fashion, would serve as a launching pad for the reassertion of Crown authority over the rest of Ireland. Essentially Richard envisaged the Pale as the basis on which the successful conquest of Ireland could finally be completed.

The vision for the Pale, despite the warm reception which the Irish afforded Richard, was never realised. By the 1450s the area covered by the Pale, rather than expanding into Ireland as envisaged by Richard, had actually shrunk back towards Dublin. The reasons for this failure were many, but Richard's own actions contributed. Rather than remaining in Ireland and making his vision work, Richard, as other monarchs before him, hurried back to England. He did not summon a parliament to discuss his plans, and as had happened before, the justiciar was left with a mammoth task, but no real authority to complete it. External events also added to the difficulties of the Pale and its relationship with the rest of Ireland. Throughout the 1400s, England was locked into an almost perpetual state of war with France and was suffering major upheavals domestically as epitomised by the Wars of the Roses. English finances were in a state of chaos, and against this backdrop, the dreams and desires of Richard for Ireland had little chance of realisation. How could any English monarch be that interested in Ireland, a problematic and expensive lordship with an aggressive native population, when he had problems of such magnitude to deal with at home?

Against these wider themes of the fifteenth century, events in Ireland were largely allowed to follow their own course. There was no major intervention from England, and thus Ireland became a battleground between the forces of the Pale, representing the seemingly distant and uninterested monarchy, and the forces of the various Anglo-Irish kings and chieftains. The many Englishmen who travelled to Ireland to take up the post of justiciar had a difficult time. The government in England was demanding increased revenues to fight foreign wars, while the justiciar was finding it harder to collect taxes in Ireland. Those people who worked on Crown projects, such as the soldiers and artisans, found themselves unpaid. The Irish who lived on the fringes of the Pale could not be controlled, and those who lived within the Pale were forced to pay black rents (protection money) to the Irish to ensure their safety. The only strong figure to appear from England during the fifteenth century was Richard, duke of York, who arrived in Ireland as lord lieutenant in 1447, a post he would hold until 1460. Richard's main desire, however, was to overthrow Henry VI, the Lancastrian king, and Ireland was to form the launching pad for his campaign.

Richard gained much support in Ireland for the Yorkist cause. He was drawn from Anglo-Irish and Irish families, and as such commanded much respect. He was not very active in Irish affairs in their own right, as he was always driven by the bigger goal of securing the crown for the House of York. In 1460, however, the activities of Richard brought about a declaration from an Irish parliament which served to illustrate how far the Pale experiment had failed and how far Ireland had moved away from England. Richard summoned an Irish parliament to Drogheda, where it gathered in early 1460. The parliament first granted Richard sovereign powers, an act which clearly allied Ireland behind the Yorkist cause and further distanced it from the English crown. More important than this, however, was a constitutional declaration by the parliament of Ireland's position with relation to England. The parliament declared its legislative and judicial independence from the English crown, choosing to recognise instead the compromise system of law and culture developed under the process of assimilation between coloniser and native Irish, which had produced, by this date, an Anglo-Irish elite. This process of assimilation, having followed invasion, now produced a situation of resistance. The Anglo-Irish were choosing to define themselves as distinct from the English and were recognising their land, Ireland, as removed from English jurisdiction. Importantly, Richard, although a contender for the English crown, supported the claims of the Irish parliament.

Richard died at the Battle of Wakefield in England at the end of 1460, but his Yorkist campaign was ultimately successful, as 1461 saw the coronation of his son, Edward IV (reigned 1461–83), as king. At first it appeared that Richard's support for the declaration of the Irish parliament might be honoured by his son. One of his first actions was to remove land and titles from all those families in Ireland who had backed the Lancastrian cause. It seemed as though Edward, in remembering the loyalty of those who had favoured his father's cause and actively punishing those who had digressed, was aware of the events which had taken place in Ireland.

The practical embodiment of Edward's removal of land from the Irish Lancastrians came in 1463, when Thomas, earl of Desmond, a Yorkist, defeated Butler of Ormond in battle. Desmond, now all-powerful, took the job of deputy for Ireland. Edward, however, was not prepared to sit idly by and allow the Irish to think of themselves as independent and he called a parliament to Drogheda in 1468 with the aim of tackling that preconception. Desmond, as the most powerful man in Ireland, arrived at Drogheda only to be arrested and charged with breaking the statute of Kilkenny. He was found guilty and beheaded. The aim of this charge, and the subsequent execution of Desmond, was to break the grip that the biggest Anglo-Irish families had on power. Edward was attempting to destroy them and thereby reinforce royal control over Ireland. As with the machinations of so many holders of the English crown before him, Edward demonstrated a woeful ignorance through his actions. Desmond's son James, rather than bowing down to the might of the English crown, rose against Edward, attacked royal lands and refused to attend parliament ever again. Effectively, Edward had forced one of the most important Anglo-Irish families away from the English crown and into the opposing Irish camp by executing Desmond.

THE HOUSE OF KILDARE AND THE DOMINATION OF GEARÓID MÓR

The vacuum left by the execution of Desmond was filled by the earl of Kildare, who was appointed as justiciar, and then deputy in 1470. Kildare's role, as with deputies before him, was to run Ireland on behalf of the King. It was a post he would hold for seven years, and one his family would retain until the time of Henry VIII's intervention in Irish affairs. Despite Edward's attempt to remove the overbearing influence of a sole Anglo-Irish earl in the shape of Desmond, he effectively made the way clear for one more powerful and enduring.

When the earl of Kildare died in 1477 he was succeeded by his son Gearóid Mór, who was confirmed by the Irish Council as justiciar and deputy. The new Kildare, although only twenty-one, was immensely powerful and highly regarded by his fellow Anglo-Irish. His extensive family connections that linked him to many of the major Irish and Anglo-Irish families of the time, the immense wealth his family possessed, his influence, which spanned both the Pale and beyond, and his private military strength made Gearóid powerful. Edward was aware of the level of Gearóid's popularity and sent Lord Grey to Ireland to replace him as deputy in 1478. Gearóid refused to step down, and in the face of his intransigence Grey returned to England. Gearóid, having successfully rebuffed Edward's attempt at replacing him, was left unmolested and unchallenged as the sole effective power in Ireland.

The course of English politics conspired to reinforce Gearóid's position as court intrigue turned English eyes away from Ireland. The death of Edward in 1483 was followed by the murder of his successor, the twelve-year-old Edward V, by his uncle Richard who then acceded to the throne as Richard III (reigned 1483–5). He in turn was killed in battle and the victorious Henry VII (reigned 1485–1509), a Lancastrian, took the throne. The whole period left the English crown in a position of relative weakness. On the back of such division and infighting within England, which had to be smoothed over by Henry, it was initially easier for him to allow Gearóid to continue in his position of deputy unmolested. This was far less problematic than attempting to remove him by force.

Gearóid fed off Henry VII's initial reticence to immerse himself in Irish affairs. He involved himself in a plot to replace Henry with a Yorkist in 1487, and in 1488 treated the King's envoy with utter contempt. The message which was emanating from Gearóid, for which he received great support and popularity in Ireland, was that the declaration of 1460 was still operating. Ireland under Gearóid, it seemed, could not be dictated to or controlled by the English crown. Henry decided to take action against Gearóid. In 1494, he chose the military option and sent Sir Edward Poynings to Ireland to replace Gearóid as deputy. Poynings was initially successful; he arrested Gearóid and forced English rule on the Pale and certain areas beyond by military force. The problem however, as had so often been the case before, was cost. Although Henry wanted to control Ireland, the threat of James IV in Scotland was far greater and more immediate. To waste money on a man such as Gearóid, who in comparison with James was a minor irritation, was pointless. The Poynings experiment was brought to a close in 1496, and Gearóid was reinstated as deputy.

For Gearóid, however, the departure of Poynings did not mean a return to business as usual. Before he left, Poynings had called together a parliament at Drogheda at the end of 1494, and passed the Poynings' laws. These laws removed the legal rights of Ireland to legislate for itself and to control its own destiny. In future, any meeting of the Irish parliament had to be sanctioned by the English monarch and his council. All laws to be put before that parliament had to be approved in a similar fashion. Finally it was made clear that English law had to prevail in Ireland. The basis of Poynings' laws, and the level of control this allowed the English monarch over Irish affairs, remained largely unchanged until the late eighteenth century.

On the back of Poynings' laws and the reinstatement of Gearóid, Ireland was mostly peaceful until the earl's death in 1513. Gearóid, despite earlier misdemeanours, remained unquestioningly loyal to the English crown, in that he did not allow Ireland to be used as a launching pad for challenges to its authority. He also largely managed to abide by Poynings' laws. The area within the Pale, small though it was, remained relatively safe, although the conditions of those living within it were far from pleasant. There were incursions into the Pale by the

Irish, and many Irish chieftains still forced those who lived within the borders of the Pale to pay black rent. Areas beyond the Pale were chaotic and rife with warfare. These Gearóid could not control, nor did he attempt to. He was content, as his successor would be, to remain powerful within the area of the Pale and run it, albeit in the name of the English crown, in his own interest. On his death Gearóid was succeeded by his son Gearóid Óg as deputy. Whereas Gearóid Mór had deterred Henry VIII (reigned 1509–47) from taking too close an interest in Ireland, Gearóid Óg would have no such luxury.

THE TUDOR INTERVENTION

Henry VIII's advisor Cardinal Wolsey was not enamoured with Gearóid Óg. He believed that the power the young Gearóid exerted over the Pale was too great and that, in effect, he had become a self-appointed king. Henry VIII was well aware of Wolsey's views and equally concerned that his Irish subject did not become over-powerful to the extent where he could challenge the established order in Ireland.

In 1520, Henry dispatched the earl of Surrey to Ireland in yet another royal-sponsored attempt at bringing the Irish into line. The aim was for Surrey to be seen by the Anglo-Irish and Irish alike as a more impressive figure than Gearóid Óg, so that they would transfer their loyalty to him, and thus to the English crown. Surrey's mission was a partial success. Many Irish chieftains came to Surrey, and the invasion of the Pale by O'Neill from Ulster was repelled by him. Despite the financial difficulties that Surrey himself encountered, he stressed his belief to Henry that a force of 5000 men could take the whole of Ireland for the Crown. Henry was not keen to embark on the expenditure which would accompany a plan to subdue the whole of Ireland. Surrey's smaller trip had been expensive enough. The Irish exchequer was broke and Surrey's own budget was quickly spent. The year of his visit was also a year of plague and famine in the Pale which harmed its fragile economy still further. Surrey asked to be recalled home as he was at his wits' end.

The Surrey excursion made clear three important facts to Henry. First, the power of Gearóid Óg could not be easily broken. Within two years of Surrey's departure he had to be re-appointed as deputy, as no one else had the ability to make the position work. Secondly, any involvement in a plan to place the whole of Ireland under crown authority would be hugely expensive. Finally, despite Surrey's estimate that only 5000 troops were required to take Ireland, it was evident that such a task could only be accomplished by large-scale military action. In a world of constant warfare on different borders, Henry had to decide whether he could stomach another campaign.

It was the removal of Wolsey from a position of power within the English court in 1529 that would bring about a fundamental change in the fortunes of Ireland. His replacement, Thomas Cromwell, believed that the English monarchy should be as strong as possible. Any force which stepped out of line, or was seen to be operating independently, had to be defeated and brought back into a position of subservience. For Cromwell, Gearóid Óg was such a force. In 1533, the Irish Council had Gearóid Óg imprisoned in Maynooth for stealing Crown property, from where Cromwell had him brought to London and placed in the Tower. In his absence, Gearóid Óg's son, Lord Offaly, popularly known as Silken Thomas, was made deputy. It was Silken Thomas who would face the full force of English power as Cromwell and Henry VIII acted to complete the Norman invasion of Ireland.

2

....

Early Modern Ireland, 1534–1691

The challenge for Henry VIII was whether or not he had the steel to subdue Ireland finally. His predecessors had tried a variety of techniques, ranging from warfare to diplomacy, but Ireland had never fallen fully to the English Crown. Henry VIII was certainly a more single-minded and aggressive monarch than many of those who had gone before him. He was a successful military campaigner elsewhere across the Tudor world and his struggle with the Papacy over his first divorce certainly showed strength of determination. Ireland though remained a problem. Put simply, did Henry need to conquer Ireland? Many of the previous holders of the crown had been too preoccupied elsewhere, or had been happy to allow Ireland to take care of itself, to bother themselves with conquest. For Henry, his whole attitude towards the strength of monarchy and the need to cancel out all opponents put him in a different position from those who went before. He would actively wish to, and indeed would, successfully subdue Ireland.

THE DEFEAT OF THE KILDARES

With Gearóid Óg in the Tower of London, the fortunes of the House of Kildare were left in the hands of Silken Thomas. Whereas Gearóid Óg was now familiar with the intrigues involved in being the King's deputy in Ireland, the role of the Irish Council and the constant meddling of the English faction within the Pale, Silken Thomas was more impetuous and less experienced.

In 1534, a rumour gathered momentum which suggested that Gearóid Óg had been beheaded by the English in the Tower. Rather than taking the time to investigate such rumours, Silken Thomas took direct action. He gathered what allies he could and set off for Dublin intent on avenging his father's death. In front of the Irish Council, and surrounded by an armed guard, he withdrew his support for the crown, as had James, son of Desmond in 1467. Effectively Silken Thomas was calling on those across Ireland to join him in open rebellion against the English. He knew that he must either submit to the Crown, or else stand against it. Considering the power of the Kildare family in Ireland, the prospect of Silken Thomas utilising all their resources against the Crown and its agents in Ireland was a troubling prospect for Henry.

Silken Thomas was as good as his word and attacked the area of the Pale with impunity. As a result of Thomas's attacks on the Pale, and on Dublin in particular, the Archbishop of Dublin, John Alen, decided to flee. Unluckily for the Archbishop he was captured and killed by Thomas's men. Within the context of the 1500s, the murder of a fleeing enemy was far from being a terrible crime. The fundamental difference in this case was that Alen was an Archbishop. The murder of the holder of such a high office meant that people from outside Ireland were bound to take an interest in the activities of Silken Thomas. In due course news of Alen's murder reached the Pope, who had no hesitation in excommunicating Silken Thomas, and damning all Christians who had any contact with him.

For Thomas, his rebellion had got out of hand. Rather than rising against the Crown and damaging the Pale, he had outlawed himself in the eyes of the Church. Although now fully earl of Kildare, as Gearóid Óg had died in the Tower at the end of 1534, Thomas desperately needed allies. He tried to make an alliance with the King of Scotland, and with the Emperor Charles V, and also attempted to encourage other Irish kings and chieftains to join with him. Time, though, was running out.

In March 1535, Sir William Skeffington, Henry VIII's new deputy in Ireland, used his large army to capture the Kildare castle at Maynooth. In the face of Skeffington's success and the skill and number of his army, any allies whom Thomas had collected evaporated. As he marched from Connacht to confront Skeffington, Thomas's army quickly reduced in size. Once in contact with Skeffington he was arrested and taken to London to his father's former resting-place in the Tower of London. Thomas was not allowed the luxury of a natural death, which his father had experienced. Instead, Silken Thomas, rebellious earl, was hanged, drawn and quartered. Soon after his death a number of his uncles who had taken part in his rebellious activities were also hanged.

The suppression of Silken Thomas's rebellion, and his death, ended the role of the Kildares as major power brokers in Ireland. Whereas his father Gearóid was allowed to retain power and influence for years, as the English monarch had no interest in Ireland, the intrigues of Silken Thomas were challenging and dangerous to the throne. While other monarchs had accepted such a state of affairs, Henry was prepared to confront it. Skeffington was sent to Ireland with one goal alone, to destroy the Kildares' power base. Once it had been swept away and Thomas was dispatched at Tyburn, the way was clear for Henry to decide what he might do with Ireland.

THE EFFECT OF THE REFORMATION

In 1536, while Thomas was languishing in the Tower, an uneasy peace fell over Ireland. During that time an Irish parliament was called together. The parliament was not only played out against the backdrop of Thomas' recent rebellious outburst, but was firmly grounded in the context of English Church and State relations. Henry VIII had married his brother's widow, Catherine of Aragon, in 1509. The marriage did not produce a male heir, and Henry began to argue that he should be granted an annulment of his marriage by the Pope. Such an annulment was not forthcoming, and Henry, now in love and wishing to marry the expectant Anne Boleyn, searched for more radical alternatives to Papal annulment. Henry took the decision to turn away from the Catholic Church and establish an alternative Church as the religion of state. In 1533, he appointed the Protestant Thomas Cranmer as Archbishop of Canterbury. Cranmer annulled

Henry's marriage to Catherine and crowned Anne as Queen. In December 1533, Henry VIII established the English Church as the state religion and broke with Rome. The English parliament duly recognised the step and appointed Henry as the Head of the Church of England. These events were the true context for the Irish parliament of 1536, the Reformation parliament.

The parliament predictably stripped the traitor Silken Thomas of his lands and titles, but this was minor business. The main business was how Ireland would deal with the process of the Reformation and whether such a fundamental change in the religious status of the country was acceptable. The first step taken by the parliament was the dissolution of the monasteries, a process which followed on from what had been happening in England. The dissolution of the monasteries was a step which, in all likelihood, would have been opposed by the parliament. There were within the Anglo-Irish families, however, supporters of Henry who had already accepted the Reformation as a reality and embraced the process, and who accepted Henry as Head of the Church. These included the Butlers of Ormond, who, taking the proposal of dissolution as an actuality, set about taking Church lands, properties and wealth. In the face of so aggressive a dissolution of the monasteries, which was being effected by families such as the Butlers, the parliament passed the bill.

The legislation, which would confirm Henry as Head of the Church in Ireland, thereby replacing the Pope, was keenly contested by the Irish parliament. All Church members of the parliament opposed the bill of supremacy. The solid opposition from the clergy was a potential stumbling block to Henry's transformations of the state religion, and their intransigence might have become a focus for a more sustained challenge to royal authority. The Butlers, who had been so instrumental in forcing through the dissolution of the monasteries, came to the rescue of the supremacy bill. By attacking and holding the different bishoprics around the country to ransom, and through a systematic policy of intimidation, the Butlers convinced the archbishops of Cashel and Tuam, and eight other bishops, that they should vote for supremacy. With such a switch in voting, the bill of supremacy was passed and Henry VIII confirmed as Supreme Head of the Church of Ireland. The Reformation parliament, whose religious members gathered in opposition to the changes envisaged by Henry, was ultimately, through a process of intimidation at the hands of the loyal Butlers, bullied into servility. The process had been underpinned by a liberal redistribution of monastic lands to both Anglo-Irish and Irish families. A gift of land, as had often been the case in Ireland in the short term at least, ensured loyalty to the Crown.

THE KINGDOM OF IRELAND

Following the successful acceptance of the religious policies which underpinned the Reformation, Henry turned his mind to the more substantive issue of how to rule Ireland. As a result of the fallout from the process of Reformation in England and on the continent, Henry was unable and unwilling initially to undertake the military conquest of Ireland. The aim of his policy would be to ensure that those Anglo-Irish families within and beyond the Pale were brought directly under English control. In itself this would be the easier task as these groups knew that their primary allegiance lay with the Crown. The more difficult and delicate task would be to reach a peaceful settlement with the native Irish kings and chieftains. Their relationship with the elements of English rule in Ireland had always been problematic and their links with the Crown itself ill defined. For Henry the task was to settle the Crown's relationship with the Irish and place it on a sound footing.

To tackle the thorny problems posed by Ireland, Henry dispatched Sir Anthony St Leger to Dublin as the new deputy. St Leger knew Ireland well, had travelled widely in the Pale and beyond, and had attended recent Irish parliaments. In St Leger, Ireland had been given a deputy who had prior knowledge of the country and a degree of empathy with conditions there. Arriving in Ireland in 1540, St Leger set about his new job with enthusiasm. One of his first actions was to tackle the question of Ireland's constitutional position in relation to the Crown. Ireland had long had the status of a lordship. St Leger argued that this was no longer relevant to the contemporary situation. Not only had Ireland and England changed hugely since the lordship had been introduced, but the recent revolutionary upheavals of the Reformation had made the lordship irrelevant. St Leger

suggested that Ireland would be better served if Henry, in light
of the Act of Supremacy, was not only Head of the Irish Church,
but also King of Ireland. This would clearly settle the question
of where Crown authority stemmed from. The lordship had
legally been underpinned by the power of the Pope. In the days
following the Reformation, the Pope had no say over any other
aspect of English or Irish life, so why should he define the
'constitutional status of the country? If Henry were made King of
Ireland, authority would rest solely with the monarch and would
not be underwritten or guaranteed by any other party.

St Leger called an Irish parliament together in June 1541 to
seek approval for the change to Henry's status in respect of
Ireland. After the continued benevolent re-granting of monastic
lands to leading Anglo-Irish families, the vote in favour of such a
change was never in any doubt. The legislation was read in
English to the Anglo-Irish, the clergy, nobles and gentry who
were present, while the large number of Irish chiefs present
necessitated another reading in Irish. Within days, Henry's new
title was proclaimed at a service of celebration in St Patrick's
Cathedral in Dublin. Officially Ireland had become a kingdom.
The wide range of interests which were represented at the 1541
parliament, and which so freely gave their consent to Henry's
new title, suggested that Ireland might finally be on the verge of
a peaceful and successful conclusion to its long history of failed
conquest.

Henry's main policy, carried out by St Leger, was to integrate
all those who lived in Ireland under English rule. The segrega-
tion that had been crystallised in the statutes of Kilkenny was
abandoned in favour of a policy of integration. All populations,
be they colonisers or natives, were to be ruled by English law, a
system which would be universally enforced. The place of
Henry, as the giver of law and the ultimate judge, underpinned
the whole system. In the context of the parliaments of 1536 and
1541, where Henry had been confirmed as Head of the Church
and King of Ireland, the rule of law under Henry had effectively
become supreme and regal. To bring together the Irish under his
rule, Henry had to break the links between the Irish and their old
system. To achieve this, Henry enforced a system of surrender
and re-grant. The idea centred on Irish landowners voluntarily
surrendering lands to the Crown. These lands had been held

under Irish law and were therefore invalid holdings under English law. By instantly re-granting the surrendered lands back to the Irish with a new title underwritten by English law, the link with Irish law was broken. In return for entering into such a process, the Irish were promised royal protection from their enemies and, at the time of the re-granting of their lands, they were given noble titles, as was the common practice in England. The whole process located the Irish firmly under Crown control. If they were prepared to accept the re-granting of their lands, then they had to accept English law. Effectively the Irish were being offered the opportunity to relinquish Gaelic law, and transform themselves from chieftains to nobles. Within a short time, the process of surrender and re-grant had brought some forty Irish chieftains under the control of the Crown. Accordingly some forty Gaelicised titled chieftains, such as Conn Bacach Ó Néill, were transformed to become Anglicised with titles such as earl of Tyrone.

As peaceful an ideal as surrender and re-grant was, and no matter how eagerly some Irish chieftains embraced it, the scheme did not work in the long term. It was not that the logic behind the plan of Henry and St Leger was in any way wrong. To offer the Irish a reason to come under the control of English law seemed in itself quite a coherent aim. The flaw in the plan was that the Irish were not making the clear-cut decisions as to which scheme of law they lived under that Henry had expected. In taking the surrender and re-grant option, the Irish chieftains were more than happy to accept the protection of the Crown. Such protection and recognition afforded by the Crown also allowed them to settle old scores with their fellow Irish who had not come under Henry, in an aggressive manner. The Irish were therefore using their royal recognition, not as a way of leaving behind their Gaelic customs or as a means of relinquishing inter-Irish struggles, but as a method of improving their status. An English title and royal protection was a new weapon to be used in the old system of Irish struggle.

In abusing the system into which they had entered, the new Irish nobility encountered dual problems. First, if they entered into feuds and alliances as a way of furthering their interests in Ireland, they failed to understand that those feuds or alliances were now considered to be against the Crown. In such cases they, as subjects, were charged with treason and dispossessed of their land and title in accordance with English law. Secondly, in refusing to accept the right of the eldest son in the inheritance process as dictated by English law, and sometimes relying instead on the Irish system of electing the successor, the new Irish nobles were creating countless power vacuums. In the event of the death of an Irish noble there were branches of the family who would operate the succession under Irish law and there were those who would choose to follow the English way. As the two were incompatible, the competing branches of the family would inevitably take to the battlefield.

Henry's attempt at a peaceful conquest of Ireland thus failed. The uneven application of English law created a mass of problems as the Irish, even those who took Anglicised titles, could not submit themselves completely to Tudor rule. To further their interests and to settle disputes they reverted, as they had always done under their own laws and customs, to warfare. If Henry were to subdue the Irish then he, or his successors, would ultimately have to utilise the same methods as they had traditionally used themselves.

THE CONTINUING REFORMATION

Alongside the process of surrender and re-grant, the powers of the Crown in Ireland still had to continue Henry's work in attempting to carry through the process of Reformation. Although the Irish parliament in 1536 had accepted the dissolution of the monasteries and that Henry should be seen as Head of the Church, religious affairs continued relatively unchanged. In Ireland the formal system of religion was in a bad way. Churches and cathedrals were in a poor state of repair, religious offices were left unfilled and the intellectual investigation into points of theology was years behind that elsewhere in Europe. Religion was undoubtedly popular amongst the people of Ireland, but they relied on local friars for their spiritual guidance. Thus, although the Irish were a religious people, they were distanced from the formal Church. For them the initial changes brought about by the Reformation in Ireland had little practical effect.

The lack of change brought about by the Reformation probably helps to explain why the Geraldines, and other rebellious Irish family groups through the 1530s and 1540s, had so little success in attempting to use the religious upheavals as a rallying call. By the time of Henry VIII's death, Ireland, although having officially been part of the Reformation, had not substantially changed. The people had learnt to accept that Henry was now Head of the Church, but as the practical changes were so small and the organised Church so weak, Ireland had effectively developed a system that adhered to Catholicism but with no Pope. Fundamental changes to the substance of religious practice began to emerge at the end of Henry's reign, and were carried on by his successor, Edward VI (reigned 1547–53). Whereas the early years of the Reformation had not brought about any changes to the nature of religious doctrine or liturgy, these were now to be challenged. What is so fascinating about the Irish situation is that the fundamentally religious aspects of the Reformation were introduced into a land not fully under the control of the Crown, and that lacked a native party or power block which firmly believed in the theological value of Protestantism. There were few reforming zealots present in Ireland. Those who would challenge accepted religious doctrine in Ireland would have to be brought in from outside and they would inevitably face opposition.

Edward VI was only ever an adolescent king. He died in 1553 at the age of sixteen. Whereas Henry's policies towards Ireland can be examined in the light of his own actions and ideas, it is far harder to understand which forces within the court drove along Edward's Irish plans. The reality of his policies arrived in Ireland in book form. In 1549, the first book ever to be printed in Ireland was published in Dublin. The book, which had the force of royal prerogative behind it, was an English edition of the Book of Common Prayer. The book was an attempt to change the doctrine and liturgy of the Church in Ireland. It symbolised a reforming Protestantism, which sought to replace the understood norms of Catholicism. The reception of the Book of Common Prayer spoke volumes, not only about the religious nature of Ireland, but also of the lack of Crown control which still existed. Outside the area of the Pale, and a few other minor pockets, the book was rarely used. The book was rejected equally by the Irish and Anglo-Irish, and firmly objected to by the Irish clergy. At the ecclesiastical level, the arrival of the Book of Common Prayer, which seemed to be being forced on the Irish, brought about stiff opposition and a rethinking of previous actions. Whereas the bishops and archbishops had acquiesced at the Irish parliaments held by Henry, and accepted the removal of the Pope as Head of the Church, they now travelled in the opposite direction. As Edward VI did not call an Irish parliament, the clergy had no direct vehicle for challenging the introduction of the Book of Common Prayer, so instead, they showed their objection through their actions. Primarily the process of opposition was voiced in the refusal to use the new prayer book, but some, such as the Archbishop of Armagh, left Ireland rather than change their services. In taking such action, and refusing the new prayer book and order of service (such as the abolition of the holy Mass), the Irish clergy were implicitly rejecting Edward as Head of the Irish Church and returning their allegiance to Rome. By enforcing the Reformation in Ireland in a way which challenged the doctrines of the Church, in a practical way Edward ensured that opposition to the Crown became stronger and more widely felt.

For the rebellious Irish clergy, relief from the Reformation came with the death of Edward. His place on the throne was taken by his eldest half-sister, Mary (reigned 1553–8). For Mary, the turn away from Catholicism under her father and half-brother had been an abomination. As a Catholic, she sought the restoration of the Catholic Church and wished to reinstate the Pope as Head of the Churches in England and Ireland. The Irish rallied firmly behind her and the reversal of the Reformation was applauded by clergy and laity alike. Under Mary those few bishops in Ireland who had supported the Reformation were deprived of their powers, while those who had stayed true to Rome were reinstated. However, Mary's reign was curtailed by her death in 1558 after less than five years on the throne. The ease with which the Irish had entered into the spirit of Mary's counter-reformation demonstrated how poorly the actual process of Reformation had worked across the country. For the Irish, little really changed. There were few genuine Protestant believers among them, and as a result the charges of heresy that were witnessed in England under Mary never materialised in Ireland. Despite the mammoth undertaking which the counter-reformation was for Mary (especially in England), hei other policies were largely a continuation of those of her father and half-brother. In this, the state of affairs in Ireland barely changed. The Pale still had to be supported and secured by military activity, the deputy and Crown authority across the country were weak, and the Irish involved themselves in warfare and intrigue with impunity. Mary's counter-reformation undoubtedly placated the Irish clergy and laity, but did nothing to alter the relationship between the Irish and the Crown. That relationship continued as poorly as ever.

Elizabeth I (reigned 1558–1603) succeeded Mary to the throne and set about reversing all that she had done. Elizabeth was a firm believer in the Reformation. For her, that process was incomplete, but she understood that the reversals under Mary had caused damage and division. To achieve the Protestant State which she aspired to, Elizabeth would have to act with a heightened sense of political reality, and ideally introduce changes through compromise not coercion.

In Ireland she allowed Mary's appointee as deputy to continue in his post. Lord Fitzwalter was thus duly re-appointed and promoted to the title of earl of Sussex. In England, Elizabeth had used the powers of parliament to introduce the ecclesiastical changes she desired. The parliamentary seal of approval on the process of renewed Reformation instilled some degree of wider agreement upon it; thereby making the changes seem less autocratic. In England the changes that parliament approved brought into being a revised Protestant Church which was widely accepted. Although there were still Catholic dissenters in England, the more secular nature of Elizabeth's Church, compared with that of Edward VI, won many of the doubters over to the new Protestant Church. In Ireland, the Elizabethan reforms brought about further division and dissent. In 1560, the earl of Sussex was empowered to bring together an Irish parliament which would establish the Church. The parliament met in Dublin and was faced with bills similar to those presented to the parliament in London. The parliament met for only three weeks, and in the face of some stiff opposition did the Queen's bidding and passed the required legislation. The Acts of 1560 imposed Protestantism on Anglo-Ireland through an act of uniformity. The Irish Church was compelled to use the second Book of

Common Prayer. The language of that book, as with all the church services, had to be English.

The Acts of 1560 mark a watershed in Irish history. They effectively legislated for the enforcement of an alien religious system, that of Protestantism, on an unwilling Catholic population. To enforce such legislation on an unwilling population was bound to create problems. These problems were, however, compounded by the condition of Ireland at the time, and the scope of the legislation. The 1560 Acts were only to be applied to the Anglo-Irish, effectively those living within the Pale. The remainder of the population of Ireland, the other two-thirds, did not come under the jurisdiction of the laws and were thus able to retain their allegiance to the Pope. This meant that the Acts were faced by a varied opposition. The Anglo-Irish in the Pale would oppose the legislation as they did not believe in the nature of the religious reform it advanced. The population outside the Pale would, if the legislation was successful and Protestantism took hold, increase their adversity to the Anglo-Irish. It was bad enough for the Irish that the Pale existed, considering all that it encompassed: royal authority, foreign troops and such like. In future it would also represent an alien and oppositional religion. How could Elizabeth reconcile all these differences? There seemed no way to force the practice of Protestantism on the Anglo-Irish, and could she even risk such an enforcement considering that it might produce resentment within the Pale?

Elizabeth was effectively dealing with many of the conundrums faced by her father. For her, though, the situation was more extreme. Her decision to reinvent the Reformation, following the death of her Catholic half-sister, brought her into conflict with all the major royal families across Europe. They saw Elizabeth as a pariah and would seek any opportunity to weaken, if not destroy her, so that England and Ireland could once more return to the Vatican. Elizabeth was only too aware of the views and intentions of her European opponents and had to watch carefully for any sign of a Catholic plot which could destabilise her rule. In this, Ireland offered her nothing but a sense and source of insecurity.

REBELLIOUS IRELAND AND THE ELIZABETHAN CONQUEST

The earl of Sussex had been open in his concern over how easily Ireland could be used as a base for foreign intervention in English affairs. In the first instance, however, it was the Irish themselves who came to cause Elizabeth problems. In 1559, the earl of Tyrone, O'Neill, died. O'Neill had been a beneficiary of Henry VIII's policy of surrender and re-grant. Members of his family refused to accept the letter of English law, which O'Neill had signed up to in being granted his title, and turned instead to Irish law. They elected his younger son as his successor. Shane O'Neill, who became more popularly known as 'The O'Neill', was flouting English law and, in doing so, was bringing himself into conflict with Crown authority. The problem was that Shane O'Neill saw himself only in the context of his own surroundings and did not deal with the larger political landscape in which he existed. He saw himself as an Irish chieftain in the traditional sense and identified with the norms of Gaelic culture. His main interest was to control and dominate Ulster.

The Crown could not force Shane's hand and failed to act immediately on the question of his succession. The problem for the English was, as so many times before, that they were occupied elsewhere and could not spare the necessary troops and money to deal with a difficult Irish situation. Instead the English chose to negotiate with Shane, and although he travelled to London and submitted to Elizabeth, his power in his part of Ulster was left unmolested by the Crown. Shane was symbolic of Elizabeth's difficulties. Not only was he a loose cannon within Ireland, and a powerful one at that, but he refused to bow down in any way to English law, authority or influence. Instead he had a long-running dialogue with Elizabeth's enemies on the continent in Spain and France, and also kept himself in touch with those rebellious elements in Scotland.

In an effort to control Shane's power, and reduce the impact of his potential intrigues, the earl of Sussex advised Elizabeth to support the weaker groupings in Ulster. Shane, however, could not resist the opportunity to use his freedom to take other parts of Ulster into his command. The O'Donnells of Donegal and the Scots of Antrim were the focus of Shane's campaigns. For some years, he was successful and managed to expand his territory and influence at the expense of his neighbours. In 1567, the O'Donnells, who were supported by the forces of the Crown, finally defeated Shane, who was beheaded by the Scots. They dispatched his head to the earl of Sussex who displayed it outside Dublin Castle.

The treasonous activities of Shane were duly discussed in 1569 when a parliament was called. As with many a rebel before him who had displeased the Crown, Shane's name was attainted and his lands removed. The parliament installed Hugh O'Neill on part of Shane's lands and recognised him as the rightful heir to Shane's father in accordance with English law. Despite this legal step in Parliament, the English forces did nothing to challenge Turlough, Shane's cousin who had claimed the bulk of Shane's land after his death.

The establishment of Hugh O'Neill in Ulster would, in time, have important ramifications, but for the time being it was the least important part of the parliament's business. The parliament, called by Sir Henry Sidney, Elizabeth's new deputy in Ireland, laid down legislation which would have a fundamental effect on the future of land ownership across Ireland. Tenants would have to pay for their land in cash, rather than in return for their services. This transformation, included as it was in a changing formula for funding the army in Ireland, put the administration of the country in line with that in England. The most important piece of legislation was the one which removed the Irish chieftains from their positions of power. In future, there would be no chieftaincies. The traditional power structure in Ireland, which had taken years to evolve, had been, in legal terms at least, swept away overnight.

The problem for the English was whether they could actually divest the chieftains of their traditional rights and powers without bringing Ireland to the point of complete chaos. The Anglo-Irish did not believe that was possible and attempted to block Sir Henry Sidney's legislation. The attempt failed and the Crown was set on a collision course with the Irish chieftains.

Sir Edmund Butler led the opposition to the removal of chieftaincies. He, as did many other members of the Anglo-Irish element, believed that the attack on the chieftaincies would bring about a destabilisation of Ireland. In the face of such destabilisation, the Irish would break out of the lands they held and challenge their Anglo-Irish neighbours. It was feared that all the compromises and accommodations which the Irish and Anglo-Irish had reached over the years would be destroyed. Imperfect though the accommodation was between the two groups, as it had never ensured genuine peace in Ireland, Butler and his followers were convinced that the alternative being pursued by Sir Henry Sidney was infinitely worse. Butler had personally been a victim of the fluid new system. An English adventurer, Sir Peter Carew, had claimed lands from an Irish chieftain in Munster. An English court upheld his claim to the land, thereby evicting an Irish family who had held their lands for nearly half a century. The chieftains of Ireland were outraged by the implications of such legislation, while men like Butler, who had lost part of his barony as a result of Carew's court case, felt equally insecure.

Munster became the initial battleground in the fight for the control of Ireland. On one side were the Irish and old Anglo-Irish, while on the other were the forces of the Elizabethan crown and the new English adventurers who were looking to Ireland as a source of new riches. The Crown forces, concerned as they were that Ireland would be the launching pad for a Catholic insurrection, were aware of Munster's strategic importance. The ports of Munster traded regularly with France and Spain, among others – the very powers that Elizabeth feared. To control Munster was to block the easiest entry point of the Catholic invaders.

In the face of English intrusion into the affairs and traditional power balances of Munster, the Irish defence of the area fell to the Geraldines of Munster. The seventh earl of Munster had been executed in 1468, and since then, the family had refused to be seen as anything but Irish, and had spurned contact with the Crown. In the 1560s the head of the family was Gerald FitzGerald. Gerald was a weak man in both mind and body. After a minor but far from unusual argument with his neighbour Sir Edmund Butler had ended in warfare, Gerald was summoned to London. He was punished by Elizabeth for taking a private army into battle and sent to the Tower. Into the void left by Gerald's imprisonment stepped Sir James Fitzmaurice.

Fitzmaurice was driven to take action not only because of the imprisonment of his cousin Gerald. He was also a vehement opponent of Protestantism and was thoroughly ill disposed towards any English government intrusion into the affairs of Munster. Although Fitzmaurice's opposition to Protestantism may have been more of a personal driving force, he knew well enough that he could not galvanise popular support around his cause on that issue alone. Initially he recruited support around the issue of the removal of the land by the Crown. The emotions of his supporters were boosted in 1570 when the Pope excommunicated Elizabeth, and absolved her subjects from the duty to obey her. Fitzmaurice could now lead a force that was united in its desire, related to both land and religion, to drive the English from Munster.

The Fitzmaurice campaign was successful while it faced only pockets of resistance. They took land and property easily, but seemed intent on destruction rather than acquisition. Hurt by the failure of Philip II of Spain to help him in his rebellion (Philip did not believe such an escapade could be successful), Fitzmaurice was then faced by the force of Sir John Perrott. Elizabeth had dispatched Perrott to Munster with the expressed aim of regaining control of the region. Despite the skill of Fitzmaurice and his troops, and their superior numbers, Perrott, like Strongbow before him, had the advantage of superior technology. For Strongbow in the 1170s it had been suits of simple armour; for Perrott in 1571 it was the use of the most modern cannons and guns. Perrott quickly subdued the whole of Munster and defeated Fitzmaurice's men. By 1572 the Irish troops had been forced to submit to those of the English.

Desmond FitzGerald was released from the Tower in 1573, and, once back in Munster, became a focus for renewed protest; but it was to be a short-lived outburst of dissension. Faced by the forces of the new deputy, Sir William Fitzwilliam, Desmond, like Fitzmaurice before him, submitted. In 1759 there was another brief outburst of Munster intransigence when Fitzmaurice landed at Dingle with a small foreign force. As before, Fitzmaurice failed and this time was killed in battle. In 1580, Desmond sacked Youghal in one last defiant act, but he, like Fitzmaurice, was defeated. He was beheaded by his captors and the rebellious province of Munster fell quiet.

The defeats of Fitzmaurice and Desmond effectively ended

any dissension against English rule in Munster. In 1580 and 1581 the area was plagued by a terrible famine. This, combined with the cost of the Fitzmaurice and Desmond campaigns, and the harsh nature of English justice once it had taken control of Munster, reduced the province to servility. The sheer human cost to Munster of its sufferings reduced the number of its men to a bare minimum. Munster could no longer fight. With such a depleted and servile population to control, the English could finally enact legislation which had been on the statute book, yet ignored, for years. A president was appointed to control the province, with a council and court of its own. The rule of English law and the religion of the Protestant Church were rigidly enforced. Munster offered a model for how Ireland could be subdued.

The suppression of Munster, although a victory in the military sense for England, brought about many transitions which would shape the future of Ireland in the long term. Although many of the Anglo-Irish families and some of the Irish sided with the Crown during the Munster rebellion, the process of conquest by the English predominantly forced the two groups closer together. In the face of the new English who were arriving on the back of the Elizabethan campaigns, it became clear to the Anglo-Irish and the Irish that they had more in common with each other, and that neither of them had any commonality with the invaders. The two groups had so much that was shared with respect to culture, values and history that to fuse fully was only natural. Of great importance in this fusion of the two races was the question of religion. Although both the Anglo-Irish and the Irish had, at different times, proclaimed their loyalty to English monarchs, the one constant in that ever-changing relationship had been their adherence to the Papacy. With the onset of the Reformation, especially the manner in which it was enforced during the Elizabethan years, links with the Vatican and the preservation of Catholicism became increasingly important. This was now rein-forced by the arrival in Ireland of Jesuits from the continent who went out into the communities and brought about a committed devotion amongst the Irish, a sense of devotion and belief that had always been missing from the process of Anglicisation. As opposition to the tactics of the Elizabethans grew over issues such as land ownership, military incursion and law enforcement, so the practice of Catholicism became an important part of resistance and a way of preserving cultural traditions. The experience of Munster during and after its rebellion was that religion served to both define and widen the differences between the Irish and the English.

Following the suppression of Munster, only Ulster provided a major stumbling block on the path to Elizabethan domination of Ireland. Connacht came to Elizabeth without any strong resistance. Connacht was dominated by one family, in the shape of the earl of Clanricarde, who accepted English rule. Despite occasional resistance, Clanricarde stayed loyal throughout his life, and on his death in 1582, was succeeded by his son, Ulick, who continued the allegiance to the monarchy. In the mid-1580s the development of English rule in Connacht was made complete when the English system of land ownership, titles and succession were introduced and accepted.

Ulster was far more problematic than Connacht. Like Munster, Ulster had to be won by the English, and the battle for control was especially long and bloody. Following the demise of Shane O'Neill, a twin system of rule had developed in Ulster. The Irish parliament had accepted the succession of Hugh O'Neill to parts of Shane's lands, which he ruled from 1569 as the baron of Dungannon, and as the earl of Tyrone from 1587. Hugh O'Neill was seen to represent loyalty to the English crown in Ulster and had connections with the English court. The remainder of the land was in the hands of Shane's cousin Turlough, who ruled in the manner of an Irish chieftain and who was observed by the English with a wary eye.

Hugh O'Neill, on the basis of his actions following the granting of lands to him, was a loyal English servant. He had done nothing to upset the rule of the Crown in Ulster. He had never challenged the position of Turlough, had attended the parliament when called, and had even travelled south to fight against the Munster rebels. But, O'Neill, despite the veneer of loyalty and respectability, had other plans. He understood the English well, having been educated in Kent, and yet had an affinity with the Irish. No matter what his title may have been, baron or earl, Hugh owed his position and his support to the Irish. He lived his life in the style of an Irish chieftain and did not develop English manners or customs. The use of his troop-raising powers was evidence of his attitude to his rulers. Elizabeth had granted him a force of six hundred men, which she would pay for, after his help with the Munster situation. If Hugh had been as loyal as was supposed, then these troops would have been kept ready only for use in support of the Crown. Hugh, however, used his powers and the finances provided by the Crown to develop an Irish army. He drafted a new group of six hundred men into his army every year and trained them all in the use of modern weaponry. As each year passed his potential army became bigger and better trained. Since he was seen as loyal and compliant by the English, they failed to realise that a potential force of resistance was developing in their midst.

In 1591, Monaghan was taken over and divided, under the rule of English law, after the local chieftain had been executed for taking cattle. Fermanagh was the next county to come under pressure from the forces of Elizabethan expansion into Ulster. The local chieftain, Hugh Macguire, rebelled when they attempted to force a sheriff on the county. In the face of such a rising, which was at first on a small scale and highly localised, O'Neill was expected to support the Crown and assist in putting the rebels down. With the massive forces which he had developed, Hugh's army would have easily and quickly completed such a task. The difficulty for the English was that Hugh did not want to unleash his army against a fellow Irish chieftain and such a near neighbour. By 1593, Hugh was in a powerful and, for the English, potentially dangerous situation. He had an army that numbered over fifteen thousand, connections with the Scots and close contacts with Philip of Spain. The connection with Philip was especially symbolic. It placed any intrigues which O'Neill might enter into on a far higher plane than the local rebellion being carried out by men such as Hugh Macguire. To seek contacts with Philip brought Ulster into a situation where it could pose a serious threat to England – especially as such connections were driven by a mutual loathing for the English Crown and a mutual belief in Catholicism.

The Macguire rebellion was given extra force by the intervention of Hugh O'Donnell, from Donegal. Red Hugh, as he was known, fought his first engagement against the English who had been sent to subdue Macguire near Enniskillen in summer 1594. Red Hugh's troops were victorious and Ulster entered a period

of genuine, province-wide rebellion. It was still unclear what
O'Neill would do, but the actions of the English pushed him into
making a decision. He learnt that the English were sending a
massive force to take control of the situation. For O'Neill this
provoked real concerns. A large English force might subdue the
whole province, enforce the strict rule of English law and bring
about the effective end of his power in the area.

O'Neill made his decision and threw in his lot with his fellow
Irish. He used his massive force to destroy large parts of Ulster
and to drive the English colonists to the safety of the towns or
back into the Pale. The English troops sent against the rebellious
Ulstermen were easily defeated and appeared ineffective against
the tactics of the forces under O'Neill. The chaos created by the
rebellion was added to when Red Hugh took his forces west in
Connacht, attacked the resident English and encouraged the Irish
to rise. The people of Connacht, who had seemed so peaceful
and acceptant of English rule, had no qualms in rejecting their
masters and returning to traditional ways.

With most of Ireland to the north of Dublin in open rebellion,
and with English forces seemingly powerless to stop the destruction which Hugh O'Neill and his allies were causing, the twists
and turns of events in the late summer and autumn of 1595 seem
incredible. As the most successful fighting Irish chieftain for
generations, who had managed to bring about a unity of purpose
amongst his fellow countrymen which had never previously been
witnessed, O'Neill gave it all up and requested that the English
grant him a pardon for his ruinous activities. However, he used
the smokescreen of his suing for peace to transport even greater
numbers of arms and weapons into Ireland, many of which came
from his Spanish allies. In August 1596, royal officials met with
O'Neill and granted him his pardon. Amidst the celebrations of a
successful peace, a dangerous situation was coming to a head.
Hugh O'Neill, using his allies in Ireland and beyond, was
becoming a direct and dangerous threat to Elizabethan power in
Ireland. The English did not have the forces or the resources to
defeat him and could not risk deposing him. Any power vacuum
would be far more destabilising. O'Neill was growing stronger
with each passing day. Unlike many chieftains who had gone
before him, O'Neill was patient and understood the nature of the
power with which he was confronted.

Crown forces, who were only too aware of the threat posed by O'Neill and his allies, especially the threat of a resurgent and well-armed Catholicism supported by the Spanish, regrouped and waited to attack. They made the decision to attack in 1597 under the guidance of the deputy, Lord Brough, and were again roundly beaten by Hugh O'Neill and his fellow chieftains. Constant victory was all very rewarding but what did O'Neill actually want and what did he hope to achieve? In discussions which followed the defeat of Brough's forces, O'Neill outlined his demands. He wanted the removal of all English officials and forces from Ulster, the restoration of all lands to their rightful and traditional owners, a full pardon for himself from the Crown, and the recognition of Ulster as a county palatine, which he would rule. All these demands related to conditions on the ground and were essentially to do with land and power. If the demands had stopped there it is possible, although perhaps not likely, that the English would have agreed. If O'Neill had never again stepped outside of this Ulster which he envisaged, then such a situation might have been considered as a way of ensuring a lasting peace. The demands were, however, underpinned by an idea which meant, in all likelihood, that O'Neill would face perpetual opposition from the English. He demanded that the Irish be given freedom of worship, which meant the right to practise Catholicism. In stating such a demand O'Neill was repudiating the work of the Reformation in Ireland and allying Ulster with the religion of England's sworn enemies. Such a cancerous body could not be allowed to exist within Elizabeth's Ireland. While O'Neill championed Catholicism, he threatened not only the security and safety of Ireland, but also that of England.

Such demands, as abhorrent as they were to the English, had to provoke a response. In the summer of 1598, the English sent four thousand men into Ulster. Near Armagh, O'Neill's forces killed three thousand men of the English force, and trapped the remainder. Simultaneously the Irish rose in Connacht, Leinster, in the Pale and in Munster. Ireland was in a state of full-scale rebellion against English rule, and all those who rose pledged themselves to the support of O'Neill. He had placed himself in a position where he could be considered as strong and as powerful as one of the traditional High Kings. He had united Ireland behind three clear goals: the rejection of English rule, the defence of Catholicism and a reinstatement of Irish traditions.

In the face of such opposition from her Irish subjects, Elizabeth had to take steps to retake the country. Her problem in previous campaigns against O'Neill was that her commanders had always misjudged the strength and skill of the Irish forces. It had also been difficult for Elizabeth to commit the high level of resources necessary to defeat the Irish, as she had been at war with Spain since 1585 and this had entailed the dispatch of forces first to the Low Countries and then to France. However, by the second half of the 1590s, the situation was so severe that Ireland had to be a priority. The earl of Essex, Robert Devereux, was appointed the deputy for Ireland and dispatched to retake control from O'Neill. Heading the largest army ever to enter Ireland, numbering some sixteen thousand, Essex still had an intensely difficult task. A problem was quite simply where to start? The Irish Council members demanded, quite selfishly, that he begin his campaign in Leinster and Munster as that was where the bulk of their land was. These two areas, although in need of recapture and in rebellion, were not the strongholds of O'Neill and his forces. In travelling south to recapture these two provinces, Essex opened the Pale up to attack from O'Neill, and he plundered it with impunity. The journey south also depleted Essex's own forces. O'Neill and his followers had done such a thorough job in destroying the land and the crops that an army the size of Essex's, which relied on plundering local fields and stores, could not survive. Desertion and sickness were the norm for Essex's soldiers, and thus, from the day of his arrival, his forces became increasingly inefficient and unlikely to succeed. He was victorious in the south and managed to retake control of most of Munster and Leinster, but resistance here was weakest as he was not fighting his true enemy. When he turned north, on the orders of Elizabeth, Essex had only four thousand men left in his army.

Once faced with the reality of O'Neill, the size and skill of his army and followers, Essex knew that he could not force a military victory. The two men met near Dundalk after O'Neill had sent Essex a message requesting, yet again, a pardon for his behaviour. Essex, believing that he had won back enough of Ireland to please his Queen, felt that a truce with O'Neill would be the best he could achieve. He travelled back from Ireland to the court in London where he was sent straight to the Tower. Elizabeth believed that Essex had not followed her orders and in failing to remove O'Neill was effectively guilty of treason.

Following the departure of Essex from Ireland, O'Neill and his followers retook most of the lands liberated by Crown forces. Elizabeth had no choice but to honour the truce granted by Essex, and O'Neill used the period of truce to strengthen his forces still further. Despite the calamity which had accompanied Essex's mission to Ireland, and the abject failure with which it had ended (O'Neill was still in power unmolested), Elizabeth felt compelled to try again. This time it fell to Lord Mountjoy to attempt to win Ireland for the Crown. Mountjoy realised that simple military conquest through a series of pitched battles in the open was not going to work in Ireland anymore. O'Neill was too strong and too firmly entrenched for those tactics to be successful. The Irish had to be conquered and then dominated, if the recapture of Ireland was going to be anything other than short term.

Mountjoy began by capturing and building forts at Ellogh, Cullmore and Derry. The forces used to capture these sites were large, and strongly backed up by a fleet of ships. The forts, once built, were quickly peopled so that they became strong and oppressive symbols of the English presence. These early successes in 1600, achieved as they were without major battles, had the effect of breaking the Irish alliance. Those living under the large garrisons, such as the previously troublesome Red Hugh, had no choice but to surrender to Mountjoy.

It was not only the building of strong garrisons in the heart of Ulster that caused the coalition, which had formed around O'Neill, to collapse. Alongside the campaign of Mountjoy, two other English armies attacked Ulster, one from the direction of the Pale, the other from Connacht. The English were ruthless and stopped at nothing. When O'Neill's forces attacked the Pale in an attempt to divert attention from Ulster, the English allowed the Pale to suffer so that the breaking of Ulster was not slowed down. Crops and livestock were destroyed, so that O'Neill's forces could not be fed, and the morale of the domestic population was dented.

O'Neill's allies became fewer by the day and more of Ireland,

and more importantly, increasing parts of Ulster, were placed under English jurisdiction. The only hope for O'Neill was that his Spanish allies would come to his rescue. The Spanish did arrive, but rather than joining directly with the remaining areas in Ulster or Connacht where O'Neill was strong, they landed in Kinsale, too far to the south to have any real impact. Once they were established in Kinsale a standoff developed. The Spanish remained in their camp, surrounded by the waiting forces of Mountjoy, who were in turn ringed by the men of O'Neill and Red Hugh (who had once more taken up against the English). On 25 December 1601 the situation came to a head when Mountjoy's forces, half starved and demoralised from such a long siege, broke out from their camp and attacked O'Neill. The Battle of Kinsale was over by mid-morning. The English surprised and defeated the waiting Irish and decimated their number. The Spanish stayed at Kinsale and did not enter the fray, leaving the Irish to their fate.

Red Hugh left Ireland and travelled to Spain, whereas Hugh O'Neill went to ground again back in Ulster. He finally submitted to the power of Elizabeth in 1603 in front of Mountjoy, and he was later granted his lands back and restored to his title of earl. This time, however, he and all other Irish chieftains had to live under English laws as noblemen. The day of the Irish chieftain had finally passed. The old customs and laws of Ireland, which had ruled the different chieftains and kings, became obsolete and only English law ruled over the country. That law was underwritten by the royal administration in Dublin Castle. The destruction of the chieftains meant that many aspects of Irish life, which they had guaranteed and perpetuated, slipped into obscurity. The brehon laws were left unused, and the lifestyle which accompanied Irish local courts, the bards and harpists, became fewer in number. There were some continuities which survived the defeat of the Irish under O'Neill. The Irish language remained the most commonly used form of the vernacular, the Catholic religion remained as the most practised amongst the population and violent dissent against English rule, although muted, did not disappear. In one of those quirky coincidences which plague history, the submission of O'Neill to Mountjoy as the representative of Elizabeth took place on 30 March 1603, shortly after the Queen had died. The Elizabethan era had, almost in its last minutes, witnessed the submission of Tudor Ireland to the English crown.

THE PLANTATIONS

The English had long realised that they could not merely suppress the Irish and hope to rule by force alone. The only true way to dominate a country was to settle it with their own people. In the years following the Strongbow excursions, the English had sent adventurers to Ireland with a view to settling it, but these settlers adopted Irish habits and eventually became disloyal to the Crown. For the Tudors the situation was even more complex than that of their Norman predecessors. The state had to find, and then encourage, people to move to Ireland. Not an attractive prospect considering the country's reputation for warfare and chaos. The investments of those who might try to settle had to be made secure by the Crown. Again, there was enough evidence for any prospective settler that land ownership and investments were far from secure in Ireland. The greatest difficulty was religious. In pre-Reformation Ireland, the settlers and Irish, as different as they were culturally, at least had religion in common. With at least a degree of commonality, it is easy to understand how, and why, integration eventually took place. For the Tudors the situation was totally different. The English were Protestant, the Irish were Catholic. To settle in Ireland was to settle amongst a different people who held directly opposing religious beliefs. In such a situation it is difficult to see how there could ever be a process of integration. If the settlement of Ireland was to be seen as a success by the English crown, then enough loyal subjects would have to be placed there, so that a critical mass of self perpetuating Protestants could translate any conquest of Ireland into a situation of permanent control.

The process, which was known by the term 'plantation', began in a systematic way after the suppression of Munster. The defeat and death of Desmond meant that an astonishing 500,000 acres of land were placed in the hands of the Crown. To pass that land on to another Irish chieftain, even one who had an English title and promised to obey English laws, was to risk the emergence of another disloyal Catholic chieftain in Munster. It was deemed safer to divide the lands between English settlers. The plan for Munster was that the land would be split into 2000-acre plots, each of which would support 86 houses. In theory this would produce a loyal and Protestant population in Munster which would obey English law and follow the state religion. The population would number in excess of 8000 people. The problem in Munster was that the theory and the practice were far apart. The land was divided up unfairly, and speculators who were interested in money, rather than in the defence of the realm and religion, dominated. Also, many of those who were granted lands were absentee landlords, thereby perpetuating an all too common problem. By the time of Hugh O'Neill's rebellion, there were fewer than fifteen hundred people settled as a result of the plantations. They were too few in number and too weak to defend themselves and many were quickly driven off by O'Neill.

The defeat of O'Neill heralded a quite different, and more dynamic, process of plantation, which would have an enormous impact on the future history of Ireland. The scale of plantation at this time would be far greater than that attempted in Munster. The main reason why such a large-scale attempt at plantation could take place was as a result of an episode known as the Flight of the Earls. Despite having his lands and titles returned to him, O'Neill remained understandably suspicious of how the Crown might treat such a treasonous subject in future. In 1607, he was summoned to London. Acting on his supporters' fears that such a trip would lead to his imprisonment or execution, he was persuaded to flee from Ireland. In September 1607, O'Neill, accompanied by ninety other leading members of Ulster's elite society, left the country and settled on the continent.

This act of self-preservation, driven though it was by paranoia, meant that all those who left Ireland in the Flight of the Earls were charged with treason and had their lands confiscated. The government began to think about using this land to underpin a process of plantation, but was driven into action by the abortive and minor rebellion of Cahir O'Doherty in 1608. Despite the absence of O'Neill and the other earls, there were still those in Ireland who would rise up against the Crown. The only permanent way to secure the future stability and peace of Ireland for the Crown was to colonise the country through a full-scale process of plantation.

In 1609, the Articles of Plantation were passed by Parliament. The legislation allowed all land which had been forfeited by men such as O'Neill and Cahir O'Doherty, and other land that was forcibly taken from those Irish who had remained, was to be used for plantation. In effect some 500,000 acres were made available. The actual plans drawn up to facilitate the process of plantation were similar to those used previously in Munster. Land was defined as either that which could be cultivated, and was therefore profitable, or that such as bogs, which was not. Those planters who undertook to move to Ulster were to be granted 2000 acres of profitable land and whatever else they needed of non-profitable land. Within their boundaries they could construct a castle or some other defensible structure. Below these undertakers, there were two further groups who could take land: loyal servants of the Crown, who received 1500 acres, and the deserving Irish, who were granted 1000 acres. The granting of the actual land was the practical act of plantation, but was not the core principle. It was not worth giving away land to planters unless their ownership and cultivation of it was in the long term, and their allegiance while on that land was to the Crown. Assimilation with the Irish was not the aim of the plantations: distinctiveness and control were. The planters had to swear an oath to the supremacy of the Crown and the Protestant religion, which thereby made them ideologically loyal. They were allowed to raise an army and form a garrison. Their army was, like themselves, loyal to the Crown. By being able to raise an army the planters were being given powers to preserve their own position in the face of Irish incursion or challenge to the holding of their plantations. No Irish tenants were allowed on plantation land, indeed they were supposed to be driven off the land. This step again reinforced the purity of the plantations and reduced the risks to their continuation.

As with so many English schemes, the plantations did not develop exactly as envisaged. Despite the Flight of the Earls and the military victory over the Irish, the government found it hard to persuade either English or Scottish families to cross the water to Ireland and settle there. The old fears of Irish rebellion, and the insecure tenure of land, discouraged many potential planters. To try and bolster the situation and not rely so heavily on individuals, the newly crowned monarch, James I (reigned 1603–25), turned to business to save the plantation process.

In 1609, the City of London formed a company specifically to carry out the plantation of the area between, and including, Londonderry and Coleraine. The favourable deal which the City was given afforded them an easy route to riches. The City turned to quick and easily maximised profits, rather than endeavouring to fulfil the political function of the plantations. While they got rich, the plantation was left incomplete. By 1619 corruption was rife within the City plantation, the two towns were only partially built and defended, and the land between them poorly settled. The families who did make the journey to Ulster were far from confident, and preferred to take rent from Irish tenants, rather than work and people the land themselves, a step that flew in the face of the whole idea behind the plantations. Quick cash profit was more secure than any long-term investment in the land. Outside the comparative security of the cities the process of plantation fared even worse. The land between Londonderry and Coleraine had been divided into twelve units; one for each of the City livery companies. Across these lands the colonists were thin on the ground. Irish tenants were the norm, and many of the colonists chose to hold their lands as absentee landlords. The plantation in this area, although a rigorous process in the legal sense of granting land ownership to new settlers, did little to change the actual situation on the ground. The Irish, although dispossessed of title, still occupied their lands as tenants and those colonists who chose to settle their lands faced the constant threat of attack from those disaffected Irish who had taken to the woods. These wood-kerns, as they were known, grew steadily in number following the period of plantation, as many of the Irish tenants could not afford the excessively high rents that many of the absentee landlords had chosen to charge. The more their number grew, the more unstable they made the whole area of the City of London plantation.

While the area remained unsecured, the prospects of attracting a greater number of colonists were unlikely, as the risks were too great. If it were to succeed, plantation needed to be a complete process, one that altered the land-ownership patterns across Ireland, but also brought about the peace and stability necessary to ensure its long-term future. For this to happen, the leaders of plantation schemes, and their political overlords, had to decide whether they would achieve the necessary peace by accommodating the native Irish and the Old English, or by violent suppression of those dissident groups.

The only successful model of plantation that existed at the start of the seventeenth century was that which spread across Antrim and Down and had been undertaken unofficially by Scots. The relationship between the Scots and the north-eastern tip of Ireland had been constant since the arrival of the gallow-glasses. In the mid-fifteenth century the McDonnells had established themselves in Antrim. The presence of the McDonnells in Antrim and Down became important in the context of wider British monarchical politics at the turn of the seventeenth century. Those Protestant Lowland Scots who had fled the 1599 and 1607 rebellions of the Highlanders, sought refuge with, and were welcomed by, the McDonnells. On his accession to the throne, following the death of Elizabeth, James I recognised the welcome that the McDonnells had afforded the Lowland Scots. He confirmed their ownership rights over all their lands in Antrim, and in 1620 made the head of the family, Sir Randal McDonnell, earl of Antrim. Despite following the Catholic faith, the McDonnells were the embodiments of successful planters. They governed their region successfully, they were loyal to the Crown and were welcoming to members of the Protestant faith. An obvious reason behind their success was the sheer longevity of their presence in the area. The planters of the 1600s could not afford such a luxury. They had to make an immediate impact.

The need for immediate success was best demonstrated by Hugh Montgomery and Sir James Hamilton. They were given royal support in the pursuit of a private plantation that covered other parts of Antrim and Down. Within a few years of their arrival, Montgomery and Hamilton had created a model plantation. For those who considered travelling to Down or Antrim from Scotland and elsewhere, Montgomery and Hamilton could offer them a peaceful landscape, free from local opposition, dominated by Protestants and with a network of flourishing markets and industries. The reason for their success? Between 1602 and 1603, the English army led by Sir Arthur Chichester, that had been sent by Elizabeth to quell the Irish, had systematically killed all the Irish in large parts of Antrim and Down. This meant that when Montgomery and Hamilton arrived, they occupied and planted a vacant landscape. For them, plantation was a secure and prosperous process; completely at odds with the experience of their fellow settlers in Derry.

In May 1613, James called together an Irish parliament, the first to be held for many years. There were many issues that James needed resolving, and he wanted the whole process conducted with as little opposition and displays of rancour as possible. The issues that brought the parliament together were representative of the future of Ireland: the debates surrounding land and religion. In 1613 the most straightforward issue for Parliament was to secure the Acts of Attainder against those earls who had fled in 1607 and to ratify the changed nature of land ownership across large parts of Ireland. The more complex issue, was that of religion. Elizabeth had failed to alter the religious beliefs of Ireland. The Protestant Church had failed to make inroads into the hearts and minds of the Irish population, and its only true strongholds were amongst the settlers. Despite the regressive legislation that had been passed against Catholics during Elizabeth's rule, such as fines for attending Mass, and the expulsion of all priests in 1585, Catholicism was as strong as ever. Priests continued to work amongst their communities, and the population observed Mass. The failed attempt by Elizabeth to destroy Catholicism in Ireland had produced an important realignment: both the native Irish population and the Old English settlers had the Roman faith in common. In the face of religious persecution they had become one and the same. Despite any differences that may have existed between them historically, the Irish and Old English were driven together by the attacks on their religion and by their displacement at the hands of the new settlers. In line with the general spirit of anti-Catholicism and the growing Puritanism of the established Protestant Church, the 1613 Parliament was expected to place on the statute book a new, and increasingly regressive, penal code against Catholics.

The previous parliaments called in Ireland had included a majority of Catholics, both Irish and Old English, but in 1613 such a parliamentary makeup was untenable for the Crown. In the lead up to the 1613 Parliament new boroughs were created, especially in Ulster, which would generate new seats for Parliament. By taking such a step the Crown administration in Ireland had effectively rigged the parliament so that it would have a Catholic minority in a country whose population was overwhelmingly

Catholic. When assembled, the new parliament was comprised of 24 Protestants and 12 Catholics in the Lords, and 132 Protestants and 100 Catholics in the Commons. If the parliament went ahead on those terms it would have a free hand to pass any legislation, no matter how regressive, that the Protestants wished it to.

The coalition of the persecuted, between the Irish and the Old English, came fully together in the face of such provocation. The Catholic members of the Lords and the Commons refused to recognise the new boroughs that had elected many of the Protestant members, or the government-selected speaker. Under- standably, they walked out of Parliament. In the face of such an impasse the parliament was prorogued and the issue of the new boroughs readdressed. While the forces of the Crown wanted to establish Protestant supremacy in Ireland, they realised that they could not do so without some attempt to work with the Catholic majority. A new parliament was called together in October 1614. The Protestant majority in the Commons had been reduced to eight seats. While the Acts of Attainder were passed, the regres- sive and blatantly religious legislation was not even included in the parliament's business.

The parliament had clearly demonstrated that the elite Catholic population of Ireland, Irish and Old English, was still a powerful bloc that could not easily be defeated. It was also quite transparent that James, in proroguing the parliament, was unwill- ing to force through legislation that would completely alienate the Catholic population. The government had no choice but to look again at plantation. If the Irish could not be defeated legislatively, and there was no stomach for another attempt at military suppression, then they would have to be swamped by a planted Protestant population.

In an attempt to revive the plantation scheme, James unleashed the lawyers. Crown claims were made against large tracts of land across Ireland. The idea was simple. The Crown would legally prove that any given land had formerly existed as Crown land. The current owners would be removed if their claims were found wanting. To placate those who could not satisfactorily prove their ownership of the land and to compensate for their losses, the Crown gave them a new title and re-granted three-quarters of their land back to them. The net result was that the Crown had a quarter of the land available for plantation. As with so many other schemes, it failed to achieve the desired results across Ireland. Many of the Irish and Old English landowners were understandably nervous about the prospects, and then the reality, of losing a proportion of their lands, and this did little to endear them to the planters. As other schemes before it, the James plantations were seen by many potential settlers as solely a means of making a quick profit. They did not remain in Ireland to nurture their lands, but instead accepted Irish tenants, thereby defeating the very object of plantation: to produce a Protestant population. Some of the schemes, such as in Munster, were successful. Those plantations that worked relied on the driving force of a key individual – in the Munster case Richard Boyle – but such men were few and far between.

The death of James in 1625 ushered in a key period in Irish history. The various intrigues that would lead the English into Civil War, and the short-term rejection of monarchy, would have a profound and lasting effect on Ireland. Although the external forces that would shape events in Ireland were many and varied, the key issues remained the same: land and religion.

An ongoing theme of the rule of Charles I (reigned 1625–49) was the war between England and Spain that James I had begun. A constant fear for Charles, as for Elizabeth before him, was the loyalty of Ireland: would they choose to support Catholic Spain over Protestant England? Rather than deserting the cause, the Catholics of Ireland, and in particular the Old English, saw a great opportunity. They offered Charles a subsidy of £120,000 that he badly needed to continue with the war. As well as offering clear proof of their loyalty to the Crown, the Old English seized the opportunity of winning favours from Charles that had been denied them in previous decades. Charles agreed that in return for his subsidy, the Old English would receive benefits, which were known as the Graces. These ensured that claims for land would not be pursued, the habit of charging Catholics recusancy fines would be dropped, and the demands made by the Oath of Supremacy would be relaxed. For Catholics, Charles's problems had afforded them an opportunity that shored up their position within Irish society. The Protestants were understandably horrified by the Graces. For them it undermined the position they were slowly establishing, and halted their opportunities for self-enrichment and the expansion of their land holdings.

The nature of the deal that Charles had offered the Old English meant that it could have altered the progress of the Protestant incursion into Ireland. In offering the Graces to the Old English population, Charles had intimated that the Graces would become an article of law. This was not, however, to be the case. In 1634, Charles's deputy in Ireland, Thomas, Viscount Wentworth, called a parliament ostensibly to place the Graces on the statute book. Wentworth was not interested in the Graces. He saw Ireland as a potential source of huge wealth, and as a country that should be Protestant and subservient to the greater interest of England. He followed the pattern of the 1613 Parliament and made sure that the Protestant members of the Commons and the Lords were in the majority. The business before the parliament was straightforward: first, the granting of a subsidy to the Crown, and secondly, the legal recognition of the Graces. Wentworth's thinking was equally direct. He believed, quite rightly, that the Catholic members would vote heavily in favour of the subsidy in the belief that they would then, having proved their loyalty, have the Graces ratified. In the event, the Protestants voted en bloc, and only a small number of the minor Graces were made into law. All those that were considered central to the Old English, and dealt with the land, were denied.

Having achieved the result he desired in Parliament, Wentworth set about changing Ireland into the country he had envisaged. The key ideal that underpinned all Wentworth's thinking, was that the process of plantation had to succeed if Protestantism was to become the major religion in Ireland.

Wentworth was well aware that previous attempts to colonise Ireland had failed, and that he had to act in a far more systematic manner if his plans were to succeed. He had a meticulous eye for detail, and no part of the Irish administration was ignored during his time as deputy. His first major action following the parliament was to begin the plantation of Connacht. Using the legal system to his own advantage, Wentworth pursued the Crown's claim to the lands of the earl of Clanricarde. In a one-sided court case and with a jury that had been threatened, Wentworth won the day, and half of Connacht was taken for plantation.

Alongside the gathering of land for plantation, Wentworth set about challenging many of the established power bases in Ireland so that they would pose less of a threat to the smooth running of his programme for Ireland. Richard Boyle, the earl of Cork, was ordered to return land he had taken from the Church for himself. In addition he had to pay a large cash fine. Lord Mountnorris, a leading figure in the collection of Irish customs, crossed Wentworth. For his troubles Mountnorris lost his job as vice-treasurer.

In 1639 Wentworth was recalled to England by Charles so that he might deal with a prospective threat to the Crown from Scotland. Wentworth was a much-disdained figure. He was impeached by the English parliament, and the London mob demonstrated against him. As a pawn in the struggle between Charles and his parliament, Wentworth was expendable. He was executed on the King's orders in 1641. While Wentworth had been hugely unpopular amongst many segments of the Irish population, he had at least managed to keep the country in order. With his departure there was no equally strong and willing figure that could take his place in governing Ireland.

In 1641 was witnessed the most serious outbreak of violence and rebellion across Ireland for decades. The obvious difficulties that Charles was facing in his Crown–Parliament relationships, and the long-simmering resentment that the Irish felt towards English rule, was a lethal brew. In October 1641, the Irish in Ulster rose against the English planters. The rising was a bloody and brutal affair. It took on a life of its own, and it became clear from early on that the Irish had no sustained plan of campaign. Planters' homes were attacked, their goods taken, and the Planters themselves were killed or driven off the land. Many towns in Ulster were taken and sacked by the rebellious Irish. By the end of the 1641 rebellion it was estimated that approximately 10,000 planters had been killed by the Irish. The very factor that had given rise to the rebellion, Charles's problems with Parliament, conspired to lengthen the rebellion. The parliament was unwilling to send an army to Ireland to quell the rebellion. It feared that such an army might show loyalty to the Crown in any future Crown–Parliament struggle. The fight against the rebellious Irish was left in the hands of the Protestant earl of Ormond, who raised a small army in Dublin from those men who had fled Ulster. They were finally joined, before Christmas 1641, by just over 1000 English troops, and in April 1642 by a force of 2500 Scots. This force, slowly, but surely, was able to reclaim the land that had been lost in the rebellion, and slowly began restoring order.

Despite the military successes of the combined English–Scottish forces in Ireland, the situation was to take a profound turn for the worse. Charles's struggle against parliament had finally broken out into civil war in England. Alongside the struggle in England, there were three major forces at work in Ireland. The first was the army led by Ormond, that had put down the rebellion. He was a dedicated royalist and constantly attempted to use Ireland as a way of bolstering the fortunes of Charles. Second, were the Ulster Scots: they were driven largely by their religious beliefs and demanded that the supremacy of Protestantism and their own political might be enforced on Ireland. The third, and most complex group were the Old English. While they had taken no active part in the 1641 rebellion, they had been harshly punished because of their adherence to Catholicism. In October 1642, the Old English established the Confederation of Kilkenny and demanded the recognition of their religion, the restoration of their land, and an independent Irish parliament. From the ending of the 1641 rebellion, until the execution of Charles in London in 1649, these three elements were locked in battle. They were not solely fighting an ideological war between each other in Ireland, but were active players in the overspill from the English Civil War. At different times throughout the 1640s, Charles made promises to each group in a desperate attempt to win support, and to secure troops for his own campaigns against the Parliamentarians in England.

In retrospect it is clear that the 1640s were a disastrous period for Ireland. So many of the forces of division that had bubbled under the surface for decades were allowed to emerge in an angry torrent. The debates over land, religion, the rights of an Irish parliament and the nature of plantation all became the watchwords of the campaigns of the 1640s. These campaigns were, however, futile. No one group emerged victorious, and all sides lost thousands of men, women and children in vicious fighting. The constant dislocation of people and property meant that there was no stability, and the only safety that people could find was among their own kind. Lines of division were sharpened rather than blurred.

It was for the figurehead of Parliamentarian authority, Oliver

Cromwell, to try and stamp his authority on Ireland. The first Parliamentarian soldiers, the Roundheads, had arrived in Ireland in 1648 and taken control of Dublin after the surrender of Ormond. In the late summer of 1649, Cromwell himself arrived in Ireland with 3000 cavalry. His mission was a simple and straightforward one: the destruction of the barbarous and Catholic Irish and the promotion of the hardworking Protestant population of Ireland.

Cromwell's first task was to take Drogheda, which was defended by 2000 troops under Ormond's deputy, Sir Arthur Aston. Cromwell's use of the most modern forms of warfare, and his long experience gained in fighting a civil war, meant that Aston had no chance of victory. By the end of the siege of Drogheda, little remained of the city; over a thousand of the inhabitants and those who had sought refuge lay dead. In the wake of the collapse of Drogheda most Irish towns and cities freely surrendered to Cromwell. There was some resistance, such as that in Clonmel, but the defence of Ireland was a futile exercise. By 1652, Henry Ireton, who had been left in charge of Ireland after Cromwell's departure, had taken control of the whole of Ireland.

Once Ireland had been subdued, the Cromwellians had to return to the same issue that had long taxed the previous English rulers of Ireland: how to ensure a lasting peace? Their plan was a reinvention of plantation. This time however, there would be no legal machinery that would attempt to tease segments of land away from the Irish or the Old English. The Cromwellian plan, epitomised by the 1652 Act of Settlement, directly took two-thirds of the Irish landmass for plantation. Put more simply, all land, with the exclusion of Connacht, was reserved for English planters, with Connacht reserved for the Irish. Ireland was mapped and the plans for plantation meticulously drawn up. The Old English and Irish who had played any part in resisting Cromwell were ordered to be across the river Shannon and in Connacht by March 1655 at the latest. The depleted population of Ireland that emerged from the chaos of the 1640s numbered no more than half a million. By the middle of 1655, a tenth of that population had been forced to leave their homes and journey to Connacht to make way for the new planters.

Despite such a rigorous and blanket removal of the dissenting

Irish from the best land, the new planters envisaged by Cromwell did not arrive and his scheme largely failed. Those of Cromwell's soldiers who had been granted land at the end of the campaigns in 1652 preferred to sell their land to their superiors. For them, cash in the hand was preferable to a hard and uncertain life trying to make a living in Ireland. For others, who might have been tempted to Ireland, the opening up of the colonies of the New World offered far rosier prospects and greater wealth than travelling to Ireland. Despite the reorganisation of land ownership by Cromwell, and the sweeping changes he made in Ireland to allow plantation to succeed, it failed in the short term because insufficient numbers of Protestant planters were prepared to risk living in the uncertain surroundings of Ireland.

The long-term prospects for Cromwell's plans were finally dashed in 1658 when he died. The English experiment with non-monarchical rule quickly foundered, and in 1660, Charles II was brought from exile to sit on the throne (reigned 1660–85). Rather than attempting to drive through Cromwell's changes in Ireland and endeavouring to make plantation work, Charles opted for a policy which restored the pre-Cromwellian position. Much of the land that had been granted to Cromwellian soldiers was returned to its former owners. The anti-Catholic legislation that had been enacted by Cromwell, including the notorious £5 reward for anyone bringing the authorities the head of a Catholic priest, was reversed. Much of the legislation enacted by Charles was clearly an attempt to bring his Irish citizens back in from the cold; to ensure their position within their own country. Unfortunately for Ireland, many of the positive aspects of Cromwellian Ireland were also cancelled out. Cromwell had introduced legislation that allowed Ireland to trade freely with England. Free trade had brought about a level of prosperity for many Irish farmers that had previously been unattainable. Such legislation, by changing the nature of the economic relationship between Ireland and England, also offered Irish agriculture an incentive to build for the future. Charles reversed this legislation in 1666 to protect the English farmer. In doing so he destroyed the developing Irish cattle business at a stroke.

Charles had no legitimate male heir of his own, and on his death in 1685, his brother James II (reigned 1685–9) succeeded to the throne. Usually transition from monarch to monarch offered few prospects to the bulk of the Irish, but James II was different. James was a Catholic. For the Catholics of Ireland, James offered great hope. The period prior to the death of Charles had suggested a portent of what might be to come. In preparing Ireland for James's succession Charles had instructed that Protestants be replaced in the major civil posts by Catholics. Unfortunately for the Catholics, the signs of great hope amounted to nothing.

Opposition to a Catholic monarch in England was near absolute. Protestants in England invited James's Protestant son-in-law, William of Orange, to travel to England and claim the throne (reigned 1689–1702). In the winter of 1688 William landed in Newton Abbott in Devon with a large army of men. The reaction to his arrival was swift. By the start of 1689 William had been proclaimed King, and James had fled to exile in France. England, Scotland, and thus by implication, Ireland, were once more parts of a Protestant kingdom.

James did not accept his fate lightly. He chose the lands of his faith to make his stand against the Protestant challenger for his crown. In March 1689, James gathered his French allies along-side his Irish followers in Cork. He travelled quickly to Dublin, where he gathered more support and a yet larger army. His arrival in Dublin, and the rapidly changing situation, brought together an Irish parliament to discuss the issues of the moment. For the first time in living memory, the parliament was domi-nated by Catholic members. With the apparent security of a Catholic monarch marching with an army behind him, the Catholic Parliamentarians set about cancelling years of anti-Catholic legislation. The Patriot Parliament, as it became known, denied the right of either the English parliament or its law courts to legislate for Ireland. Free religious choice was established across Ireland. In practice this legislation completely under-mined the legal place of the Protestant Church of Ireland within the country. Beyond establishing its own freedom from England and from the Protestant religion, the Patriot Parliament attacked the various pieces of land legislation that had been put in place since the mid-seventeenth century. All Acts of Settlement that had allowed for the large-scale appropriation of land to the Protestant settlers were cancelled, and the land of 2000 Protestant landowners was taken away for redistribution.

The Patriot Parliament, while enacting legislation that is perhaps understandable in view of the history of its members' treatment at the hands of Protestant-dominated parliaments, was hugely problematic for James. It was one thing for the deposed monarch to be taking arms in open rebellion against William, but at least he could claim some legitimacy: he had legally succeeded to the throne. James had always been careful to couch his campaign in terms of reclaiming what he saw as rightfully his. He did not portray his campaign as a religious one, and avoided making public pronouncements that were openly antagonistic towards Protestants. The Patriot Parliament, however, could only be viewed by Protestants and forces in England as violently opposed to them, and openly embracing of Catholic domination. If there were any doubts before the parliament sat of Irish motivations, and the nature of James's campaign, the legislation put in place sealed their collective fates. The Irish generally, and James specifically, were pro-Catholic, and thus by definition treasonous.

For his campaign to succeed, James needed military successes in Ulster, thereby striking at the very heart of Protestantism. In search of such a symbolic victory James marched his army on Londonderry. The citizens of that town, despite being offered terms by James, elected to resist and the siege of Londonderry began. The 30,000 residents of the city had dwindling food stocks and no chance of breaking out from the city. The forces besieging the city were equally immobile. They were a largely untrained force, and certainly did not have the military knowledge or ability to break a city as well fortified as Londonderry. The only ways that the siege could be broken were either if an outside force relieved the city, or if the city residents were broken by starvation.

In besieging Londonderry, James drew William to Ireland. If William was serious in his intention of ruling Britain and Ireland as a Protestant kingdom he would have to come to the aid of his loyal servants; in doing so he could also destroy his enemy. The siege of Londonderry had an important effect on the military campaign between James and William. For James it meant stalemate and immobility. He could not concentrate on capturing and dominating the rest of Ireland while he was stuck beneath the walls of Londonderry. William, meanwhile, was afforded vital time by the siege to collect an army together and to plan his campaign. William's forces first arrived off Londonderry six weeks after the siege had begun, but their progress down the river Foyle to the besieged city had been blocked by James. William's forces stationed on the river had brought the necessary supplies to break the siege and feed the population of Londonderry. Without access to the city and the ability to break the siege, the English had to idly wait. The siege dragged on for a further seven weeks. The sheer length of the siege, and the dwindling resources available to all involved, meant that the siege could go on no longer. In the face of their own shortages, the presence of the English forces on the Foyle, and the resolve of the city dwellers, James and his army withdrew from the walls of Londonderry. It was a major, and highly symbolic, victory for the forces of Protestantism.

In June 1690 William finally arrived in Ulster in person. He was able to survey an army over 35,000 strong. James had reinforced his army with 7000 French troops and the two large forces met on 1 July 1690 by the river Boyne. It was a landmark battle in the history of Ireland, and one that became a legend that still lies at the heart of Ulster Protestantism. James lost the battle, and finally, after centuries of effort and failure, the forces of Protestantism finally established their supremacy over the ranks of the Irish Catholics. James fled Ireland quickly and quietly, and any organised resistance against William was complete. The battles that dragged on into 1691 were predominantly local affairs that allowed William's forces, step by step, to control the whole of Ireland and defeat all the different Irish regional leaders. In October 1691 the last stand, made by Patrick Sarsfield, earl of Lucan, at Limerick, came to an end. He surrendered and made terms with William's forces.

The surrender of Sarsfield produced the Treaty of Limerick. The agreement had two main clauses. The first allowed any of the forces that had fought for James and the Catholic cause safe passage from Ireland to the continent. Many thousands of Irish troops, and the bulk of the Irish gentry, took advantage of this part of the treaty. The Flight of the Wild Geese was more catastrophic than the Flight of the Earls at the start of the century. The numbers involved in the Flight of the Wild Geese were far higher, and the sheer range of Irish gentry who decided to leave

Ireland meant that there was no elite force of potential Catholic resistance remaining in Ireland. Their land was formally confiscated and made available for plantation. The second part of the treaty made allowances for religious toleration for all remaining Catholics in Ireland. Although William was quite amenable to the idea, the Irish parliament, now a uniformly Protestant body, was not. When law confirmed the articles of the Treaty of Limerick in 1697, the nature of religious toleration envisaged by Sarsfield was radically altered and did little to benefit Catholics or secure their position in Irish society.

The twists and turns of sixteenth- and seventeenth-century politics proved ruinously damaging to the Irish. The Old English had been left alienated by a crown to which they claimed allegiance, yet could not reconcile with its religion. The Irish held a declining position across the period, and what little status they had continued to deteriorate. The process of plantation that brought Protestants to Ireland went in fits and starts, and was often unsuccessful or poorly executed. By the close of the seventeenth century, Protestantism, although in no way numerically superior, held all the key cards. Catholics owned only a small fraction of the land, the bulk of their elite had banished themselves into permanent exile and their religion was barely tolerated. Protestants held the best land, had access to the wealthy English financial and trading markets, had proved themselves loyal to the Crown and occupied all the positions of political and judicial power. Ireland was a changed nation, yet it would continue to transform itself and offer new challenges throughout the next century.

3

. . . .

From King William to the
Act of Union, 1692–1800

The period that followed the Flight of the Wild Geese ushered in a century of Protestant ascendancy in Ireland. Throughout the seventeenth century the administrative and legislative machinery of Ireland had slowly been built up to replicate the English model. Although severely dislocated at times by the instability that existed in Ireland, the machinery did slowly take hold and replace all other forms of administration and law. Those English and Scots who were located in Ireland were loyal to their crown, faithfully followed the Protestant religion and celebrated the Battle of the Boyne as the symbol of all they represented and all the stood for. The problem for the Protestant settlers in Ireland was that they were slowly marginalised by their London-based parliament and crown. Throughout the eighteenth century, the Protestant settlers in Ireland took control of the country and, to all intents and purposes, prospered. Although not becoming Irish in the manner of the Old English, centuries earlier, the settlers developed a sense of nationalism during the century that allied them increasingly to an ideal of Ireland as somewhere separate and distinct. They preserved their religion and their belief in the monarchy, and did not go native through intermarriage or religious liberalism: they did, however, develop a Protestant nationalism that sought legislative independence from the interfering London parliament.

The period of the Protestant ascendancy is a complex part of Ireland's history, and one that explains many of the subsequent ideological themes that informed and shaped the development of separatist Irish nationalism in the nineteenth century. One of the most central problems for the ascendancy, a problem that will be constantly evident throughout this chapter, was how to square the developing ideal of a separate Irish parliament with a firmly held belief in the British crown and the Protestant religion. Would two such apparently opposing beliefs lead to fractures in the developing strength of the ascendancy?

The story of the ascendancy is one that stretches across the whole of the eighteenth century. Following the upheavals of the 1690s, the more immediate concern for the Protestant population of Ireland was to secure their safety and dominant position in the long term. That Protestants controlled the land, in the wake of the Flight of the Wild Geese, was without question. What they looked for, in the short term at least, was an ending to the signs of toleration that had been evident in the Treaty of Limerick and that appeared to be a feature of William's early years on the throne. The first Irish parliament since the ending of the threat from James, met in 1692. The parliament was vociferously anti-Catholic, and pushed such an agenda relentlessly. All members of the parliament took an oath that denied any vestiges of Papal power in Ireland, and they refused to accept the articles of religious toleration that were part of the Treaty of Limerick.

THE PENAL LAWS

The parliament of 1692 set the standards for the succeeding years. At parliaments in the later years of the seventeenth century and at the start of the eighteenth, penal laws were instigated against Catholics. The aim of such legislation was to ensure the subservience of the Catholic population in Ireland. They were laws that sought to hinder, rather than destroy, the Catholic religion. Under legislation passed in 1703, all priests had to be registered. More generally, all Catholics were excluded from politics, the army, the legal professions, the civil service and local corporations. Education was also tightly controlled so that all Catholic children had to be educated in Ireland, and only at institutions belonging to the Protestant Church. The aim of all this legislation was to place Catholics in an inferior position within society, and to deny them any access to power. One problem for any potential success of the seventeenth-century plantations had been that Catholics, in the shape of the Old English, had always retained access to political and judicial power. Such access was now denied them.

One of the key issues in Ireland had always been the control of the land. In the wake of the Flight of the Wild Geese, there was little land that was still held by Catholics, as the bulk of the gentry had fled to Europe. There were, however, some Catholic landowners who had refused to leave. It was against them that the legislation of the post-1690s period weighed most heavily. Catholics were prevented from gaining land from a Protestant. Any land that was held by Catholics could not be bequeathed as a single block: it had to be divided up between all male heirs. Such a process effectively meant that any Catholic-owned landed estates of any size, that could have been a launch pad to a level of political influence, could be broken up within two generations. As a result of the legislation many Catholic holdings were quickly reduced in size, so that they degenerated from being a sizeable interest, to being merely a holding of subsistence land. In the process of land transfer, religion became of the utmost importance. If the eldest son converted from Catholicism to Protestantism, he could inherit all the land as a single block. Equally, in any intermarriage between Catholics and Protestants, it was the Protestant relatives who would inherit the land. The laws relating to land ownership, and land transference, meant that throughout the eighteenth century the amount of land available to Catholics steadily decreased. As this happened their wealth, power and influence also diminished.

The penal laws, in their entirety, were aimed at preventing Catholics from being able to gain entry into the political power structure in Ireland. As a series of laws, they were largely successful in their stated aims. Although the laws were not strictly enforced across the board, and Catholics retained, throughout the eighteenth century, a huge numerical supremacy, their position was totally undermined. At the elite level, the Catholic gentry were excluded from public life, and they found it difficult to provide any resistance to the Protestant ascendancy by way of political leadership. At the common level, Catholics followed their faith, despite the legislation, by utilising the services of the thousands of Catholic clergy who inhabited the length and breadth of the country. Economically, Catholics took whatever work was available on the large estates, many of them travelled around the country looking for work, others eked out a living on small plots of land, while large numbers emigrated to distant shores. The Catholic population did not provide any sustained or effective resistance to the political power of the ascendancy in the eighteenth century, and neither did any size-able sector of it emerge as a distinct political grouping with an ideology or power base. The most important form of social resis-tance was the continued observance of the Catholic religion and a belief in the power of the clergy.

As a result of their obvious success, it is easy to see the penal laws as being solely aimed at the Catholic population of Ireland. The Catholic Irish were the biggest group in the country, and for the Protestants, had, traditionally at least, always been the most problematic. However, it has to be remembered that there was a third religious grouping in Ireland alongside the established Protestant Church and the Catholic faith: the Presbyterians. Located mainly in Ulster, and having origins that predominantly lay in Scotland, the Presbyterians remained outside of the estab-lished Church as dissenters. They had long been under suspicion in wider English society, and had been excluded from politics and local government in the second half of the seventeenth century. In Ireland the position of the Presbyterians had always been slightly easier. While the established Church remained suspicious of them, they could always be counted on for support against the Catholics. Throughout the upheavals of the seven-teenth century, the Presbyterians had proved themselves resolutely anti-Catholic, and were thus tolerated by established Protestantism as another bulwark against Catholicism. Despite their supportive anti-Catholicism, the Presbyterians were seen as a direct threat to the established Church and the Protestant mission in Ireland. The Presbyterians had a solid geographical power base in north-eastern Ulster. They had built and occupied many imposing and comparatively wealthy towns. They excelled in their businesses and were emerging as a powerful and successful mercantile class. These facts in themselves were enough of a challenge to the Protestant ascendancy based around the parliament in Dublin; a group more familiar with the linkage between land and power. The most serious aspect of the

Presbyterian success story was its religious separateness and fervour. The Presbyterians followed an independent creed, did not follow the teachings of the established Church, and were numerically strong. The ascendancy had to decide between toleration or repression.

Following victory at the Battle of the Boyne, the Flight of the Wild Geese, and the apparent lethargy of the Catholic population, the established Protestant population, those who dominated parliament, were in confident mood. They freely applied the penal laws to the Presbyterian population. The aim, as with the laws against the Catholics, was control and domination of any competing religion or ideology. The Presbyterians were excluded from public office and from sitting on municipal corporations. Their ministers had any elements of legal force that lay behind their services removed from them: they could not celebrate the Lord's Supper, they could not marry couples and nor could they conduct burial services.

The period following the upheavals of the 1690s witnessed a strengthening of the position of the established Protestant order within Ireland. At its most basic level, such a strengthened position was a direct result of the Flight of the Wild Geese and the sense of defeat amongst many Catholics. The penal laws reinforced the subservient position of the oppositional religions in Ireland, as both Catholics and Presbyterians were marginalised through the force of law. With the way cleared of any substantial opposition in the first half of the eighteenth century, the Protestant ascendancy tightly controlled Irish life so that their position as the most powerful group within society was unchallenged. The Protestant Church of Ireland was in a healthier state than it had ever been previously. There were few converts to the established Church from the ranks of Catholics or Presbyterians however, and it is clear that the Church of Ireland was never in a position whereby it claimed the majority of churchgoers across the country. Even the demands of the penal laws, and the active use of religious adherence as a yardstick for bequeathing land, did not produce a rush to join the Church. Despite all this, the church prospered because of its links with the English Church and its innately political nature. The government controlled the Church by constantly sending English bishops to take control of Irish sees. By involving itself so clearly in the activities of the

Church, the government reinforced the security of the Church of Ireland. There was no repeat of the confused and uncentralised control that was such a common feature of earlier years.

Alongside the emergence of a strong ascendancy Church in Ireland during the eighteenth century, was the development of a forceful and increasingly independent minded Irish parliament. This too was ascendancy dominated. Although the parliament was not representative of all shades of opinion and belief in Ireland, and its members were the products of many 'rotten' borough elections, its constitutional position was far clearer in the seventeenth century than it had ever been before. With the exclusion of Catholics and Presbyterians from public and political life, the only members of the parliament were Protestants. Despite this uniformity of religious identity, the Irish parliament of the eighteenth century was a highly complex body. There were no clear dividing lines between different interest groups along what would now be understood as party affiliation, although this was slowly developing in England at the time. Instead the Irish parliament was a body built around local groupings, short-term alliances and personal interests. Its main function within its constitution, and with respect of its relationship to Britain (as formulated under the terms of the 1707 Act of Union between England and Scotland) and the British parliament, was to heed the advice of the lord lieutenant who oversaw it, and to pass the biannual supply bills. The Irish parliament did not, unlike the British parliament, choose its own executive body.

As Ireland, although a monarchical democracy, was effectively a colony within the kingdom, it had the lord lieutenant as the representative of Britain imposed on it. This, in effect, curtailed its independence. The parliament also had no real independence of meeting. It was called together every two years primarily to approve the supply bills: grants of money from the Irish that contributed to the royal coffers. At the meetings of parliament the Irish gathered to do the bidding of the lord lieutenant, but also to pursue their own agendas and their claims for titles. The parliament, although a body that derived its powers from Britain, and whose allegiance was to the Crown and state religion, was not a blindly loyal institution. Within the parliament, indeed within society at large, there was an overriding interest in the Irish dimension of any legislation or activity that might emerge from within its walls. The Parliamentarians did not seek to serve only British interests they sought also to preserve their own areas and spheres of influence and to take care of Irish interests. The eighteenth-century ascendancy parliament, although hemmed in by the demands of the lord lieutenant and the requirements of Britain, was a fiercely independent body with Ireland high on its agenda.

THE EIGHTEENTH-CENTURY IRISH ECONOMY

One of the major concerns for the Irish parliament and the ascendancy, indeed all sections of Irish life throughout the eighteenth century, was the poor state of the Irish economy. There was a belief that there was nothing fundamentally wrong with the Irish way of conducting business, nor was there anything amiss with the actual structures of industry and agriculture. What the majority felt ailed Ireland was the effect of undue interference of British business demands on the Irish market. The concerns of Ireland were seen as secondary to those of Britain; as such, the interests of the Irish economy also came second. Why was there such a state of affairs? Following the accession of William to the throne, there had been a belief that the Irish economy would recover from several years of dislocation, and begin to prosper. After all, Ireland had a good range of natural resources, a potentially profitable land stock, an easy access to the trading lanes of the sea and a geographical closeness to Britain: it should have entered the eighteenth century as a rapidly growing economy. However, in the same manner that it controlled Irish parliamentary powers, Britain controlled and restricted Ireland's economic potential.

In 1699 the London parliament passed legislation that would allow the export of woollen goods, an important part of Irish economic production only, into England. Irish woollen goods could not be sold to any other country. Such legislation would have been damaging enough to the Irish wool trade if the traders were openly allowed access to the English market as the law suggested. This was not the case. Any Irish woollen exports into England paid such excessive duties that the English market had been effectively closed for years. The 1699 legislation destroyed

the Irish woollen industry at a stroke, as it was left without any
openly viable markets for its wares. The spirit of the legislation
set the scene for English attitudes towards Irish economic affairs
for the new century.

The 1699 legislation was a cause for concern to the ascendancy powers for a variety of reasons. There were the straightforward concerns that such a heavy blow to a growing industry
would have a wider economic effect on the country. This was
coupled with an increased realisation of how far the English
parliament would interfere directly in the affairs of Ireland. If
the English parliament, or at least powerful groups that exerted
influence on it, believed that the Irish posed an economic threat
to England, then the imposition of legislation would be swift. In
the case of the woollen trade, the English seemed driven by
commercial interests, that is, the threat to the English woollen
trade, but also by the prospect of an affluent Irish economy
providing an independent income for the ascendancy group in
the Irish parliament. To counter the dismay felt by the Irish over
the loss of their woollen industry, the English parliament encouraged the establishment of an effective, and mass scale, linen
industry in Ireland. The industry grew steadily over the eighteenth century and was helped by the influx of Protestant
refugees from France who were highly skilled in the trade, and
by the lack of competition in that particular sphere from
England. While contributing a large proportion of the total value
of Irish exports, and thus replacing the revenue that had been
lost with the demise of the woollen trade, the linen trade
possessed one important difference from the old textile trade.
Wool production had been a genuinely national business, and
had covered most of the country. While linen produced as much
wealth as wool, and employed a similar number of people, its
production was centred on the north of Ireland. This meant that
the effects of a prosperous linen industry were only felt on a
local, rather than a national basis. The wealth and power that
emerged from such an industry was concentrated in the hands of
the large, non-Catholic population of Ulster.

Despite the relative success of the linen trade in Ireland, its
concentration in one area, and the loss of the woollen trade,
effectively symbolised the problems of the Irish economy in the
eighteenth century, although this was not a situation that was

unique in Europe. In Ireland as elsewhere, there was no industry or business that could be developed rapidly that was truly national, and could bring about sustained levels of common prosperity. As a result the Irish were heavily dependent on agriculture; not only as a way of feeding themselves, but also as the sole method available to produce wealth for the country. This did not, indeed could not, happen. In the chaos and lack of direction that was such a feature of eighteenth-century Irish agriculture, lay the seeds that would produce, in part, the devastating famine of the mid-nineteenth century.

One problem that Ireland faced as the eighteenth century progressed, was common across Europe: a rapidly growing population. At the time of the Battle of the Boyne, and all the dislocations that had preceded it, the Irish population totalled no more than two million. By the end of the eighteenth century it had more than doubled to nearly five million – a figure that would grow even more rapidly in the first half of the nineteenth century. To support such a growing population, in the context of the eighteenth century, was not impossible. It is clear, from the experience of countries such as England and Holland, that an increased population, when accompanied by a modernising agricultural system, could feed itself and, for the most part, prosper. Why didn't this happen in Ireland? Surely a country that had good lands, a hard-working population, and one that was so geographically close to the modernising influence of England, should have been able to prosper. The problems in Ireland that prevented the land from feeding its population and creating a surplus of wealth were numerous. The single most important problem was the sheer scale of absenteeism.

THE LAND ISSUE

Absentee landlords had long been a common feature of the Irish landscape. The difficulties that had accompanied the process of invasion, repression and plantation meant that residence in Ireland was not an attractive prospect for those who had bought or had been granted land in Ireland. It was easier for them to appoint a middleman to administer the land. This usually meant that the estates of landlords were broken into smaller plots and rented out, at a very high charge, to the Irish. The absentee land-lord was then assured of an income, but free of the problems of developing the land, investing in it or having to live off it directly. By the eighteenth century, the problem of absentee landlords had reached a crisis point. Whereas the land in England was being improved and modernised in the eighteenth century, there was no concomitant development in Ireland. Those improving landlords that there were, formed the Dublin Society in 1731. They matched the developments in England, investi-gated new farming and land-management techniques, and sought to maximise profitability and yield. Their message, however, was not taken up on a mass scale. The absentee landlords did not care for such new techniques, as they involved investment, and the tenants were so unsure of their tenure, and so constantly close to the bread line, that the issue of improving their land was not an option for them.

With little or no improvement to the land, and an increase in the amount of land given over to pasture rather than arable farming, the agricultural conditions in Ireland in the eighteenth century continued to decline. A greater number of people, and less available land, resulted in smaller and smaller plots. What land was available for rent was subdivided to such an extent that tenant farmers were trying to make a living, and feed their fami-lies, on the basis of two or three acres of land. To meet their rent, tenants would have to work in paid employment, something that was not freely available, and sell the best of the crops they produced on their own land. In turn, such a state of affairs meant that the Irish tenants looked to potatoes as the major source of their diet. It was a crop that could be easily, and plentifully, farmed off a small plot of land. There was no margin for error however. With the tenants' labour and their best crops sold, the potato crop had to succeed. It was the lifeline of the tenants and their families. When the potato crop failed, as it did in the late 1720s, and again in the early 1740s, the effects were devastating. The tenants were dependent on single-crop agriculture and there was no available alternative. The failure of the potato crop in the 1740s cost tens of thousands of lives (contemporary reports talk of 400,000 dying of starvation), and offered a terrible portent of what was to come a century later. In the eighteenth century, a dwindling amount of land available for cultivation, an increasing population, the profit-driven perspective of absentee landlords and middlemen, and a lack of scientific application, all combined to make the condition of Ireland far worse.

In the face of such conditions of wretchedness, and the seeming unaccountability of the absentee landlords, it is perhaps unsurprising that the Irish began to take matters into their own hands. For some, the agrarian protests of the eighteenth century have been viewed as the first stirrings of nationalist protest within Ireland. Such a reading is to credit the various demonstrating groups with too much of a national vision. Eighteenth-century agrarian protest was concerned with issues relating to the land, and all the protests took place on a local basis. Although there were similar time-frames for many of the protests, and quite often a commonality in the methods of demonstration, there is nothing to suggest a national leadership or a unified cause behind such struggles.

The major originating focus for the agrarian demonstrations was the decision in 1759 to open the British market to Irish cattle. By the mid-eighteenth century, the growth in the British population and increasing demand on their own agricultural industry meant that it could no longer keep pace. Ireland offered a nearby, and easily controllable market, and so the previously high duties that had severely restricted the Irish cattle market were removed. Such a decision had a profound effect on Ireland. Landlords saw the opportunity for higher yields from the land, and a growth in profitability. The amount of pasture was increased massively and tenants were removed from the land. Many of the common lands that existed across Ireland, and probably ensured that families were able to make ends meet, were cleared and enclosed. In the middle years of the eighteenth century, Ireland was rapidly transformed from a land of cultivation into a land of pasture. The process only served to exacerbate the problems that already existed. The decision to open the British market to Irish cattle, and change with one action the very nature of Irish land management and usage, demonstrated once more the power that the London parliament had over Ireland. Sixty years previously it had chosen to destroy one Irish industry, wool, because it threatened English profitability; in 1759 it chose to create an Irish industry, cattle, as England needed more food.

Ireland was held and directed, economically at least, by the needs of Britain.

The response to the move to pasture, and the removal of tenants from their land, was the rise of the Whiteboy movement. Initially the Whiteboy movement, which in many ways mirrored similar agrarian uprisings in England, directed itself against the process of enclosure. However, it is clear that the move to pasture farming and the resultant creation of enclosures, was not the only grievance that the tenant farming population of Ireland had. The Whiteboy movement quickly developed a wider agenda against all agrarian grievances, which displayed itself in attacks on individual landlords, their agents and property. The Whiteboy movement spread rapidly across the south-west and midlands of Ireland. It was met with fierce and stiff resistance by the authorities, and was quickly extinguished as a form of potential mass movement. In mid-Ulster, the Oakboys, and in Antrim, the Steelboys, followed a similar course, and were met with an equally steely resolve. While the process of agrarian demonstration did not alter the course of the changes that were taking place across the countryside, it did show the tenant peasantry of Ireland that protest was possible. It was the lesson of protest that the nationalist movement of the late nineteenth century would learn from the Whiteboys and others, not any ideological or organisational methods.

Alongside the abject poverty that was such a feature of eighteenth-century Irish rural life, there was the steady growth of an affluent ascendancy lifestyle that was centred on the rapidly developing Irish towns and cities. Much of the revenue that was created in Ireland went straight out of the country, and into the hands of the absentee landlords. That which remained was centred in the hands of a small sector of the population. Because of the cheap availability of labour, and many raw materials in Ireland, as they were not being swallowed up by either the embryonic industrial or an intensive agricultural market such as existed in England, the wealthy in Ireland were able to indulge their whims on a grand scale. They built large and impressive Georgian mansions, planned-out town and city areas set around beautiful squares, maintained the leading city, Dublin, so that it could compete with many in Europe, and developed Trinity College Dublin as a centre of refinement and intellectual development. While many of the leading lights of Irish intellectualism left the country for England and elsewhere, others, most notably Jonathan Swift, remained in Ireland and articulated many themes that would become central to the political debates of the late 1700s. In the eighteenth century the bulk of Dublin's most appealing buildings, and its basic shape, that still exists to this day, was laid out by the elite ascendancy class. A similar process, albeit on a smaller scale, was witnessed in Belfast and elsewhere in Ireland.

The development of a wealthy, talented and well-to-do ascendancy class in Ireland was important in the creation of many artistic, literary and architectural forms that were central to Irish life. Such riches contrasted sharply with the extremes of poverty that existed across many parts of the country and created, in social terms at least, two Irelands. One was wealthy, educated, and began to demand power and recognition for Ireland and the Irish parliament; the other was poor, weak and concerned solely with the maintenance of life, not the attainment of political power. Such social division was not unique to Ireland – indeed, it was a common feature of contemporary Europe. In many parts of Ireland, however, such inequity would lead to changes and upheavals in the long term that were original. Despite the myriad of changes that were taking place in Ireland throughout the eighteenth century, and the small pockets of wealth that were being created, two important issues were clear and remained to be addressed by the Irish elites: finance and political power.

By 1770 it is estimated that the annual revenue created by all the different sectors of Irish economic activity amounted to approximately £1 million. It was clear that the bulk of such revenue was in the hands of a small number of people, but the problems of absenteeism, and royal and government allowances, made the situation with respect to the potential distribution of wealth across the whole of society far worse. After the revenue of the absentee landlords had been creamed off, and the commitments to royal and government pension lists met, only £300,000 of the total revenue remained in Ireland. While the remaining revenue allowed for the evolution of a high standard of living amongst the ascendancy class, it was not spread throughout Irish life. Financially, Ireland was little more than a colony. The British crown, its parliament, and its adventurous landowners and businessmen were using Ireland to create wealth, and then removing it to their own coffers elsewhere. Financially Ireland had no real self-determination, and neither could it take charge of its own affairs.

The other major unresolved problem was political. While the members of the ascendancy class were undoubtedly loyal to the crown of Britain and to the state religion, they were less than enamoured with their relationship with the British parliament. The Irish parliament had no real freedom to direct its affairs, was largely viewed as a revenue-raising house for the British, and as the experience of the wool, linen and cattle episodes had shown, was constantly undermined by the agenda of the London parliament. Any consideration of the difficulties between the British and Irish parliaments, has to be underpinned by an awareness that such difficulties, serious and complex as they were, consisted of a battle between members of the same ideological grouping. Those of the ascendancy class in Ireland were aggrieved because they did not have the same access to power as their counterparts in the British parliament. Beneath the ascendancy class in Ireland were other groups, the Catholics and the Presbyterian dissenters, who were initially excluded from the struggle between the two parliaments.

A DISTANT PARLIAMENT

The actual collision between the parliaments in the eighteenth century revolved around two parliamentary and legal issues: the right of the Irish parliament to legislate for Ireland; and the right of the Irish parliament to draw up its own supply bills, rather than having them dictated from England. The right to govern their own affairs had long been problematic for the Irish. While the lord lieutenant remained at the head of the parliament, as the agent of the Crown and the British parliament, Ireland could have no parliamentary independence. It could however, as it did in the 1720s, provoke a crisis.

In the 1720s Ireland was short of copper coinage. The contract for producing the extra coinage was granted to one William Wood of Wolverhampton. Owing to the poor quality, and the limited amount of the coinage that Wood produced, the initial

problem was not solved, and arguments over the way he had
been granted the contract began. The Irish parliament went into
open rebellion over the issue. It may seem strange that such a
relatively minor problem as the minting of coins could provoke
such excitement and sense of grievance. The whole episode,
however, has to be contextualised in the same way as the wool
issue: Britain's interference in an Irish matter. The coinage issue
was represented by many of the independently-minded ascendancy class as an illustration of Ireland's position of comparative
weakness in the face of Britain's legislative might. In the case of
the coinage issued by Wood, the Irish won the day. The complete
opposition to the lord lieutenant's desire to continue with the
grant, led to an inquiry, the revoking of Wood's contract and the
eventual recalling of the lord lieutenant. The crisis of copper
coinage demonstrated both the essential strength, but also the
inherent weakness, of the Irish parliamentary and ascendancy
cause. They could, when they operated as a single bloc, defeat
the will of the British parliament and thus act independently:
that was their strength. However, once the copper crisis was
over, the Irish Parliamentarians no longer operated as a single
bloc against the British parliament, and returned to their usual
routine of serving their personal interests and seeking self-
aggrandisement: that was their weakness.

The defeat of the lord lieutenant over the copper issue in the
1720s changed the way that the Irish parliament was to be run.
The British parliament, by altering the manner in which the Irish
parliament would be managed, secured, in the short term at least,
a higher degree of control. They relegated the position of the
lord lieutenant, so that although he still remained the most
powerful political figure in Ireland, he would no longer be
responsible for the maintenance of the government grouping
within parliament. This task was handed to a group of undertakers. These men were drawn from the leading figures in the Irish
parliament, and it was their job to see that the government's
work was done, and that the supply bills were passed. Although
such a change in the management of the Irish parliament may
appear to favour moves towards independent action within the
parliament, this did not initially happen. The undertakers were
given, in return for managing the parliament, the control of large
sections of the royal patronage in Ireland. For the Irish this

seemed a real advance on the old situation. In a period where the bulk of public, and patronage-based, posts in Ireland were being granted to Englishmen, the undertakers had some control, enabling them to switch direction and appoint Irishmen to positions of power. In all this, the Irish were blinded by their new power. For a period they were content to use the undertaker system to promote their own people, and pursue personal interests. What they did not seem to realise was that while they were given crumbs of power, they were quietly passing and agreeing to the bulk of legislation sent over from Britain. The switch in the style of management was assisting the British in their control of Ireland, while denting the ability of the Irish to form an independent-minded body politic within the parliament.

The failings of the undertaker system were demonstrated in the 1750s, when the Irish parliament demanded that it should have the power to distribute any surplus revenue that Ireland had created. The issue created great excitement across Ireland, and particularly in Dublin, while the parliament sat. The ascendancy class within parliament demanded independence of action, while the popular mass on the street backed their parliamentary leaders, as the revenue issue was symbolic of all that ailed the Anglo-Irish relationship. The undertakers led the campaign in the parliament, and joined with all the other members of the House in defeating the government in a vote. In this, the undertakers demonstrated how their position could be used to generate independent action, and how they, as a group, offered the parliament, indeed the whole of Ireland, an embryonic leadership for national independence. This was not, however, the case. The undertakers, as so many other potential Irish leaders before them, operated in selfish interest, not for the common good. The undertakers had been concerned that the primate of Ireland, George Stone, was becoming too powerful and was bypassing the Irish parliament as the central authority in the land. By stoking the fires of the revenue issue, and backing the mobs on the street, the undertakers demonstrated to the lord lieutenant, and to the government, how powerful they were. In the event, the undertakers struck a deal with the lord lieutenant, the revenue issue was solved and the popular masses were left without leadership or focus. Rather than bringing into question the nature of the relationship between the two parliaments, and pushing for

reforms that were favourable to the Irish, the undertakers acquiesced in the name of personal interest. They demonstrated to the
lord lieutenant not just how powerful they were but how they
could be trusted to control Ireland for the government, and were
duly rewarded with titles and land grants. Faced with such a self-
serving and self-interested undertaker system, Ireland, if it was
to achieve the parliamentary independence that sectors of its
society badly wanted, needed an independent-minded, patriotic
leadership.

The crisis in the 1750s over revenue, although settled in their
favour, demonstrated to the government that the undertaker
system could not continue. It was decided to replace them with a
resident lord lieutenant; someone who would be in Dublin on a
permanent basis and who would administer Ireland. By introduc-
ing such central control, the government hoped that the continued pressure for Irish parliamentary independence could be
thwarted. The first important resident lord lieutenant was Lord
Townshend, who arrived in Dublin in 1767. Townshend set about
his work with enthusiasm, and immediately broke the undertaker
system. In an attempt to engender some popular support for the
change in the parliamentary order, Townshend introduced a
parliamentary Act in 1768 that limited the life of the Irish parliament. Previously, elections had only been held on the death of a
monarch, and parliaments had then sat for as long as the new
monarch reigned. Such a system was not conducive to any idea
of accountability, nor did it engender popular enthusiasm for
apparently stale parliamentary affairs. The new system brought
about a greater interest in the business of parliament and
favoured the evolution of clearer political groupings within the
house: most notably the patriots.

The change in electoral process was well received, but would
ultimately count against the lord lieutenant, indeed against the
whole English system of administering Ireland. With a greater
interest in parliamentary affairs, the electorate generally, small
as it was, and the ascendancy class particularly, became acutely
aware of the injustices involved in the way Ireland was governed
and controlled by the demands of the British parliament. With
the arrival of a resident lord lieutenant, who was so visible
within the governance of Ireland as acting in the British interest,
the whole situation reached a point of potential crisis. The lord

lieutenant was symbolic of all that ailed Ireland from the patriot perspective: an Englishman governing Ireland in the interest of another parliament.

THE RISE OF GRATTAN

Townshend departed Ireland in 1772, having broken the power of the undertakers. His successor, Sir John Blaquiere, ruled the Irish parliament with a firm hand, and, from the English perspective, the resident lord lieutenant system appeared to be working as intended. The situation could not, and did not, remain static. In 1775, Henry Grattan entered parliament as the new leader of the Patriots. Grattan was a lawyer by profession, a member of the ascendancy and a man with a clear political vision. Grattan argued, as many members of the ascendancy did, that Ireland needed independence in its parliamentary affairs. This did not mean that he wanted complete independence from Britain, and he stressed the usual loyalty to the power of the monarch and the religion of state. Where Grattan was more aware than many of his counterparts, was in his attitude to the Catholic population of Ireland. He saw that no matter how wretched the condition of the Catholic masses, and how acquiescent they appeared to be, an independent parliament for Ireland could not simply ignore them. The potential for popular discontent, as shown by the earlier agrarian outrages, was always present. The parliamentary independence that the ascendancy dreamt of, could not exist in the face of a religiously divided Ireland. Grattan did not believe that Catholics should have political power; such thinking would have been untenable for a leader of any ascendancy party. He did accept, however, that Catholics should be free from the worst aspects of the penal laws, that they should have freedom of worship, and that their economic position should be improved.

Against the rise of Grattan and his reformist agenda, events overseas were beginning to shape opinions in Ireland. Throughout the 1770s legislation had been passed by the Irish parliament that improved the positions of Catholics, and for some at least, made their access to the land easier. Despite the attempts of the Irish parliament, the position of the Presbyterian dissenters was not improving at all. A bill in 1778, that had sought to remove the sacramental test, thereby improving the lot of the Presbyterians, was blocked by the Privy Council. In the face of such regressive action, which was part and parcel of a long tradition, many Presbyterians had chosen to look outside Ireland for their futures. In this many Catholics joined them. Representatives of both the marginalised religious groups in Ireland travelled across the Atlantic throughout the 1700s and settled in America and the Caribbean islands. Once overseas, many of them found wealth and power, which had been unobtainable in Ireland, and, most importantly for many, they found religious freedom. America became, as it has remained to the present day, the Promised Land for many Irish people. In the eighteenth century, letters from the American continent carried news back to Ireland of a new and better way of life. One of the reasons that America in particular was seen as a preferable location was for its sense of independence. The ideal of American political independence from England had grown throughout the 1700s, and had come to a head in 1775 when the American War of Independence began.

The American War of Independence is fascinating in terms of the effects it had on Ireland. It is clear from newspaper reports, public speeches and the declarations of the Patriots in the Irish parliament that the American cause struck a chord. Here were the Irish Patriots' fellow travellers: a group who had laboured under the same restrictive and financial demands of the British parliament, and had chosen to free themselves. For men like Grattan and many other Patriots the Americans were an inspiration. However, desiring parliamentary independence and fighting a war against the Crown were different things. While admiring the independent streak in the American action, and recognising many of the issues that had driven them to war, the bulk of the Patriots wanted to defend Britain and Ireland in such a potentially difficult situation.

During the late 1770s the British allowed the Irish parliament to pass a welter of legislation that they had long fought for: extra fishing rights, greater access to sea trade, extra relief for Catholic hardship, the removal of the sacramental test and the right to raise a militia. Britain was responding directly to Irish demands, in an attempt to head off any outbreak of pro-American or anti-British feeling. It was easier for Britain to offer

Ireland concessions to secure their loyalty in the war, than to lose their support. The allowance made by the British that the Irish could raise their own Protestant militia, was of key importance. France and Spain had joined the American War of Independence on the American side. For Irish Protestants and Presbyterians, any sympathies that they had for the American cause were held in check by a greater, and older, fear. Would the Catholic nations of Europe use Ireland as an entry point into Britain? Would such a threat stir up resistance to the Protestant ascendancy amongst the Catholic population? The ability to raise a militia, something that the British parliament had always disallowed for fear of rebellion, meant that the Irish Protestant population could meet any threat by itself.

The raising of the militia was a huge success, and was carried out with a religious fervour. By 1780 the membership of the militia, mostly armed and uniformed, numbered approximately 80,000. The militia brought together Protestants and the Presbyterian dissenters under the same flag, and many Catholics, despite their exclusion, chose to support the militia for the cause of the greater common good.

The rise of the militia demonstrates, yet again, the complex nature of the ascendancy's loyalty to Britain. The militia was raised and funded, with great speed and great enthusiasm, across Ireland so that the Protestant population could protect themselves and demonstrate their loyalty to the royal cause in the war. Once in place, the militia, and the unified sense of purpose that it engendered, was used as a tool of the Patriots to move against the British parliament, and strike for a better deal for the ascendancy. In 1779, the Irish parliament, led by the independently-minded Grattan, granted taxes to Britain only for six months, as opposed to the usual two years. He followed such a bold act by demanding that Ireland be granted free trade. In all this, Grattan was supported by his own Patriot party and the whole of the Irish parliament, many sectors of the Irish population, and, for the first time, sections within the British parliament. For Britain, Grattan's demands were unanswerable in any way but the positive. Fighting a war in America was draining enough; they could not risk open rebellion in Ireland, especially as the Irish parliament now had the massed ranks of the militia standing behind it. Ireland was granted free trade: all restrictions on wool, glass and hops were lifted, Ireland was free to trade with any country in the world that was not a British colony, and there they would only have to pay the same duties as goods from Britain.

It was a tremendous victory for Grattan. He realised, however, that he had to keep pressing his advantage home. What would happen when Britain completed her war against America? Would she suppress the demands of the Irish ascendancy once more? In February 1782, Grattan brought together 250 leading delegates from amongst the militia, now commonly known as the Irish Volunteers. The meeting, held in Dungannon, asserted Ireland's right to parliamentary independence. A week after the Dungannon meeting, Grattan put a Declaration of Independence before the parliament. There was no real hope that the Tory administration that held power in London would agree to such a bill. However, the Tory government fell, Grattan went back to Parliament, again presented his Declaration of Independence and demanded that it be recognised by the British parliament. In May 1782, the parliament accepted Grattan's arguments and repealed all the Acts that prevented Ireland being administered solely from Dublin. The Irish parliament would be the sole legislative body for Ireland, and no more could its sister body in London interfere. The Irish House of Lords was the supreme lawmaker in the country, and the only way that Irish legislation could be altered in future was by the King himself.

GRATTAN'S PARLIAMENT

The years 1782–1800 are commonly referred to as those of Grattan's parliament. It would be the last time that the whole of Ireland would have a single Irish-based parliament which governed over all thirty-two counties. As a result of the opening, overnight, of free trade with the rest of the world, Ireland entered a period of relative prosperity after 1779. Industries that had previously been stunted by customs duties and infringements on trade, such as the woollen industry, boomed and provided income and jobs. The change in Ireland's trading relationship with outside nations had a dramatic effect on the Irish landscape. Lands that had been used for pasture were turned over to crops, and more and more land was used for the growing of corn. Throughout Ireland, prosperity, in the context of what had gone before, appeared the norm. Some absentee landlords returned to their lands, and took an active interest in their estates, and the major cities continued to grow in size and splendour. For those in Ireland who benefited from the transformation in fortunes that Grattan's parliament oversaw, independence became firmly equated with prosperity.

The picture was not all rosy. Across Ireland, those poor tenant farmers, mostly Catholics, who farmed one- or two-acre farms continued to live in abject poverty. The prosperity that free trade engendered, only reached as far as those who had something to produce or sell on a large scale; for those who lived hand to mouth, nothing changed. The Whiteboys made a reappearance in Munster, and violent sectarian clashes were commonplace in Ulster, as Catholics and Protestants fought over the ownership of the land. These social problems were large-scale and common across Ireland. In the context of the improved status of the ascendancy class in Ireland under Grattan's parliament however, such problems appeared to be taking place only on the margins of society. Catholic tenants, although numerically the largest group in society, were largely invisible. As long as the ascendancy chose to ignore the conditions of the tenant farmer, and focus instead on their new-found freedom and prosperity, it merely postponed the inevitable moment when the degrading social conditions would encroach, with devastating results, on their world.

Inside Grattan's parliament the spirit of consensus that had won reform from the British parliament quickly disappeared. Henry Flood, who had lost his position of power with the rise of Grattan, led a vociferous campaign to push the reform programme further than Grattan and his supporters envisaged. While the demands of Flood were legitimate – he wanted to ensure that Britain had no power to bind Ireland, his campaign was imprudent as it only served to further alienate the British. Flood's demands did win a Renunciation Act from the British parliament in 1783, but there was little that he, or anyone else, could ever do to ensure the permanency of Irish parliamentary freedom. Britain was simply too powerful. While it was expedient for the British to agree to any reforms demanded by the Irish while they were waging a war in America, they could always return the status of Ireland to its original position if they wished. For all the advances that the Patriots made in the late eighteenth century, men like Flood never grasped the simple point that the Anglo-Irish relationship was not an equal one. In addition to illuminating the inherent difficulties in the Anglo-Irish relationship, Flood also alluded to one of the other central issues of Grattan's parliament: Who did it serve? Irish parliaments had, for too long, been driven by the demands of those that sat within them, and did not appear to have the interests of those outside at heart.

With the winning of the parliament and the concessions in 1782, Grattan had asserted his view that the Irish Volunteers should be removed from politics. They had, Grattan accepted, played a key role in winning freedom, but they should not play a political role in influencing the policy of his parliament. Flood argued against this. In 1783 there had been a Volunteer convention in Dublin. It made demands for a new constitution, in a manner that matched the Dungannon Declaration a year earlier. The calls for reform were presented to parliament by Flood, but the members refused to discuss any further liberalisation of parliamentary membership or accountability. The rejection of the Volunteers' demands demonstrated how quickly an apparently radical body had turned in on itself, its members preferring to pursue self-interest above the wishes of those men in the Volunteers who had supported them in their initial struggle.

Any discussion of reform would have to tackle a myriad of issues that had been subsumed in, and disregarded by, the whole history of the ascendancy throughout the eighteenth century. The Volunteers, although a movement of a uniformly Protestant membership, had been embraced by a wide range of support groups within Ireland, and contained an ideological agenda that stretched beyond the ascendancy mindset. Foremost amongst the supporters of the Volunteers had been the Catholic aristocracy, gentry, and slowly emerging middle classes. They had openly supported the cause of the Volunteers, and embraced their success and the establishment of Grattan's parliament. By the 1780s Catholics were in an anomalous position. With the slow repeal of the penal laws, the elite members of the Catholic faith had found it easier to rise to a position of financial security and many more of them were able to hold onto their land. Despite this, the laws that prevented Catholics from voting in parliamentary elections, standing for election or taking a seat still remained, as did restrictions on the right of worship or freedom of educational choice. Catholics, despite any economic progress that they may have been making, were disenfranchised.

The Volunteers had been broadly supportive of their Catholic backers and followers. The majority of them believed that any restrictions on Catholic worship, and education, should be revoked; but they were divided on the issue of granting Catholics political rights. Grattan, for example, believed in granting political concessions to the Catholics. However, such apparent liberalisation was underpinned by a constant reiteration of the ideal that the Protestant ascendancy should always be maintained. It was not difficult to see, in the context of the late eighteenth century, how such a seemingly contradictory belief as Grattan's could be accommodated. True, there were a number of Catholic landowners that would qualify for political rights, but these were a minority. While land remained the yardstick for entry into parliament, and the bulk of the Catholic population lived in abject poverty with no access to the land, the ascendancy position could not be challenged. The issue of Catholic representation, and of their rights to access to political involvement, would become a feature of Irish politics for the next century.

Alongside the possible turmoil that the issues of parliamentary reform and the status of Catholics threatened, and the continued existence of the Volunteers as a potentially populist and armed force, was a more basic and legalistic problem that Grattan's parliament had to face. What power did it actually have? In pushing for the reforms of 1782, Grattan and his followers had become centred solely on the issue of the Irish parliament, and its rights to make and pass legislation in a manner that was not answerable to London. What they had achieved in winning their 'freedom' in 1782, was the legislative independence of Ireland. What they had not secured, nor, it seems, understood, was the need for executive independence. Even during the apparently halcyon days of Grattan's parliament, the lord lieutenant remained. The lord lieutenant was the executive officer who effectively still administered the Irish parliament on behalf of the Crown and the London parliament. The lord lieutenant could still grant titles, offer bribes and call in favours so that important legislation, or rather legislation that was important to London, was passed.

On some issues, the lord lieutenant could not control the Irish parliament, and at times it proved a fiercely independent body. This again provoked problems. There were two parliaments in one kingdom. Bodies that should have been pulling the same way for the mutual greater good of Britain, involved themselves in petty gestures and point scoring. Such behaviour benefited no one and served, at times, to provoke a sense of crisis. In 1785, a commercial treaty that could have brought about increased wealth for Britain and Ireland was lost because the parliaments could not agree. Equally combative, was the Irish parliament's decision, in 1789, to recognise the Prince of Wales as the Irish regent when faced with one of George III's first lengthy bouts of apparent madness. Understandable as such action may have been in the face of the evident loss of the monarch to the demons of his mind, the Irish parliament's decision pre-empted a reciprocal piece of legislation by the parliament in London, and the recovery of George III. Grattan's parliament had effectively provoked a constitutional crisis before one existed.

Without engaging in counter-factual history, it is impossible to say whether the Anglo-Irish parliamentary relationship could have continued weathering such problems. It is clear that Ireland's parliament did face a serious problem while it did not have executive control of its own affairs. It is doubtful, however, that the parliament in London would have humoured the Irish for any length of time if the creation of potential constitutional crises had become the norm. None of these difficulties had to be faced. As so often in Irish history, events outside the island conspired to transform the situation completely. By 1800 the position of Ireland, constitutionally and legally, had changed in a manner that would have been unimaginable to Grattan and his followers in the 1780s.

REVOLUTIONARY FERVOUR: THE UNITED IRISHMEN

The event that changed the course of Irish history, in the late eighteenth century, was the French Revolution. The effects of events in France were cataclysmic for Ireland. The ideological underpinning of the Revolution, including demands for democracy, exerted a powerful pull on groupings in Irish society, who demanded similar reforms at home. On a wider level, the French Revolution pulled Britain into another European war; a war that necessitated extra troops being called from Ireland, and heightened military demands that Ireland be made secure. In such a period of emergency, Ireland faced a dilemma: to revolt and reform along the lines of the French experience, or to stay loyal to the Crown and the relationship with Britain. With such a stark choice facing Ireland, it was unlikely that Grattan's fragile experiment with legislative independence could weather the storm.

The reformist model that emerged from France in the 1780s and 1790s was most keenly embraced by the Presbyterians of Ulster. The key figure in the moves to duplicate the French experience was Theobald Wolfe Tone. The news from France enabled Tone, and many other Presbyterians, to see a new way forward for Ireland. They argued that the republican experiment in France, which challenged the established Church, should be duplicated in Ireland. In 1791, Tone argued that Catholics and Presbyterians should join together, refuse to pay tithes to the established Protestant clergy, and campaign for complete political reform which would, amongst other things, lead to the enfranchisement of the Catholics of Ireland. Tone's call to action found a practical outlet in Belfast. At a meeting of the old Volunteer clubs, led by Samuel Neilson, Tone's ideas were translated into a straightforward call for a union between Catholics, Protestants and Presbyterians, to be known as the Society of United Irishmen. On a practical level, Tone's political ideology should have appealed to all groups in equal measure. In the early years of the French Revolution however, this was not the case. While Presbyterians understood the appeal of French Revolutionary Ideology, they could not square this with the prospect of sharing land or power with Catholics.

In the 1780s, Ulster had witnessed the unfolding of a new wave of agrarian violence. In the wake of Presbyterian emigration to America, Catholic peasant farmers had rented the vacant land in many parts of Ulster. The remaining Presbyterians were outraged by the presence of Catholics on what they considered

to be their land, and demanded, through the intimidating force of
societies such as the Hearts of Oak, that landlords think twice
before renting their land to Catholics. The Hearts of Oak were
joined by the Peep o'Day Boys, who openly attacked and intimi-
dated Catholics who rented land. In response, the Catholics of
Ulster formed an organisation called the Defenders, to protect
themselves. Intercommunal violence continued unabated
throughout the late 1780s, and continued into the early 1790s.
The Defenders organisation spread across large parts of Ireland,
the Peep o'Day Boys flourished where they had local support,
and into all the chaos were thrown local militias, as the landlords
attempted to restore some semblance of order. The effects of the
agricultural depression, which accompanied the Anglo-French
war of the period, exacerbated the levels of intercommunal
violence of the 1790s.

In 1795, a key event took place in Armagh which, although
having a limited impact at the time, was of central importance to
the future history of Ireland. In September that year, the
Defenders attacked a much smaller force of Peep o'Day Boys. In
spite of their numerical weakness, the Peep o'Day Boys won the
day and the battle left many Defenders dead. To celebrate their
victory, the Peep o'Day Boys renamed themselves the Orange
Society, in honour of William of Orange and his similar victory,
as they saw it, over the forces of Catholicism a century earlier.
The Orange Society, or Orange Order as it is most commonly
known, was to become a key feature of Presbyterian resistance to
the forces of Catholicism in the nineteenth and twentieth
centuries. In sum, the period of the 1780s and 1790s witnessed
the first outpourings of organised and reciprocal sectarian
violence that would become such a feature of Ulster life. From
such chaos and bitter infighting, could Tone bring about any
semblance of unanimity for his cause?

The establishment of the United Irishmen in Belfast in 1791
had been mirrored by a similar development in Dublin. The
United Irishmen, although driven by the republican idealism that
was a feature of the French Revolution, and arranged around a
commitment to co-religious organisation, was primarily
supported at the elite political level by senior Catholic figures.
The fluid situation in Ireland, indeed across Europe, warranted
some immediate response. The British Prime Minister, Pitt, was

well aware that the position in Ireland needed addressing so that he could secure support against his greater enemy, France. In 1793 Pitt restored the parliamentary franchise to Catholics, by means of a Catholic Relief Act. In its entirety the Act swept away many of the regressive pieces of legislation that denied socially elite Catholics, at least, an equal place in Irish society. His thinking was simple. Although recognising that an ascendancy parliament would always resist the Catholic claim to franchise, the need to prevent a popular, active and dangerous organisation such as the United Irishmen from creating problems, and possibly allying itself to France in the war, was far more pressing. Following Pitt's wishes, the Irish parliament passed the Catholic Relief Act, with a two-thirds majority, but they voted against a motion that would have allowed Catholics to take a seat in the parliament. The passage of the Act, which restored parliamentary franchise to those Catholics who were qualified to vote, had ensured one thing above all else: the sole control, by the ascendancy, of an Irish parliament free from Britain, had ended. To resist British interference in Irish affairs, in the face of war against France, would be to ensure the rise of the United Irishmen and possible separation from Britain as a republic. To allow Pitt's direct involvement, as happened in 1793, was to signal the end of the ascendancy period.

The battle of the last years of the eighteenth century was between an Irish parliament that was desperately trying to preserve the rule of the ascendancy for an elite and minority group of the population, and a revolutionary group that wanted to change Ireland in its entirety. The war against France only served to heighten the problems in Ireland. The French saw Ireland in the same way as the British, as the possible weak link in the British chain of defence. In 1793, a French agent was dispatched to Ireland to make contact with the United Irishmen, in the hope that they could be turned to the French cause. An agent acting on behalf of British intelligence accompanied the French agent, William Jackson, throughout his trip to Ireland. Jackson was duly arrested and tried for treason in 1794. At his trial, Jackson implicated Tone as a leading light in the United Irishmen, and stated that Tone had been open to the idea of a French invasion of Ireland to assist his cause. On the basis of Jackson's testimony, Tone was seemingly guilty of treason. Tone struck a deal with the British, and rather than face trial himself, went into exile in America. Prior to his departure for America, Tone had one last meeting with his old colleague Neilson. The outcome of the meeting was that Tone was to pass on a message to the French Ambassador in Philadelphia, announcing the formation of a new and larger revolutionary force in Ireland that would be a combination of United Irishmen and Defenders. The hope was that the French, suitably impressed by such a large-scale force, would commit themselves to an invasion of Ireland.

In America, Tone contacted the French Ambassador. He was given the necessary introductions, and travelled to France to convince the powers there that Ireland was ripe for invasion. Tone spent nearly all of 1796 convincing the French that his scheme for an invasion of Ireland could be successful. His plan was quite simple. A large French invasion force would be met, and supported, by the United Irishmen. Once conquered, Ireland would form the launching pad for a French invasion of Britain, from which French domination of Europe would ensue. Tone was successful in his quest for support, and on 16 December 1796 he left France with a French fleet of ships and an army of 14,000 troops. Ireland was to be invaded.

The invasion became, as with so many threatening situations in history, a farce. Bad weather was a feature of the French fleet's journey to Ireland, and by the time the fleet arrived off Bantry Bay on 21 December, nearly a third of the fleet had returned to France. Once off Bantry Bay, the invasion force was spotted, and a messenger was dispatched to Cork to warn the authorities of the immediate threat. The bad weather continued throughout the Christmas period. As each day passed, more and more of the ships turned for home. The last of the fleet left Ireland's shores on the final day of 1796, having failed to put a single man ashore. Tone's French invasion was stillborn.

Tone had managed to organise the French fleet, and gather all the troops together without news leaking out. His arrival in Bantry Bay was a complete surprise. The simple fact that Tone had been able to amass such an impressive force, coupled with the inadequacy of the reaction in Ireland (a militia of 400 men was all that could be raised quickly), sent shock waves through-out the British hierarchy. The government had to ensure that they would be better prepared for any future invasion. One factor that had surprised them in 1796 was the apparent lack of support for Tone's fleet amongst the Catholic peasants. It appears that the peasantry, one group who might have been expected to find Tone's call for a republic appealing, had more basic fears in mind. They suspected that the French force were in league with the Orange Societies, and were bent, not on the establishment of a republic, but on driving Catholics off the land.

In some respects the suspicions of the Catholic peasantry were understandable. The United Irishmen's support was mainly based in Ulster amongst the young, radicalised and educated middle classes. They were drawn from all three of the main religious groupings, and were those individuals who had been denied access to any of the existing political power structures. In Ulster, the combination of the United Irishmen and the Defenders had produced a lethal brew that had, by the start of 1797, reduced the area to chaos. Members of the United Irishmen and the Defenders all wore national colours and proclaimed their support for the cause of a republican Ireland, yet many of them chose to use their radicalism to settle old scores and to claim land. In response, the government put huge numbers of troops into Ulster. These were regular troops, as well as Catholic militia and a Protestant yeomanry. Rather than solving the problem, and calming the Ulster countryside, the government forces became part of the difficulty. Instead of simply arresting and restraining known members of the United Irishmen and Defenders, the troops attacked all those they suspected. The cycle of violence in Ulster became utterly destructive through the course of 1797. In an attempt to ease the situation, Grattan introduced a bill that would allow Catholics to take seats in parliament, so long as they were eligible to stand, and were then successfully elected. The British, now fighting a European war, facing constant intercommunal violence in Ulster, and still concerned that Ireland might be invaded by the French, had lost all stomach for reform and refused to indulge Grattan. In an age when Parliamentarians were open to bribery, they bought the necessary votes and Grattan's reform was lost. He subsequently withdrew from Parliament. In 1797, Grattan eventually accepted what had been evident in 1793. When the stakes were high enough for Britain, his parliament in Dublin could never be independent.

THE 1798 REBELLION

At the opening of 1798, a year that would become legendary in the annals of Irish history, Ireland was divided, and in many parts was in a state of open warfare. The problems in Ireland were, with respect to personnel, internal, but were shaped by outside forces and external choices. One side wished to remain loyal to Britain. Across Ulster – the main hotbed of the violent struggle – the pro-government supporters included many Protestants, Presbyterian Orangemen and the Anglo-Irish. Ranged against them in the United Irishmen's camp were some fringe elements of the Protestant faith, many Presbyterian dissenters and a large number of Catholic tenants and peasant farmers. These divisions were echoed across the country, although the initial violence was nowhere as extreme as in Ulster.

A constant problem for the United Irishmen was how Tone and his followers could ever fashion a genuine cross-religious movement in the way they wanted. Certainly the events of 1797, and the early months of 1798, did nothing to build the necessary cross-community linkages around a common cause. Division, rather than a single anti-British and republican ideal, was the norm. In March 1798, the government arrested the main leaders of the United Irishmen, including its military leader Lord Edward FitzGerald. Considering that Tone's major French ally, General Hoche, had died in the autumn of 1797, and Napoleon had made it clear that he did not share Hoche's enthusiasm for an Irish adventure, the fortunes of the United Irishmen were at their lowest ebb. How could they ever succeed without French assistance and with their leaders absent?

The prospects of a successful rising led by the United Irishmen suffered a further blow during March and April 1798. Following the arrest of the main leaders of the United Irishmen, the government introduced martial law in Leinster. In seeking out members of the United Irishmen, the British instigated a reign of terror. Villages were attacked, men flogged and crops destroyed, until someone would name a member of the secret organisation. Once a name had been secured, the individual was rooted out and punishment freely given. In the face of such terror, the United Irishmen, the self-proclaimed defenders of Ireland, had to act. The national rising of the United Irishmen was set for 23 May 1798. The plan was for Dublin to be attacked, the machinery of government to be broken and Ireland freed. On the actual day there was only the weakest of risings in Dublin, as the local organisation was too weak, and this was swiftly suppressed. The United Irishmen did rise in Carlow, Kildare, Laois, Meath, Offaly, Wexford and Wicklow. The rising was poorly planned and weakly executed. The main targets for the United Irishmen were government troops, and anyone who was a known government sympathiser. In response, the army swept through any towns and villages that were known United Irishmen strongholds, and meted out revenge.

Ulster, the previous stronghold of the United Irishmen, should have been the centre of the rising. However, because of the ravages of the intercommunal violence, the loss of the United Irishmen's leadership to the British, and the failure of the French to assist, it appears that no one really had the stomach for the cause. Any violence that took place in Ulster was along familiar lines and across the communities, and did not contribute to the events of 1798 in any major way.

The losers in all this were the peasants of Ireland, whose cause was championed by no one, yet who suffered at the hands of both sides. The only place where the peasantry joined the rising in any numbers was in Wexford. The British believed that any French assistance for the United Irishmen would come ashore in Wexford. The county thus became labelled, in the minds of many members of the army, as the heart of the rebellion. The attacks on the locals by the army, the floggings and beatings, were far worse in Wexford than elsewhere. To defend themselves, many Catholic peasants rose. They equipped themselves with the para-phernalia of the United Irishmen, though it is not clear that they were explicitly organised behind that cause, or whether self-defence motivated them. Whatever the truth of the matter, Wexford became central to the story of the 1798 rebellion. The violence in Wexford was extreme, and often took on an inter-communal form. Many of the Catholic peasantry believed that members of the Orange Societies, and the army, wanted to destroy all Catholics, and in the minds of the other side, such apocalyptic fears were reciprocated.

In the early summer of 1798 the government forces won out. Under the command of General Lake, they acted with excessive cruelty, but such behaviour had become the norm on both sides. In an attempt to bring the rising to a close, and restore some semblance of peace, Pitt sent Marquis Cornwallis to Ireland. His job was to restore order to Ireland, and he was given the titles of lord lieutenant and commander-in-chief to enable him to complete the task. Cornwallis held executive powers that had not been witnessed in Ireland for years, but, rather than abusing such powers, he acted with clemency. He granted a general amnesty, and the chaos that had ensued in Ireland was officially drawn to a close by a declaration from Cornwallis on 17 July 1798.

Peace was not to last. Tone had watched the rebellion unfold from France and believed, or at least wanted to believe, that it had been conducted in the true spirit of the United Irishmen; all religions together in a common cause. Tone convinced the French that the rising in Ireland gave them the opportunity that they wanted. Duly, in August 1798, a French fleet with troops, supplies and arms sailed to the Irish coast. On 22 August, the first ships arrived off the coast of Mayo. French troops, under the guidance of General Humbert, took Killala. Humbert flew the green flag of the United Irishmen over Killala, and called upon the Irish to rise in the name of an independent and free Ireland. From such a promising start, the entire French expedition to Ireland descended, once more, into farce. Humbert was unable to engender an uprising in his favour amongst the Irish populace. Although the Irish greeted the Frenchman and his force, most were unconvinced that he could win any battle against forces loyal to the Crown. In the light of events earlier in the year, when acts of disloyalty met with a heavy price, most Catholic peasants were simply not prepared to risk violent retribution by joining a French campaign that was far from certain to succeed. Humbert, detecting the lack of fighting spirit amongst his supposed Irish supporters, cut his losses and surrendered. He left Dublin for France, shortly after his surrender on 8 September, with his forces intact.

Humbert was not the sole representative of French force who arrived in France during September 1798. On 4 September, James Napper Tandy arrived off Donegal, with arms and a small force of men. Hearing the news of Humbert's surrender, within days of his arrival, Tandy also chose to depart Ireland without loss of life or engagement with loyal British forces.

The final force that arrived in Ireland travelled to Donegal on 12 October 1798, and was led by Wolfe Tone himself. Tone's fleet consisted of ten ships and he had nearly 3000 men at his disposal. Tone firmly believed that if he could get ashore he could spark a rebellion where both Humbert and Napper Tandy had failed. Before he could land, however, British ships attacked Tone's fleet. While Tone stood his ground and fought, many of the French ships, perhaps understandably, turned for home. Tone was captured, and transported from Donegal to Dublin to face trial. He was accused, and found guilty of treason. Tone had wanted to be shot in the military style for his execution, but the British only offered him the hangman. Rather than face such an ignominious end, Tone slit his own throat. His wounds were not serious enough to kill him outright, but he died a week later as a result of his self-inflicted injuries.

With the death of Tone, the 1798 rebellion was finally over. The whole period of the rebellion had a profound effect on Ireland and the future shape of Irish politics. It is clear that the year of rebellion caused massive loss of life, led to the wholesale destruction of crops and villages, drove people from their homes and produced a total dislocation of Irish life. The rebellion had made sectarian and intercommunal violence a norm in many parts of Ireland, especially Ulster, and the divisions and wounds that such violence caused would be difficult to heal. Most important for the future development of an Irish nationalist ideology and mythology, was the place that Wolfe Tone, and the United Irishmen, would come to occupy in the pantheon of national heroes. The events of 1798, coupled with Tone's open embrace of violent means as a method of achieving stated goals, secured a tradition within the evolving Irish nationalist mind that exists amongst extreme Republicans to the present day. After 1798, some of the movements that would seek separation from Britain were willing to use violence to achieve their goal, 1798 was a landmark for the development of an Irish nationalist psyche. Despite its laudable appeal to all sections of the religious divide in Ireland, the actual events of the year demonstrated to many of those Catholics in Ireland who were impassioned by a fledgling sense of national freedom, that sovereignty was more simply a question of 'them' and 'us'; that when the link with Britain and the Crown was threatened, or the superior status of Protestants within Ireland was challenged, Catholics would be the losers. Despite its bucolic simplicity, such a thought process has had a lasting appeal, and 1798 remains widely perceived as one of the most important dates in Irish history.

UNION

Beyond the legacy of 1798, the immediate responses to the crises that the year's events produced were straightforward. Ireland was in a state of chaos. The action of the United Irishmen had threatened the security of Britain, and the Irish parliament had shown itself unable to govern. It was time for the British to force a settlement on Ireland. The Prime Minister, William Pitt, rationalised that the answer lay in a union between Britain and Ireland. If the two countries were drawn together as one, and governed from a single parliament, many of the problems could be solved at a stroke. Rather than having a quasi-independent Ireland, with its potentially threatening population that was half the size of Britain's, on her western flank, it would be preferable to have Ireland joined as part of the same state and unit of government. Such a new, and potentially radical direction for Anglo-Irish relations might also serve to break the singular power of the ascendancy in Ireland, and bring about a greater inclusion of Catholics and dissenters as part of the political process.

Throughout the eighteenth century, any mention of union between Britain and Ireland had universally been rejected by all sectors of Irish society. In the wake of the destruction of the 1798 rebellion, many parties were more amenable to such a suggestion. For the Protestants, union might result in a lessening of their powers, but it was preferable to be protected directly by Britain, than face domestic insurrection and external interference. Catholics were well aware that union with Britain was nowhere near the independence that some of them had sought in supporting Tone, but Pitt was offering Catholic emancipation as part of the package. Such emancipation, although located within Ireland as part of a union, would change their status within society in such a radical fashion that it was an appealing prospect. After all, how could independence ever be secured in the context of the aftermath of 1798? There was no effective independence movement on which hopes could be pinned. Advancement and emancipation within the union was a better bet. Some groups did, quite understandably, fear the prospect of union. Would Britain use union to destroy the developing Irish economy that had flourished under the free trade of Grattan's parliament? Would the onset of union lead to an economic and cultural downturn in the fortunes of Ireland? Could Britain understand and protect the needs of the fiercely independent Orange Societies within the union? All these questions were for the future. First, Britain had to formalise the idea of union into a legal and practical reality.

In Ireland the main British architects and negotiators of the union were Cornwallis, the lord lieutenant, and Lord Castlereagh, who worked as his chief secretary. Opposition from the Protestant ascendancy made Cornwallis and Castlereagh toil for their eventually successful implementation of the union. Seats in the Irish parliament were freely bought and sold so that the British could ensure their majority. In January 1799, the first votes on union were taken in the Irish parliament. Incredibly the ascendancy members who opposed union won the day, winning 111 votes, against the government's 106. Castlereagh in particular worked ever harder to secure the necessary votes. Ascendancy members who opposed union were bribed and bullied. It was made clear to any of them that opposed the government's will, that they could expect no favours in the future. On 15 January 1800, the Irish parliament again met to debate the issue of union. The debate lasted all day, but it was never a genuine contest. Despite all the passion, and even the appearance to speak against union of an aged Grattan, in Volunteer uniform, the government had secured enough votes through expenditure and intimidation. The government's will prevailed, by 138 votes to 96.

What opposition remained against union could not rouse any popular support in favour of retaining the Irish parliament. There was a massive force of British troops resident in Ireland, as if to remind the people of the might of their more powerful neighbour. The British parliament voted for union, without any great debate or excitement. As so often in Irish history, important affairs that would shape the future of the island failed to arouse any great interest or passion within the mainland legislature. The Act of Union received royal assent on 1 August 1800 and came into operation on 1 January 1801.

With its old parliament gone, how would Ireland actually be ruled under the union? Put simply, Ireland was swallowed whole by the British parliament and became nothing more than a collection of parliamentary constituencies that were part of a larger unit. As part of the union, Ireland was granted 100 members in the House of Commons. In the House of Lords there would be 28 peers and four bishops. Ireland would still retain its own legal system and control of its judiciary, but law-making powers lay in London. Despite the fears of traders and merchants, the union was built around the principle of free trade, and the former customs restrictions on the entry of Irish goods into Empire nations were abolished. The political machinery that was put into place to govern Ireland as part of the union was much as Pitt had outlined in the first instance. On issues such as trade, the union was certainly more favourable to Ireland than had been imagined in many quarters. The problem for the union, which would be an issue that would trouble it for much of the nineteenth century, was the position of Catholics. Pitt had promised, or at least hinted, that Catholics would be emancipated as part of the process of union. It was clear during the passage of the Act of Union through the Irish parliament, that Catholic emancipation was unpalatable to the ascendancy. As a result of their opposition and intransigence, the move to emancipate Catholics was dropped from the whole union debate. When the first parliament sat under the Act of Union on 22 January 1801, it still excluded Catholics. Although those who qualified were allowed to vote under the terms of the 1793 Relief Act, emancipation was as far away as it had ever been.

Ireland had entered the seventeenth century on the back of upheaval, rebellion and war. It entered the eighteenth century in much the same way. The United Irishmen's rebellion of 1798 had served as a catalyst for bloody chaos across Ireland, and had precipitated the Act of Union. While union was clearly a concept of Irish governance that had never existed previously, and placed the Anglo-Irish relationship on a definite legal footing, the whole process of union chose to ignore as many problems as it addressed. Issues such as land ownership, Catholic emancipation, intercommunal violence, self-determination and a host of others, would be central features of the nineteenth century in Ireland. The battles and tragedies surrounding these issues combined to form some of the most recognisable narratives of Irish history, and would see Ireland locked into a continuing spiral of violence, protest and upheaval.

4

The Nineteenth Century

Ireland was a place of rapid transformation, but also of terrible destruction during the nineteenth century. While the passage of the Act of Union was initially contested by many of the Protestant ascendancy, and by followers of the Presbyterian faith, the actual experience of union in the nineteenth century served to transform their opinions so that they became the staunchest defenders of the Anglo-Irish link. The Catholic population gained little from the union. In the first half of the century, they followed the campaigning Daniel O'Connell, and, in part, brought about Catholic emancipation. However, while the Protestant and Presbyterian populations of Ulster benefited from the effects of industrialisation and an upsurge in wealth, the lot of the rural-based Catholic peasantry continued to deteriorate. In the middle of the century, famine struck Ireland. The destruction of large sections of the population as a result of starvation and disease was devastating; a sense of desolation in Ireland was heightened by mass emigration to foreign shores. In the second half of the nineteenth century the relationship between Ireland and Britain was constantly questioned and challenged by those supporting independence for Ireland.

Equally problematic was the complex relationship between the religious groups in the country. These tensions were played out in the context of the forces of modernity. Although their effects in Ireland were far from uniform, factors such as increased communications and levels of literacy had a profound effect on the nature of conflict, and the development of separate and competing religious and political ideologies within Ireland. By the end of the century, Ireland was in such a state of turmoil, and had experienced so much since the inception of the Act of Union, that something would have to give. The twentieth century would usher in further transformations in the complex internal and external relationships that made up Ireland.

The Act of Union was a tactic of rapid response from a British-based legislature faced with the prospect of foreign invasion at the hands of France, aided by an apparently disloyal part of the kingdom in the shape of Ireland, and the intrigues of Wolfe Tone. The Act of Union, although forced through the Irish parliament with a high level of opposition, ensured that Ireland and Britain would act as one coherent unit against the French. What union did not achieve, however, was a lasting settlement of the Irish problem.

Throughout the first half of the nineteenth century, Ireland, far from being peaceful under union, had to be governed constantly by coercive Acts of Parliament. The Irish members of parliament, unrepresentative as they may have been of the whole population, were now distantly located in the Palace of Westminster. To most, they seemed more remote than ever. Alongside the physical distance of the parliament, was the confusing presence of an executive that remained in Ireland. The lord lieutenant still resided in Dublin, as did the legal system, and the whole machinery and symbolism of British rule that was contained in Dublin Castle. It was a complex picture that produced confused and contradictory messages as to who, or which group, governed Ireland. The ascendancy had given up their parliament under the Act of Union, and had been subsumed into a larger body, where they seemingly had little influence. They retained, however, control of the executive powers in Dublin.

The situation was further compounded by the attitude of the British parliament. It had taken on the Irish members, and governance of that country, so as to ensure its own security, but it was overtly interested in Ireland. The country still had an image of being backward and difficult. With the exception of parts of Ulster, Ireland did not fit alongside the British experience of rapid growth and development, and moves towards mass industrialisation. Yet it was part of their kingdom, their land, and came under their jurisdiction. For that reason, despite the apparent lack of interest that the London parliament often demonstrated with respect to Ireland, it expected and demanded that Ireland behave in a loyal manner. It was not a distant and far-flung land that was coming under the jurisdiction of Britain's growing Empire. Ireland was next door, and part of Britain. Any expressions of discontent, or moves towards independence, be they Catholic, Protestant or Presbyterian, would be considered a treasonous act aimed at destroying the developing cohesion of what could be recognised, at the end of the eighteenth century, as a British nation.

THE GROWING ECONOMIC CRISIS

Ireland was thus in a difficult situation. All its disparate groups were supposed to accommodate each other under existing laws and within the context of an unevenly developing economy. In addition, they were to be loyal to a union whose senior partners had little interest in guiding it for the benefit of all involved. From such an unsure footing at the opening of the century, it is clear that union was inevitably a relationship that could be constantly challenged, and which might potentially throw up a multitude of problems.

If the period of union had achieved a level of wealth and afflu-ence that was acceptable to the aspirations of each of the groups in Ireland, it is likely that its lifetime would have been far longer; but wealth, as with many other aspects of the union, was only open to certain groups. Under the terms of the Act of Union, Ireland was allowed to trade freely with Britain, her colonies, and any other nations of the world. In theory, such an allowance should have been the springboard to the creation of great prosperity in Ireland. As a part of the union, Ireland, in theory, had free and direct access to the markets of Britain and its Empire, which had the widest and strongest global economy. However, this was not the case. Ireland did not attract much inward investment capital after union, and few new industries developed. It is true that those industries that were in place, in Ulster particularly, flourished. Elsewhere in the country, the main form of employment and potential wealth creation was agriculture.

The agricultural structure of Ireland was not developing

quickly enough. In the first half of the nineteenth century, the population of Ireland grew from under five million to over eight million by 1841. If Irish agriculture had undergone the modernising transformation that had been witnessed in British agriculture, or if alternative sources of employment had sprung up, it might have been able to cope with the growth of population. The reality of the early nineteenth century was that Irish agriculture could not cope with the challenge of extra mouths to feed. While many younger sons chose to emigrate rather than face subdividing a small land plot still further for their inheritance, others stayed in Ireland and saw their family holdings reduced to ever-diminishing plots as each generation passed away. The standard of living in Ireland, especially for the Catholic peasantry, who relied on the land for their family income, dropped to crisis point. It is evident that many families survived on the thin line that existed between poverty and starvation. For the Irish who were locked into such a cycle, there was little chance of escape. For those who were not among the considerable number who chose to emigrate to the New World, especially to America, there was no choice but to stay on their small plot of land and try to survive. There was no alternative employment in most parts of Ireland, few of the landlords appeared interested in the peasants' plight, and the government seemed unprepared to intervene. It was recommended to the government in 1836 that they consider a scheme of public works in Ireland, to offer an alternative to agricultural subsistence; and in 1837, a suggestion was made that a full railway system be built in Ireland as a way of producing wealth and employment. Within the strict ideological confines of the 1830s, a period dominated by *laissez-faire* politics, such obvious and direct government intervention was unpalatable. The only crumb that was thrown to Ireland by the London parliament was the extension of the poor law system to the country in 1838. While a gesture of the right kind, the poor law system was not geared to cope with the strains placed upon it by the Irish situation.

FROM REBELLION TO REFORM

Against the backdrop of union and agricultural stagnation, the politics of Ireland continued to exert a powerful influence on all involved in the country's affairs and directing its future shape. Despite the garrison of 25,000 soldiers kept in Ireland by the British, to prevent French invasion, and to suppress any further attempts at rebellion by the Irish, 1803 did witness another attempt at insurrection. Although the rebellion of 1798 had been put down, the spirit of the United Irishmen had not died. In 1803, Robert Emmet led what can be described as the second United Irish rebellion. Emmet had purchased new types of explosives from an American visitor to Dublin in 1802, and set about gathering together a rebellious force. Emmet's rebellion fits the dictum that when history is first played out it is as tragedy, when it is repeated, it is as farce. Whereas Tone had at least planned his rebellion, albeit poorly, Emmet appears to have run his rising on a very ad hoc basis. In July 1803, when he rose and proclaimed a provisional government of the Irish people, Emmet, although dressed in the uniform of a United Irish general, could gather together only a handful of supporters. His new explosives, which were supposed to have torn down the walls of Dublin Castle, were completely ineffective. All that Emmet managed to achieve was to spark a riot amongst Dublin's urban poor, which took on a life of its own as a rampaging mob. Emmet's rebellion was an abject failure. It did not bring together a mass body of followers, nor did it suggest or promote a coherent nationalist ideology.

Emmet's legacy, as with so many heroes in the annals of Irish nationalism, was the manner of his death. Caught by the British, Emmet was subjected to a horrible execution. In the speech at his trial however, Emmet voiced a series of cohesive ideas that had been absent from his attempted rebellion. He demanded that Ireland be allowed to take her place among the nations of the world. In the context of the American and French revolutions, and the putative emergence of the nation-state as a recognisable form of government and national self-determination across Europe, Emmet had given Ireland a clear-minded definition of its nationalist goal; a goal that fits in well alongside the ideas of contemporary nationalist thinkers elsewhere around the world. Emmet became a hero across Ireland. Symbolic of the foolish hopefulness of youth, and a desire to change the world that he lived in, Emmet also signified the heroic abilities that many who sought freedom from London, believed would one day liberate Ireland.

After the period of Emmet's brief rebellion, Ireland went quiet for a period. It appeared that all the fervour that had unleashed Tone and Emmet had died away, and that most Irish people were either taking time to adjust to the reality of union, or merely seeking to survive in the midst of agricultural and rural poverty.

Grattan re-emerged in 1805, and managed to win a seat that would allow him to sit in the British parliament in London. He set about trying to win over the members of parliament over to policies of intervention and change, and to convince them that there were grave injustices within Ireland that urgently needed addressing. His major aim was to achieve Catholic emancipation. This was not an easy task. The majority of MPs were ignorant as to the state of Ireland, and the idea that Catholics should have access to parliament was a foreign concept for them. Grattan put three different Catholic emancipation bills before the House of Commons. The final attempt, shortly before his death in 1820, was only lost by two votes. This was an achievement, considering the crushing defeats that Grattan's bills had suffered in the past, and a testament to Grattan's ability to win over fellow MPs to his way of thinking.

The difficulty for men like Grattan, who wanted reform for Ireland, was always the question of support. Considering how the ascendancy class had been forced into the British parliament under the Act of Union, they might well have emerged in the House of Commons as a belligerent group who would express their opposition to union by acting independently. This was not however the case. It became clear at the start of the nineteenth century that the ascendancy group, although initially hostile to union, realised that it was actually in their best interest to work within the British parliament. Such practice would secure their position in Ireland in the same way their own parliament had done. As such changes in allegiance towards the London-based legislature were made by the ascendancy, indeed the majority of Ireland's Protestant and Presbyterian population, it became difficult for reformers such as Grattan to act in the interests of Catholic reform. But why was the non-Catholic population of Ireland so readily convinced that union served their best interests? The actual Act of Union guaranteed the position of the established Church in Ireland. It had not granted, as had been feared, and as Pitt appeared to have promised, Catholic emancipation. As the early years of union passed by, it became clear that contentious issues such as land ownership and tenancy laws would not be altered to favour anyone but the incumbent landowner. Those members of the industrial and trading classes, uniformly followers of the Protestant and Presbyterian faith, prospered under the move to full free trade and also possessed enough of their own capital to allow their interest to grow. The very fact that such business concerns were mainly concentrated in Ulster, an area where anti-Catholicism was normally at its most virulent, made the area's belief in, and support for the union, the strongest and most loyal of any province in Ireland.

While Protestants and Presbyterians wholeheartedly backed the union, it was not embraced so fully by Catholics. In their eyes, the Act of Union had merely served to reinforce many of the prejudices and disadvantages that had existed under the Irish parliament. If anything, the situation was worse, as many of the young radically-minded Presbyterians, who had sought an alliance with Catholics at the time of Tone, now chose personal interest and union, above radical cross-religious co-operation.

The future of Catholic fortunes in Ireland, indeed the whole future of the union, was brought into mainstream debate by one man in the period from the 1820s until the onset of the mid-century famine. Daniel O'Connell successfully advanced and elucidated the ideas of Catholic emancipation, and then proceeded to set the markers for the debate surrounding the aspirations of Irish nationalism that would dominate the second half of the century. In following such a course, O'Connell began to re-shape and define the political and religious allegiances that the Irish population would follow for many years to come. He also brought the Irish problem, as it would come to be known, into the centre stage of British politics: a problem on which many British governments, despite their ability to wage war, build global economic interests and conquer an empire, would ultimately founder.

Daniel O'Connell was a middle-class Catholic from a landowning family in Kerry. He had studied law in London, and returned to take his place at the Irish bar in 1798. O'Connell had mixed in liberal circles in London, and he found the repression of the 1798 rebellion unpalatable. In the message of Tone, O'Connell found much that he admired, but he felt that the use of violent rebellion as a tactic, and disloyalty to the parliament, were deeply problematic. O'Connell's belief in the value of law, which sprang from his profession, was replicated in his political activity. The law should not be broken, nor the authority of a legal parliament challenged by force of arms. O'Connell was the natural replacement for Grattan, following his death in 1820, as the leader of the Catholic emancipation movement.

THE CATHOLIC ASSOCIATION AND EMANCIPATION

O'Connell's first task was to reinvigorate the emancipation movement following the loss of Grattan's bill in 1819. The very real problem for O'Connell, in assuming Grattan's mantle, was that he was a Catholic. He could not take a seat in parliament and thus could not, as Grattan was able to do, present bills to the Commons. O'Connell had to embark on a non-parliamentary campaign for emancipation that neither produced violence, nor called into question the legitimacy of the parliament. To do this, O'Connell formed the Catholic Association in May 1823. The initial aim was to fund the activities of those Protestant MPs who were favourable to emancipation. Such a tactic was standard practice in the early nineteenth century for any campaigning group, and was obviously the preserve of political activists who had recourse to funds; that was normally the middle and upper classes.

In 1824 O'Connell changed, at a stroke, the nature of the emancipation campaign, indeed the whole nature of politics in nineteenth-century Britain. He brought the mass of the people, who were not represented in parliament by anyone, and whose traditional involvement in politics had only ever been as part of 'rent a mob', into partnership. The annual membership of the Catholic Association was set at one guinea a year. This was well beyond the purse of the average Irish man or woman. O'Connell reorganised the Association so those members of the lower classes could join as associate members, by paying only a penny a month. The effect of such a move was electrifying. Overnight it made the Catholic Association a mass movement. It was no longer a political grouping that was solely the preserve of the self-interested middle and upper classes, but an alliance between the Catholic peasantry and the Catholic elite. The real success of the Association was the involvement of the Catholic clergy. All parish priests were members of the Association, and it was these men, in every parish across the length and breadth of Ireland, who collected the penny subscription from their parishioners. The Catholic Association was not an abstract political grouping that demanded the support of the lower orders, but was present in every parish, and was directly joined to the people through the all-important figure of the local priest.

The landowners and other elite groups in Ireland were horrified at the prospect of such a mass movement. The Catholic Association was, within a few months of O'Connell throwing open the doors of membership, a highly organised and firmly structured organisation that was well funded, and, by virtue of the parish organisation, truly national. The government, fearful of a repeat of 1798 or 1803, took a regressive course of action and banned the Catholic Association in 1825. In the face of such proscription, O'Connell's legal skills and the ethos that underpinned his political activity became his ultimate strength. He reinvented the Association a mere four months after it had been banned. The new Catholic Association had a constitution that talked of charity and public harmony as its aims, and expressly stated that any activities which the Association under-took would be strictly within the letter of the law. The govern-ment, despite all its worst fears of the spectre of a mass Catholic movement, had no choice but to allow the Association to continue. O'Connell had proved his legal abilities, and the prudent nature of his approach ensured the continuation of his movement.

With the Association firmly established in the context of the law, its activities continued and its campaign gathered momen-tum. At the 1826 general election, those Catholics who had the vote (those whose property values afforded them the wealth and status of forty-shilling freeholders), acted independently of their landlords for the first time. Traditionally, the landowners had been able to count on the votes of their tenants, as the threat of eviction was more worrying for the tenants than the free practice of their democratic right. Supported as they were by a mass movement, and directed in their political affairs by their parish priest, many Catholic freeholders felt able to break free of their landlords and vote as they wanted. The result marked a radical shift in Irish politics. For the first time, Catholic freeholders shaped election results in constituencies in areas such as Dublin, Louth, Monaghan, Roscommon, Waterford and Westmeath. In key constituencies where there was a chance that a pro-emancipation candidate might prevail, the Catholic Association swung into action. Rather than behaving as a drunken and wild mob, the crowds supporting the Association conducted themselves with perfect gentility, and made their support for preferred candidates clear through a series of meetings and marches, all of which passed off within the confines of the law.

Despite the successes that the Association achieved in Ireland, the election of 1828 went against them on a national scale. The new Tory government that was formed in the wake of the election was led by the Duke of Wellington as Prime Minister, and driven along by the organising and political zeal of the young Home Secretary, Robert Peel. The problem for O'Connell and his Association, indeed for the whole cause of Catholic emancipation, was that Wellington and Peel personally, and their party generally, were resolutely opposed to emancipation.

The reaction of the Association was straightforward. All government candidates in any future elections would be opposed, until the Tory party changed its direction on the issue. A series of mass meetings and demonstrations were held against the government across Ireland. Despite the widespread support for O'Connell, it was difficult to see how opposing government candidates would radically alter the situation; if anything, it was likely to further cement the government's resolve and polarise the situation. O'Connell's chance for a radical change in tactics came in June 1828. A by-election was called in Clare, in a seat held by a sitting government MP. O'Connell made the decision to stand for election against the Tory candidate. Although the law forbade the presence of Catholics in parliament, it did not prevent them from contesting the election itself. O'Connell's campaign was well organised and supported. Members of the Association swept into Clare, and campaigned hard for O'Connell. They held their now familiar mass meetings, and

paraded through the town wearing their nationalistic green cloth-
ing and various accessories; all conducted without the infringe-
ment of any law. In line with the government's worst nightmare,
O'Connell won the election. He easily defeated the Tory candidate, and secured two-thirds of the vote.

The government was placed in an unenviable position by
O'Connell's success. They could, as the law allowed them,
refuse him entry to the House of Commons and face another
by-election. If they did take such a course of action, it was
unimaginable that the people of Clare would vote for anyone
other than O'Connell. If they wanted to avoid such an
eventuality, they would have to consider changing the existing
legislation, and bar all Catholics from even contesting
elections. Either of these courses of action ran the risk of bringing about wide-scale disturbances across Ireland. O'Connell had
given the government no real room for manoeuvre. It was emancipation or nothing. Facing the inevitable, the government
passed the Catholic Emancipation Act in 1829. The Act allowed
Catholics to take seats in parliament, sit as judges, and take
commissions in the armed forces. A few senior posts such as
lord lieutenant were still barred to Catholics, but essentially,
O'Connell had won the day. The government, in seeking to
salvage something from the defeat, changed the voting rights of
freeholders. The forty-shilling freeholders, who had been the
bedrock of O'Connell's campaign, were debarred from the electorate as the minimum freehold was increased from forty
shillings to ten pounds. The number of freeholders on the electoral role was reduced from over a million to just fewer than
100,000.

After winning Catholic emancipation, and again securing his
seat in Clare, O'Connell had to decide where his political future
lay. He had achieved emancipation: something that Grattan had
fought for, yet had failed to secure. As the head of the Catholic
Association, O'Connell was the most powerful populist politi-
cian in Ireland. Around him in parliament, O'Connell built up a
team of MPs who had supported emancipation, and they formed
themselves into an ad hoc party grouping. Such was their power
that they were able to assist the Whig Prime Minister,
Melbourne, in forming a government in 1835.

WHIG REFORMS

From such a powerful position it was clear that O'Connell's support for any given cause in Ireland would give it a massive boost. The question was, which cause would O'Connell pursue? In the 1830s he turned his attention to the position of the established Church in Ireland and the collection of tithes. The English and Irish churches had been united as part of the Act of Union; but it was clear that the British need to support the established Church in Ireland was not as pressing as their firmly held belief in the supremacy of the English Church. The Whigs would clearly listen to O'Connell and attempt to reform the Irish Church in line with his thinking. O'Connell's difficulty, however, was not simply that the Anglican Church was the established Church in Ireland, but that the tithe system existed. At a time when Catholics had come in from the cold and had been granted emancipation, it seemed incongruous that they should have to pay a tithe to the established Church. Even without the intervention of O'Connell, the tithe issue had taken on a life of its own. Against a backdrop of diminishing agricultural yields, rising rents and increased levels of poverty, many tenants were making the decision that they could not afford to pay their tithes. This decision meant that they were living outside the law, and that many of the established clergy were living in a state of poverty as their tithe income had disappeared. O'Connell brokered a deal with the Whigs which meant that the worst excesses could be curbed. The tithes were based on a new formula so that the charges to the tenants were not so excessive; but they were still collected, and passed to the established Church, and not, as O'Connell had hoped, to all the clergy on an equal basis.

The tithe issue was illustrative of O'Connell's problems throughout the 1830s. He wanted, indeed demanded, reform in Ireland. The Whigs were in an unenviable position. Their majority in parliament was not particularly strong, and Ireland remained, as it always had been, a minefield for British politicians and their fortunes. To reform the conditions and inequalities in Ireland too far, was to invite sustained opposition from the Protestant and Presbyterian sectors of Irish society, and to bring about the wrath of Tory MPs and Peers. If reform was not

attempted in any form at all, the Catholics would remain dissat-
isfied, and O'Connell could possibly return to populist agitation
in Ireland rather than keep working within the system. To remain
in office, and to keep Ireland at peace, the Whigs had to walk a
dangerous tightrope.

The Whigs elected for minor, although important, reforms.
Elementary education was extended to Ireland on a national
level, the poor law provisions that had been applied to England
in 1834 were extended to cover Ireland, and the system of
municipal government was reformed. While understandable,
indeed desirable in the context of the 1830s, two of the reforms
instigated held vital keys for understanding future events and
tensions in Ireland. The introduction of elementary education,
although increasing literacy and affording access to education,
especially amongst the Catholic tenancy, went a long way to
destroying Irish as the vernacular. Many of the cultural nationalist movements, which became important in the second half of the
nineteenth century, viewed the decline in the Irish language as a
critical blow to the continuance of a shared, and vibrant, sense of
common identity. Equally important was the extension of the
1834 Poor Law. The Act had been conceived as an English
answer to the problems of growing poverty that related to industrialisation, short-term unemployment and the difficulties caused
by the process of rural-to-urban migration. While its application
to Ireland was welcome, as it was a form of protection against
poverty, its very genesis meant that it was unsuited to the Irish
situation, which was predominantly agricultural and rural. The
Poor Law would be found badly wanting at the time of the
famine.

As the 1830s came to a close, O'Connell and the Whigs had
much to be proud of. Their reform programme was, in the
context of the time, a worthy achievement. O'Connell's influence, however, was on the wane. From the highpoint of the
emancipation campaign, membership of the Catholic Association
had fallen, and with it, the number of penny subscriptions. The
Whig government was in crisis, and it seemed inevitable that the
1840s would be a decade dominated by a Robert Peel-led Tory
party; a prospect that offered little succour to the Catholic population of Ireland.

THE REPEAL ASSOCIATION

In 1840, O'Connell embarked on a new direction and formed the Repeal Association. The mode of organisation was much the same as that of the Catholic Association. Small subscriptions ensured a mass membership, as did the Association's arrangement around the parish system. The aim of the Association was the repeal of the Act of Union by means that were consistent with the law. The election of a Tory government in 1841 meant that O'Connell lost his power footing in parliament. While still an MP with a body of support, O'Connell could achieve nothing from the opposition benches. The campaign for repeal would have to be taken to the people if it were to succeed. O'Connell's rationalisation was straightforward. Although the Whig reforms had been laudable, there was too much self-interest in the British parliament ever to achieve true reform in Ireland. The only way that reform of all the injustices in Ireland could be achieved, was through a self-governing independent nation. O'Connell also believed that the mobilisation of the Irish people, in a manner that was reminiscent of the Catholic Association, would produce the same results; that is, Peel would grant Ireland independence from the union, rather than face potential rebellion in Ireland.

The situation in 1841 was radically different from that in the late 1820s. Catholic emancipation, although a centrally important issue to many people at the time, was ultimately only a single issue. In itself, Catholic emancipation did not call the union into question, nor did it radically upset the established power groupings in Britain or Ireland. O'Connell's decision, in 1840, to embark on a programme campaigning for repeal was something altogether different. He was demanding the destruction of the British nation as it had been established under the Act of Union. A union that had bedded down over the forty years since its inception, to the satisfaction of the majority of those who had a stake in its administration, or who had benefited from it economically. Public opinion in Britain was behind union. Peel was supportive of union and had the weight of a secure parliamentary majority behind him. The bulk of Protestants and Presbyterians in Ireland supported union. O'Connell's only support would be found amongst small groups of radical politicians and thinkers, and the mass of the Catholic tenants. His difficulty was that for all the support he would gather in Ireland, and no matter how large-scale his support became, the power brokers in London would not stomach the destruction of union.

The Catholic Church backed the Repeal Association, and as a result the bulk of the Catholic middle and peasant classes threw their support behind O'Connell. Despite such levels of popularity, the Repeal Association struggled to engender the same enthusiasm that had been such a feature of the campaign for Catholic emancipation. What is clear, is that O'Connell's repeal campaign, although backed by some Protestants and Presbyterians, fractured for good the cross-religious ideal of an Irish nation that had been so important to Wolfe Tone. O'Connell effectively drove the Protestant and Presbyterian dissenters, such few as still existed by the mid-nineteenth century, firmly and vociferously into the camp supporting union. As a result of O'Connell's campaign in the 1840s, nationalist politics became a battle, not solely between the ideals of the Irish nation and the union, but a battle between Catholicism on the one hand, and Protestantism and Presbyterianism on the other.

Despite such schisms that were to appear in Irish life, one important factor, which did underpin and promote O'Connell's campaign, was the newspaper *The Nation*. Newspapers had spread steadily across Ireland throughout the first half of the nineteenth century, and had growing readerships. As literacy improved, the relative cost of producing and selling newspapers decreased, and their availability increased, so the various messages that the different organs promoted spread across the country. Newspapers in Ireland would become vital in the nineteenth and early twentieth century in the struggle for hearts and minds, and for either the promotion of the cause of nationalism or support for the union. It is difficult to assess how important any single newspaper can ever be in mobilising or transforming public opinion. As an example of the arrival of the press within Irish political campaigning, *The Nation* is worthy of brief examination as a single example of a growing trend; its importance, however, should not be overstated. *The Nation* threw its weight behind O'Connell's campaign for repeal, and became an important voice for the movement. All of O'Connell's speeches were reported, as were details of his forthcoming meetings. In the first half of the 1840s, *The Nation* achieved a readership in excess of

250,000: a testament to the power of the press, and an endorsement, of sorts, for O'Connell's campaign.

The campaign itself changed direction in 1843, as O'Connell sought to recapture the feeling of populism that had supported the emancipation movement, and galvanised the powers in London into action. Across Ireland, O'Connell held monster meetings in the open, where he spoke to the people about the validity of his campaign. The meetings became a legendary part of Irish politics: although peaceful, O'Connell's meetings gathered together crowds numbering well into six figures, and many commentators were willing to estimate that some meetings brought crowds of half a million to hear 'the Liberator', as he became known. Considering how many Coercion Acts had been passed against the Catholic tenant population of Ireland by the Westminster parliament, the sight of over a hundred thousand supporters of repeal gathered in one place, peaceful as they may have been, must have alarmed the government.

The monster meetings were promoted by *The Nation*, opened by a Catholic Mass, thereby linking Catholic Irish politics firmly with the Church, and addressed by an impassioned O'Connell. Peel's view of the O'Connellite meetings was less than benevolent. While many in Westminster could understand the forces that had mobilised support for repeal, they could not allow such a movement to challenge the union. There was a belief amongst many of the elite in mid-nineteenth-century Britain, a country that was mobilised at the time in the pursuit of industrial and imperial glory in every corner of the globe, that repeal could lead to the potential destruction of the Victorian Empire.

In 1843, O'Connell planned yet another monster meeting, this time in Clontarf. The potential for a huge gathering of Catholics, to hear further denouncements of the whole idea of the union, was too much for the government. The decision was made to ban the Clontarf meeting. Troops were sent in great number to quell any potential rising or rebellion in favour of the Clontarf gathering, but O'Connell, ever the law abider, acquiesced in the face of the ban. The meeting was called off. O'Connell's bluff had been called: for all the support he could gather, he was clearly not willing to utilise it in a potentially violent clash with the authority of the government.

Sensing that O'Connell's moment had passed, and his resolve

for a stand-up battle with the parliament was weak, the government pressed home its advantage. Shortly after the proposed Clontarf meeting in October 1843, O'Connell, along with his main supporters, including Charles Gavan Duffy, the editor of *The Nation*, was arrested. All those arrested were charged, and successfully prosecuted for treason, and sentenced to a year's imprisonment.

The government's aim of curbing the enthusiasm for the Repeal Association, by placing its leader behind bars, backfired. Support for, and financial contributions to, the Association grew throughout the period of the trial and with the passing of sentence. The government decided that backtracking, in the name of clemency, would be preferable to belligerence. Duly, in September 1844, O'Connell's conviction was quashed. The release of O'Connell was met with huge celebrations across Ireland: the Liberator was free. Despite such a triumphal release, the real question remained. Where could O'Connell's movement go now? His bluff had been called in Clontarf, and the government's belief in union was unbending.

In 1845 the future shape of O'Connell's campaign, or rather the radicalism that it had engendered, became clearer. The staff of *The Nation* had always been a younger and far more radical grouping than O'Connell and his movement. Although full-square behind the Liberator, as he gathered so much public support, some of the young radicals looked towards the spirit of 1798, and the use of violence, as the method by which their goals could be achieved. The radical faction came together as a group under the name 'the Young Irelanders'. The split between O'Connell and the Young Irelanders came in 1845 over the issue of education. The government had decided to fund the development of three universities across Ireland. The 'Queen's colleges', as they were known, were to be located in Belfast, Cork and Galway. In line with the spirit of inclusiveness that Catholic emancipation had engendered, the colleges were to be non-denominational. O'Connell and the Church condemned the non-denominational plans for the colleges, and demanded that they be split on religious lines. The Young Irelanders, inheritors of Tone's belief in a co-religious Irish nation, backed the government line that the colleges should be open to all. O'Connell and the Catholic Church won the day: the colleges of Cork and

Galway became predominantly Catholic, while Queen's College in Belfast drew its students from the Protestant and Presbyterian population. In response, the Young Irelanders departed company from O'Connell and the Repeal Association. Such freedom allowed them to embrace their more radical idealism, and to pursue the promotion, as they saw it, of the spirit of 1798.

The legacy of the split between O'Connell and the Young Irelanders would not clearly show itself until later. For all the potential of O'Connell's Association as a mass movement, or the Young Irelanders' radicalism, the story of Ireland in the second half of the 1840s is one dominated by famine; a famine that would profoundly alter the whole nature of Irish life, would lead to mass emigration, untold numbers of deaths, and the development of an antipathy towards British rule which would fester for the remainder of the century.

THE GREAT FAMINE

The effects of the Great Famine are difficult, if not impossible, to comprehend fully. The economic historians of Ireland have carried out much work that has calculated the cost of the famine in terms of deaths, the number of emigrants, changes in land-ownership patterns and so on, but the hardest story of all, the unquantifiable, is the human cost of the famine. In 1845, the population of Ireland stood at approximately 8.5 million. By 1851, and the nominal end of the famine, the population had been reduced by over 2 million. Roughly half of this figure died from starvation and its accompanying diseases, while the remainder left Ireland's shores for a new life in a foreign land. Each and every one of those individuals who died or left Ireland had a story to tell, as did those that remained in Ireland and observed and lived through the devastating dislocation of the famine years. Many of the individual stories were left behind in the form of letters and diaries, and there are many observation pieces that can be read in the huge number of eye-witness newspaper reports of the period, within the journals of travellers to Ireland, or inside the covers of austere-looking government and relief committee reports. From such harrowing personal narratives and official observation, the lived experiences of the famine can be, at least in part, uncovered. The difficulty for the historian of Ireland, or the impartial observer, is to attempt to understand how far the effects of the famine shaped the future course of political, social and economic life across the land. Much mythologised history, especially within the Irish nationalist or Irish-American canon, has directly linked the devastation of the famine with the presence of the British in Ireland. From the tales of death, emigration, poverty and evictions from the land, a straight line is drawn to the reawakening of Irish nationalist politics in the latter decades of the nineteenth century and the successful expulsion of the British from Ireland. The task here is to explore the facts of the famine, as far as they are known, and to attempt to understand how powerful a force such a legacy exerted on the future direction of Ireland's history.

Before exploring the events of the years 1845–51, the famine needs placing in a broader context. Many of the themes that were to be seen as representative of the famine – emigration, hunger and such like – were already common features of Irish life prior to the mid-nineteenth century. The very nature of Irish agriculture, particularly for the poorer members of society, meant that large sections of the population had been living hand-to-mouth for the best part of a century, if not longer. Small plots of land, over-dependence on a single crop (the potato), poor living conditions and high rates of fertility, had all resulted in periods of poverty and destitution prior to the 1840s. In 1816, for example, crops had failed, disease had been rife and many deaths had ensued. On the back of such a precarious existence, many Irish men and women, from a variety of social backgrounds, had made the decision to emigrate to America, Canada, mainland Britain or, in much smaller numbers, Australia. In accepting that the famine was a human disaster for the Irish, on a scale that could never have been predicted, it has to be acknowledged that the outcomes of famine were not new. These were simply exacerbated to unprecedented levels.

To understand that the effects of famine were not original features of Irish society, is also to understand much of the contemporary reaction. It has been a long-held view, of many Irish nationalists at least, that the famine was, if not engineered by the British, then certainly managed to their supposed benefit. Considering the extreme effects of the famine, and the emotional attachments that it has formed within the Irish consciousness, such conclusions are perhaps understandable. In the 1840s, the government of Robert Peel was locked in crisis. At a time when the British Empire was expanding to its Victorian heights, British industry was the most advanced in the world, and imperial competition between the British and other European nations was beginning to become an issue in political life, the future of economic policy and prosperity was a key issue. Peel's government had to decide between the ideology of free trade or protectionism. Within such a debate, centrally focused on the wealth potential of the ever-more-powerful elite industrial classes, the needs or desires of the Irish Catholic peasantry were lost in an agenda that did not encroach on their life. Victorian society, especially at the industrial, political and imperial level, was built around an ethos of competition and self-aggrandisement. Ireland, or rather rural Ireland, could not locate itself within such an ethos; though commercial Dublin and industrial Belfast were certainly part of it, and both cities played key roles in the wealth creation of the Victorian period.

In addition to Ireland's not fitting within such an economic and imperial project, aggressive questions were being asked within certain circles about the future of small-scale Irish agriculture. There was a widespread acknowledgement, even before the famine, that families could not survive and feed themselves on small plots of under an acre. The Devon Commission had been called together by the government in 1843, to investigate the distribution and usage of Irish agricultural land. Members of the commission travelled across Ireland in 1843 and 1844, the very years before the famine, when there was no portent of the disaster that waited. The Devon Commission argued that, as long as small plots remained in existence, the future of Irish agriculture generally, and the lot of the Irish peasant class specifically, were bleak. The commission acknowledged what had long been known by many in Ireland: the whole Irish agricultural system, especially in the western areas, was unstable, and would not be able to cope with any imbalances produced by a sustained period of poor crop yields. While it was clear that the state of Irish agriculture was parlous, there was not the government will, in the context of the Corn Law, and debates over free trade versus protectionism, to tackle the problems. Others within the British hierarchy welcomed such forecasts of doom. Some argued that the Catholic Irish problems of poverty and unemployment were on such an insurmountable scale that only some form of Malthusian collapse could save Ireland. In the famine years, the British Treasury Secretary, Charles Trevelyan, clung on to such thinking, and publicly spoke of the Irish problem being solved by the relentless destruction caused by the famine.

The effects of the famine, and many of the questions that it raised, can therefore be seen as being evident in the years leading up to the 1840s. What was most shocking about the famine then, was not that it happened, but its immediacy and its scale. In the summer of 1845, there was a belief that the potato crop would be plentiful, even good, and that the population that relied on such a mono-crop existence would be fed for another year. The reliance on the potato had been a product of the changes in land ownership that were such a feature of the seventeenth and eighteenth centuries. The laws that had controlled the amounts of land that Catholics could own or inherit, the lack of alternative work that was available for them, and the relative size of their family units, all contributed to the depletion of the size of plot that the Catholic peasants were working in an attempt to feed themselves and their families. The problems were further exacerbated by the rapid growth in Ireland's population in the decades leading up to the 1840s. From a population of barely three million in the 1770s, the number of Irish had peaked at over 8 million at the start of the 1840s. Such unparalleled growth in the population had been sustained without the concomitant modernisation of agricultural methods, or a major relocation of the population into urban areas and their employment within a robust industrial sphere. Much of the population was still reliant on small-scale methods of peasant farming that were little changed in over a century. The only way that such people on the margins of society could produce enough food, with only a small sub-acre plot, was to grow potatoes. By the 1840s, a third of the Irish population was directly reliant on their home-produced potato crop.

Disaster came in 1845 in the form of the potato blight. The blight, caused by a fungus in the potato, was first identified amongst crops in England in the early summer of 1845. The first recognised case in Ireland was in Wexford in September.

Overnight it seemed, the hopes of a bumper potato harvest were destroyed. Abject poverty and starvation replaced potential plenty. The blight devastated crops across large parts of Ireland, a process that would continue, harvest by harvest, for nearly six years.

The failure of crops at the hands of the dreaded blight meant that the Irish rural population had little or no food. There is a tendency to view the famine as a national catastrophe, as it undoubtedly was in the broad social and economic sense, but the specific effects of the failure of the potato harvest were regionally concentrated. The famine struck hardest in localised areas and against members of particular social groups and classes. It is clear from all the statistical information that has been gathered and assessed, that the worst affected groups were the poorest potato- dependent peasantry in the west of Ireland, particularly in Connacht, where the rate of death was nearly five times higher than in Leinster. Counties such as Wexford were barely touched by the famine, in respect of deaths from starvation and disease. The counties that fared worst were Roscommon, Sligo and Mayo in Connacht, and the southern counties of Ulster: Cavan, Fermanagh and Monaghan.

Alongside the actual deaths that were a product of the famine, was the physical cost to Ireland, and the legacy of emigration. Those who emigrated were from the poorer classes within Ireland. It has been estimated that 90 per cent of those who left Ireland's shores in the period of the famine were labourers. Whereas emigration had previously been the preserve of the well off, or those who had the ability to accumulate some capital savings, famine emigration changed the social makeup of emigrants completely. Those who emigrated were the Catholic poor who originated from Irish-speaking areas. Their flight from Ireland was assisted by the mid-nineteenth century access to comparatively cheap sea transport. Despite the low prices of sea passage, especially across the Atlantic, many Irish had to rely on assisted passage. Such assistance came either from landlord and government sponsored projects, or more normally, from family settled overseas. Once abroad, the Irish diaspora sent money or pre-paid tickets back to Ireland, so that family members could escape the famine. The family-funded route freed far more people from starvation and disease than the other 'official' schemes. Between 1848 and 1851, nearly £3 million was sent across the Atlantic to pay for sea passages to America or Canada.

As with the pattern of deaths from starvation and disease, the patterns of emigration have to be carefully analysed so that simplistic judgements are not made. Far from the situation being the same across Ireland, the picture of emigration was complex. It was not simply a case of joining the next ship out of Ireland to avoid the famine. The counties that were worst affected by the famine and had the highest death rates, also, with the exception of north Connacht and south Ulster, had the lowest emigration rates. It appears that emigration was the choice of those who avoided the worst ravages of the famine. This is not to suggest that those who emigrated were well off, they were uniformly poverty stricken. They were, however, keeping their heads above the starvation line. It is for this reason that emigration rates were highest from counties such as Limerick, Donegal, Kildare, Kilkenny and Louth, where the effects of the famine were not as extreme as in Roscommon, Sligo or Mayo. The flow of emigrants from counties that were not racked by the worst excesses of the famine was exacerbated by the widespread practice of evicting smallholders from their land, and the failure of the Poor Law to assist any but the worst off. These groups took the understandable decision of using what little money they had left, to leave Ireland.

For those who lived in Ireland during the famine years, and suffered the effects of the blight, the situation was desperate. The potato crop failed in the autumn of 1845. That winter, many of the starving Irish, those who were potato-dependent, travelled from their home districts in a desperate search for food and work. While a decision of self-preservation, such journeys meant that the diseases, especially typhoid and dysentery, which were rife amongst the starving, were spread about wider areas and amongst the non-potato-dependent population.

From 1845 the situation deteriorated still further. Not only did the blight persist until 1848, but as each year passed, the amount of actual farming that was being done in preparation for the following year's crop was substantially reduced. The Irish, it appeared, as the latter half of the 1840s progressed, were locked into a vicious circle from which they could not escape. During 1849/50 as the nightmare seemed to be finally drawing to a close, Ireland was struck by a cholera epidemic. The attack of cholera was a great social leveller: the large urban cities that had previously avoided the worst effects of the famine, were struck hardest. The cholera completed any of the apocalyptic work that the famine had left undone. The weakest were finally struck down, those who had resisted emigration finally boarded the constantly waiting ships, and the cities witnessed the horror of death on a mass scale.

In the modern age, the range of problems that Ireland suffered in the 1840s would be met with a sustained relief programme and the mobilisation of a seemingly endless supply of resources, food and medical supplies. The situation of the 1840s was radically different. Although the Victorians may have a general reputation as the originators of many charitable bodies, and for acts of generosity and philanthropy, they had little concept of how to respond to the sheer scale of the problems witnessed in Ireland in the mid-nineteenth century.

The first stages of the Irish famine were played out against the wider political battle over the Corn Laws, a battle centred on the rights of industrialists to pursue their markets, exports and business within a context of free trade. Such a philosophy was driven by a demand for profit maximisation, and thus sat uneasily with the charity that was required in the famine years.

Robert Peel, and the Conservative Party, had long opposed the abolition of the Corn Laws. During his ministry of the 1840s, it appeared that Peel would cling to the orthodoxy of his party position, and resist repeal, no matter how populist the free traders, especially the Anti-Corn Law League, were becoming. The onset of the Irish famine radically changed the direction of the 'free trade versus protectionism' debate. Despite all the ideology, and self-interest, that had informed the debate prior to the mid-1840s, the Irish situation introduced a chilling realism to the debate. The shortages of food that also existed in mainland Britain during the period meant that extra corn would have to be imported to meet demand. The British would have to continue importing the corn that was grown in Ireland for export across the Irish Sea; but then, what could be used to feed the Irish? Facing a no-win situation, Peel sacrificed principle and the support of his party, in favour of abolition of the Corn Laws and the opening of the British market to cheap foreign imports.

Peel's hope was that starvation and tragedy could be averted.

In addition to changing the law so that corn, free of duty, could be imported, Peel attempted direct intervention in Ireland in 1845 to try and relieve the worst effects of the famine. His government bought £100,000 worth of maize for distribution to the starving in Ireland, and instigated a scheme of public works to try to relieve the problems of the Irish peasantry.

Considering the repeated failure of the potato crop in Ireland over a number of years, it is impossible to say whether the attempts by Peel to relieve the situation would have had any long-lasting effects. Certainly the situation in 1845, although diabolical for the Irish peasantry reliant on the potato, was far better than it would be in succeeding years. As a result of his repeal of the Corn Laws and the apparent desertion of his party's central ethos, Peel could not retain the support of his followers. In the summer of 1846, he was forced to resign, and his Tory government fell. Peel was succeeded in office by the Whig administration of Lord John Russell. Whereas Peel had favoured intervention and aid for the Irish, to ease their collective plight, the free-trading orthodoxy of the Whigs spilled over into, and effectively directed, their policy towards the famine. All the assistance that the Irish had received during 1845 evaporated with the change of government in 1846, and with the failure of that year's potato crop.

For the first two years of the Whig administration, the policy towards Ireland was simple: there would be no direct intervention in the form of food purchases to relieve distress. The Irish, it was decided, should work their way out of poverty and starvation. The Whigs decreed that a massive public-works scheme would be instigated in the areas worst affected by the famine. Those Irish who had fallen victim of the famine would be employed on public works, thereby earning the money to buy food. In principle, many would see such a project as sensible, and worthy of praise. In the mid-1840s, however, it failed to recognise a basic reality. The numbers who were suffering from the famine were simply too large for a public-works scheme to be effective, and to feed everyone that it was supposed to.

As 1846 progressed into 1847, and another crop failed, the demands on the public-works schemes, indeed on all public-relief schemes, grew to breaking point. By the middle of 1847, it

is estimated that nearly 3 million Irish, just under half the population, were being supported, in one way or another, by the
public purse.

The government, despite any contrary ideological views,
changed direction. It was clear that their policy of public-works
schemes had failed. Death from starvation and disease was rife,
and growing ever faster by the summer of 1847. The numbers
heading for the ports, and joining the emigration ships, were
growing quickly. The government tried a variety of different
tactics, all of which, it has to be said, failed to find a solution to
the problems caused by the famine. While some of the government schemes undoubtedly kept people alive, they did nothing to
bring about any future sustainable development, halt the flow of
emigration or provide food and work on anything but the most
basic level.

Soup kitchens became a regular feature of famine life after
1847, as did the dreaded symbol of Victorian charity, the workhouse. By 1848, a seventh of Ireland's population, approximately a million people, were living in, and supported by, the
workhouses of the country. In addition to these centrally run
government schemes, there were other charitable projects that
were administered and funded by private individuals and groups,
such as the British Relief Association and the New York Irish
Relief Committee, which contributed huge sums of money to
famine relief. Alongside such well-meaning projects, ran one of
the crueller aspects of the famine. The Whig government insisted
that the Irish landlords assist in relieving the poverty that their
tenants were enduring as a result of the famine. While it is clear
that many landlords followed such suggestions, and supported
their tenants through the period of hardship, often to their own
detriment, many others did not. For all the enduring images of
the famine that contribute to its history and mythology, especially within many nationalist minds, the most powerful representation of the famine hardship and its resultant cruelty is that
of eviction. It is clear that many landlords reasoned, whether
through heartlessness or economics, that they could not support
their starving tenants. As a result, countless landlords took the
decision to evict their tenants. What emerged from such choices
was an image of broken families, often disease-ridden and potentially starving, being driven out of their homes and off the very

land that offered the only hope of self-produced salvation from the famine. Such families joined others in the workhouse, at the quayside awaiting emigration or in the grave, directly as a result of their landlord's action. As such landlords were often absentee landlords residing in Britain, or were from wealthy Anglo-Irish families, the outsider and the non-Irish would come to be blamed for many of the hardships of the famine era. The image of eviction, and the issues of land ownership would become a major feature of political debate and popular dissent across the remainder of the nineteenth century.

The legacy of the famine would have long-lasting effects that would shape the future of Ireland. One of the most important trends that had been exacerbated by the famine was the separation between Ulster and the rest of Ireland. The majority of Ulster counties had not been dependent on the potato, and thus the effects of the famine had not been so extreme. The famine does not form such a central part of the Ulster historical narrative as it does across the rest of Ireland. Ulster's industries benefited from the move to free trade that resulted from the ending of the Corn Laws, and it became an oasis of comparative wealth and prosperity. While the rest of Ireland dealt with the direct results of the famine, or else suffered through disease or emigration, most of Ulster continued to develop as a modern industrialised region in line with the common experience of many mainland British industrialised areas. The gap that existed between Protestant and Presbyterian Ulster, and the Catholic remainder of Ireland, had always been a large one, at least with respect to religious adherence, national politics and the avenues available for wealth creation. After the 1850s, the gap was much wider, and the distance between the aspirations and lived experiences of the two communities within Ireland was becoming increasingly divisive and insurmountable.

Evidence of the growing distance between Belfast along with the north-eastern counties of Ulster, and the rest of Ireland, became apparent in the years following the famine, and in the rapidly developing vocalisation of Irish nationalist aspirations. While emigration continued at a rapid rate, and the land-based and agricultural problems that had lain at the heart of the famine were slowly addressed, an increasing number of Irish political activists reasoned that the only way a prosperous and secure

future could be attained for Ireland was through self-government.

The train of emigration that was such a feature of the famine
years, continued in the decades that followed. With the exception
of Dublin, all areas suffered post-famine emigration at high
levels. In the 1880s, for example, over half of Ireland's counties
suffered population depletion through emigration, which
numbered into double-figure percentage losses. In the half-
century leading to the foundation of the Irish Free State in 1922,
it has been estimated that approximately 2.5 million people left
Ireland's shores to find a home elsewhere around the globe. The
rate of Irish emigration was so great that the percentage of
people leaving other countries considered to have had high levels
of emigration, pale into insignificance.

The chaos caused by the famine was a product of poor land
management, an outmoded system of land ownership, over-
reliance on a single crop and a generally inept agricultural
process throughout the island. It was vital, if Ireland were to
prosper, that such problems were faced, and tackled, head on.
While there was a wide-ranging debate over what had gone
wrong in Ireland, there was no sense of urgency in actually
changing the system. Those changes or improvements which did
emerge in post-famine Irish agriculture were a product of the
famine itself, rather than a sustained process of managed better-
ment. The famine vastly reduced the number of people who were
reliant on the land, and the high levels of emigration in the
second half of the nineteenth century furthered that process.
With such a massive disappearance of people from the land, the
size of agricultural holding, one of the key contributory factors
in the famine, steadily increased as more land became available.
With the advent of larger plots of land, the agricultural horizons
of the average family grew. No longer did they envisage their
plot of land, as they had previously done, as solely a venue for
potato growing, but they saw their larger plots as a place where
they could grow a wider range of crops, and also keep some livestock.

In the decade following the famine, the number of the Irish
population subsisting on an agricultural holding of over fifteen
acres more than doubled. In the 1850s, the situation seemed
hopeful for the Irish tenant farmer. First and foremost, anything

seemed better than the famine experience, but more generally crop yields improved, more land was available and work was obtainable. Despite these hopeful signs, other more fundamental structural problems would hold back those who depended on the land in the second half of the nineteenth century. In the wake of the famine, the Irish patterns of marriage and fertility declined sharply, so that reproduction rates became the lowest in Europe. While late marriage, and fewer children, might be seen as laudable goals after the famine, there is little evidence in recent historical work to suggest that such changes in marriage and fertility rates had any great beneficial effects in Ireland. In Connacht and Munster before the famine, a traditional form of employment had always been harvest migration, which provided much needed income to underpin the household's chances of survival. From the 1870s, the Irish agricultural system became increasingly mechanised, and so while yields grew in certain areas, the demands for seasonal labour simply collapsed. Households that had relied on harvest migration for their security had no option but to leave Ireland. They could not survive on their own small plots of land, and there was no work to replace that which the machine had taken.

The process of emptying the west, which the famine had begun, was taken a stage further by the destruction of seasonal employment. Those who left the west were the poorest members of society, those who could not access greater plots of land and new ways of farming. The demise in their way of life was shadowed by the slow depletion in the number of paid labourers that were needed in Irish agriculture. As plot sizes increased for the small farmer, and land holdings grew for the landowner, so the demand for paid labourers reduced. Put simply, more people were farming for themselves and did not need labouring work. The poorest sectors of society, those most dependent on such work, were the ones that boosted the emigration levels of the 1880s and 1890s. In the period 1881–5, 313,680 Irish emigrants landed in the United States, 27,480 arrived in Canada, 26,100 in Australia and New Zealand, and 46,200 travelled to Britain.

The effects of the famine would, as has been made clear, have long-lasting effects on all aspects of Irish life. One of the most profound legacies of the famine was the reawakening, during the latter half of the nineteenth century, of Irish nationalist sentiment in various guises. Many of these nationalist movements, some of them political, others cultural, looked back at the famine as a watershed, and fed off the memory of the famine period. The nationalist movement was able to promote the famine as proof that the British presence in Ireland was evil and destructive.

The first stirrings of nationalism appeared during the actual famine years, and were as farcical as the attempt of Robert Emmet to rise at the turn of the century. The year 1848 witnessed a whole series of attempts at revolution across many European states. The Young Ireland movement decided that the time was right to strike for national freedom. Ireland was in a perilous condition as a result of the famine, and the whole of Europe was imbued with the excitement of rebellion. In Ireland, Thomas Meagher, John Mitchel and William Smith O'Brien led the Young Ireland 1848 rebellion that resulted in a putative declaration of an Irish Republic. While the terrible effects of the famine might have produced a population that was open to the revolutionary demands of the Young Irelanders, the truth was that the general population was so brow-beaten by the extremes of starvation, death, illness and emigration, that there was no popular support for the rebellion of 1848. In the immediate famine and post-famine years there was a deep apathy across Ireland for political activity. The end for the Young Ireland rebellion came in July 1848, when, after government officers had infiltrated the movement, those still loyal to the cause lost a shoot-out in a cabbage patch at Vinegar Hill.

The question for Ireland when the famine finally came to an end, was how would it move forward? The devastation wrought by the famine was terrible, the decimation of population enormous, and the differences between parts of the Ulster region and the rest of Ireland (economically, politically, religiously and culturally) were wider than ever.

THE DEVELOPMENT OF HOME RULE POLITICS

In the wake of the famine it was unimaginable that the British could simply ignore the plight of Ireland. Despite all the arguments over Victorian *laissez-faire* politics, and the primacy of free trade, the scale of devastation in Ireland in the 1840s and

early 1850s, stood in sharp opposition to the Victorian character-
istics of charity and philanthropy. The chain of events that would
alter British attitudes towards Ireland, and lead to the development of a sustained and effective parliamentary movement that
stood solely for Irish Home Rule, was long and highly complex.
It relied on a series of domestic and external events, and, most
centrally in the mid-Victorian era, on the personal beliefs of key
individuals.

The two central problems facing Ireland in the immediate
post-famine years were land and leadership. Although some of
the issues surrounding land ownership and management, which
had given rise to the famine, had been partially solved as a result
of emigration, migration and death, the core problems still
remained. While such problems required a solution, political
leadership was also required to effect such a transformation.
Since the death of O'Connell in 1847, Ireland had been without
a respected, able and well supported national leader.

In the 1850s and 1860s British policy that related to Ireland
went into a period of drift. Despite many different groups plead-
ing that the Irish situation needed urgent and serious attention,
such focus was not forthcoming. The British were more
concerned with wars in the Crimea and India, and local difficulties elsewhere in Europe. The business of running and maintaining the world's largest empire, especially when so many other
world powers coveted what Britain possessed, meant that Ireland
was low on the list of mainstream political priorities. In the post-
famine period, the events of 1848 and general societal chaos had
produced a land that did not function around the norms of
Victorian order. In the years from the late famine and culminating in 1857, the government passed twelve Coercion Acts in a
vain attempt to control the Irish, and instil some semblance of
calm in the Irish countryside.

An official attempt at improving the land situation was the
Encumbered Estates Acts of 1848 and 1849. The idea was
simple. All landlords, predominantly if not exclusively Irish,
who were effectively bankrupt because of the famine, would
have their land bought by British gentlemen farmers. Such
imported farmers, with their high levels of skill and experience,
would encourage a system of tenantry in the improvement of
their land. The scheme failed miserably, as those who were

prepared to travel to Ireland were speculators who had no intention of improving their new land holdings, but merely saw the opportunity for a cheap investment. In the face of such ill-thought-out, and badly managed schemes as the Encumbered Estates Acts, and the general lack of British interest in Ireland, tenants began taking matters into their own hands and protesting on a local basis. The upshot of such protests was the formation, in 1850, of the Irish Tenant Land League.

The Irish Tenant Land League was a cross-denominational organisation that used land agitation as a method of putting across its demands. The League has been seen by many commentators as the first attempt at the creation of a national political grouping that used land agitation as its basis, indeed its *raison d'être*. In this, the Irish Tenant Land League, as short-lived as it was, can be seen as the forerunner of, and blueprint for, the Land League, which would emerge in the later nineteenth century. The Irish Tenant Land League utilised all the gains that had been won for such groupings by the reforms of O'Connell. Most notably, the organisation had forty of its nominees returned to Parliament in the 1852 election. The aim of this impressive bloc of MPs was that they would fight for an Act that would secure the rights and security of the tenant farmer in Ireland. The MPs constantly split over the issue of religion and the fierce debate that surrounded the powers of the Papacy, which was such a feature of contemporary British politics. The organisation eventually fractured at the parliamentary level, and any gains it had made and popular support that it received were lost.

THE FENIANS

The galvanising force that would enter Irish politics in the late 1850s, and end a period of political stagnation, came from overseas. In the wake of the failure of the Young Ireland rebellion in 1848, many of the believers in violent insurrection had emigrated. Two of the key figures who had played a role in 1848, and had chosen to depart, were John O'Mahoney and James Stephens. O'Mahoney had initially travelled to France with Stephens, but had subsequently moved across the Atlantic to

New York. Once in America, O'Mahoney worked tirelessly amongst the New York Irish to raise money and engender support for a future rising. O'Mahoney moved amongst the New York Irish and used the bitter experiences and stories of the famine to galvanise people into giving support to his cause. The equation was simple: few of them would even have been in New York, or ever boarded an emigrant ship, if it had not been for British policy towards Ireland. O'Mahoney offered an appealing response: successful rebellion against the British and independence for Ireland. While O'Mahoney spread his message in America, James Stephens returned from Paris, and travelled across the whole of Ireland so that he could fathom the level of support that might be forthcoming for any future rebellion. Stephens found a deeply divided land, huge levels of discontent, but no existing organisation or leadership that could free Ireland.

Stephens and O'Mahoney worked together, building on their separate experiences, and in 1858, formed the Fenian Brotherhood. The Fenians did not aim for the peaceful liberation of Ireland in the manner that had been attempted by O'Connell, through his use of orderly monster meetings and parliamentary activity. Instead they looked to the late eighteenth and early nineteenth century, and the attempted rebellions of Wolfe Tone and Robert Emmet. The choice facing the Fenians was one that would be echoed repeatedly across the years, and into the Northern Irish peace process of the 1990s. What was the best method of achieving the freedom that organisations such as the Fenians so desperately desired? Was freedom for Ireland to be won through revolutionary violence and the forcible exclusion of the British from the Irish landmass, or could it be achieved through the use of entirely peaceful and constitutional means? How far would the choice of the method of liberation govern and shape any post-independence Ireland?

The Fenians chose violent revolution, but unlike many of the organisations that had gone before them who had chosen a similar path, the Fenians did not act with undue haste. The leadership of the Fenians steadily built up a core of support amongst the emigrant Irish residing in America, Australia and South Africa, and worked hard to construct a solid following in Ireland. The difficulty for the Fenians in Ireland was that the Catholic Church resolutely opposed them. The Church had

always taken a strict line with secret societies, but an organisation such as the Fenians, organised around revolutionary cells,
and run in the utmost secrecy, was anathema to the teachings of
the Church. It is obviously impossible to state, with any
certainty, what the effect of Church opposition meant to the
movement and its chances of success. The presence of such a
clear condemnation however, at a time when pronouncements
from the pulpit carried considerable weight, coupled with the
threat of excommunication for those who did join, is likely to
have had a profound effect on levels of support for the Fenians.

In an attempt to bolster support for the organisation, the
Fenians began publishing a newspaper to spread its message.
The Irish People, under the editorship of Stephens, was first
published in 1861. It also used large public displays to impress
upon any interested party what a dynamic and popular movement the Fenians were. In the same year that *The Irish People*
was first published, Stephens used the funeral of a veteran of
1848, Terence Bellew McManus, to publicly parade Fenian
members in uniform and on horseback. Despite such displays,
the Fenians were no nearer the moment of rebellion. They
simply did not have enough large-scale support across the
country.

A diversion was offered in 1861, with the onset of the
American Civil War. Many Fenians made the decision to travel
across the Atlantic, and take part in the fighting at first hand with
the American Irish brigade. The expertise that was gained on the
battlefields and in skirmishes in America would be vital for the
Fenians if their attempt at rebellion were to be successful.
Despite any lessons that those Fenians in America had learnt,
two vital ingredients for the triumphant expulsion of the British
from Ireland were potentially still missing: the support of large
numbers of the populace, and a weakness on the side of the
British.

In 1865, the American Civil War ended, and the Irish
American veterans returned home. They were met by claims
from Stephens that the work of popularising the Fenian cause in
Ireland had been completed. Stephens boasted a huge membership amongst the general public, claimed that one-third of the
British army based in Ireland was supportive, and estimated that
the number of arms available to the Fenians exceeded 40,000.

The actual plan of rebellion was the most daring ever undertaken by an Irish nationalist grouping to date. The rebellion
would not begin in Ireland itself, but would start with a raid on
Chester Castle. The idea was that the castle would be emptied of
its armament store, a Holyhead train would be seized and the
arms transported from there across the Irish Sea. Once in
Ireland, the arms would be used for a concerted assault on the
British infrastructure in Ireland. The first attempt at the Fenian
rebellion in Chester in February 1867 was called off, as it
appeared that the British had managed to infiltrate the organisation. On 5 March, the rebellion began. Across Ireland, police
barracks were stormed, trains derailed and telegraph communications destroyed. The attack on Chester never took place, and
the organisation remained rife with British-paid informers. The
British were able to quickly bring the situation under control,
and arrest the local and national ringleaders. In May 1867, the
Americans, who the Fenians had constantly been imploring to
assist with the rebellion, sent a ship laden with arms and ammunition to Ireland. The Fenians failed to meet the vessel and take
charge of the cargo, and eventually, frustrated by the Irish, the
Americans returned home with their shipment intact.

In September, the British arrested two of the known ringleaders of the rebellion, Colonel Thomas J. Kelly and Captain
Deasey. Those Fenians who remained active planned to release
their arrested leaders by direct action. They stormed the cart that
was transferring Kelly and Deasey from prison to the court. In
the ensuing fracas a police officer was killed. In response, four
Fenians were arrested and tried for murder. They were convicted,
and hanged for their offence. The four Fenians, who became
popularly known as the Manchester Martyrs, imbued the whole
Fenian organisation with a mythologised and heroic significance.
Despite the abject failure of their rebellion both in Britain and
across Ireland, opposition to their very existence from the
Catholic Church, and the relatively small number of active
members, the Fenians came to represent an underground will of
the nation and the desire to be free from British rule.

In December 1867, the final instalment of the Fenian rebellion
was acted out in London. In an attempt to free an activist from
Clerkenwell prison, the Fenians undertook a jailbreak, using
high explosives to blast through the prison wall. The resulting

explosion tore through the wall in question, but also demolished many surrounding houses. The explosion killed twelve Clerkenwell residents residing in those surrounding houses that were affected by the blast. The government reaction to such an obvious domestic threat was swift. The presence of hundreds of thousands of Irish immigrants across Britain meant that Fenian sympathisers could be anywhere. The government recruited a large force of special constables in an attempt to control the Irish population, and the levels of mutual distrust that existed between the Irish community, in many parts of Britain, and their hosts led to much intercommunal violence during the mid-Victorian era.

POST-FENIAN ANGLO-IRISH POLITICS

That the actual Fenian rebellion failed is beyond doubt. The influence of the Fenians as a functioning group steadily declined during the remainder of the nineteenth century. Their central importance is that they acted as a catalyst of change for both British and Irish politics. Whereas many Irish emigrants, particularly Irish-Americans, clung to the ideal of violent rebellion in the Fenian model, the British and Irish both used the excesses of the Fenian rebellion, and particularly the derogatory effect that it had upon intercommunal relations, to turn their attention to constitutional means as a way of solving the problems of Ireland.

William Ewart Gladstone, Liberal leader and giant of Victorian politics, switched his focus to the Irish problem as a result of the worst excesses of 1867. Gladstone had long believed that Britain needed to take a far more interventionist role in Irish affairs, and to start acting with the Irish, as well as the British, self-interest at the heart of future policy. In 1867, shortly after the Clerkenwell explosion, Gladstone, rather than condemning the Fenians, had accepted that Irish violence was a direct product of Irish grievances. With the exception of certain MPs who had Ireland close to their heart, or the concerns of Irish constituents in their mind, this was a radical statement from a major British political figure. It marked, at the level of high politics at least, a sea change in the future of Anglo-Irish relations. In 1868, Gladstone fought his first election as leader of the

Liberals, with Ireland at the forefront of his campaign. The major issue he put before the electors was the disestablishment of the Protestant Church of Ireland. Gladstone won the election, and he was able to begin his work in Ireland, which would, in many ways, dominate the remainder of his political life.

The effect of Fenianism on the political landscape of Ireland was equally important. Whereas the initial political apathy of the post-famine years had not brought together a populist and dynamic single party grouping in the guise of O'Connell, the post-Fenian years did. It seems that the violent and destructive excesses of the Fenians galvanised those who believed in constitutional and parliamentary change into action. In 1870, Issac Butt, a Protestant barrister based in Dublin, formed the Home Government Association, which quickly became more popularly known as the Home Rule League. Butt's political thesis was simple and direct. Since the Act of Union, the British parliament had proved itself, especially in light of the famine years, unable to rule and administer Ireland without negative consequences. Butt argued that Westminster should relinquish control of Ireland, and instigate an Irish parliament, where the affairs of the Irish nation could be given the particular and 'domestic' treatment that they required. Within such a model of parliamentary independence, Butt saw the Irish parliament only overseeing Irish domestic matters. The parliament would be subordinate to Westminster, and issues such as defence, foreign policy and such like, would continue to be governed from London.

The emergence of the Home Rule League, led by Butt, exerted a powerful pull on Anglo-Irish relations. Despite the limited and quite specific aims of the grouping, the Home Rule League began to be identified in the minds of its supporters with total national self-government, and in the minds of its opponents with an attempt to destroy the union, and weaken the cohesiveness of Empire. The real political impact of the Home Rule League lay in the future. In the immediate post-Fenian era, the initiative for change lay with Gladstone and his Irish policy.

Right from the start of his first parliament in government in 1869, Gladstone took action on Irish issues, successfully pushing his Act for the Disestablishment of the Church of Ireland through both houses of parliament. The act removed all lands and properties from the Church, with the exception of places of worship, and all tithes were taken away. Gladstone's master-stroke, in the context of the Irish situation in the post-famine years, was his redistribution of the confiscated lands. Rather than simply selling them off to the highest bidder, which would have favoured existing landlords and speculators, Gladstone ensured that the bulk of available land was accessible to the tenantry who farmed it. The Act of Disestablishment allowed for any Church tenants to buy their land from the government by means of a low-interest mortgage at a fixed rate. In the years following disestablishment, over 70 per cent of the former tenants of the Church became landowners through the mortgage scheme. Such a simple piece of legislation as Gladstone enacted, ensured that for those thousands of tenants involved, relative security, prosperity and peace of mind became features of their future.

Gladstone saw the whole issue of land ownership as one of the key issues if the condition of Ireland were to be changed. In 1870, he guided the Irish Land Act through parliament, though the Act that was finally approved by the Lords was radically different from that envisaged by Gladstone. The initial bill that was proposed placed the tenant under the protection of the state. If the bill had been successful, landlords would have had to compensate tenants for any improvements they had made on their land in the case of eviction. For Gladstone, the tenant–landowner relationship was one of partnership, not solely a business transaction in favour of the landlord. The ramifications of the proposed bill for the Irish landlords, and their supporters who sat in the House of Lords, were unpalatable. When the Act was finally passed, all the safeguards that Gladstone had envisaged had been removed, and the lot of the Irish tenant was not substantially improved.

The passage of the Irish Land Act was an important precursor to Irish affairs for the remainder of the nineteenth century. While there was clearly a political will to solve the problems of Ireland amongst the British parliamentary class, there still remained powerful and well-organised self-interested groups who did not wish to see reform. Despite the support that any reformer such as Gladstone would receive from the Irish parliamentary groupings, indeed from the Irish populace at large, such support would not simply continue following blindly if the opposing parties were always able to hold back the pace of reform.

Butt's Home Rule League, which was popularly supported by a large membership across Ireland, who paid a small membership fee in line with the model of O'Connell's mass movement, would transform itself to become the voice of Ireland's consciousness. Butt believed that a better deal for Ireland could be won through co-operation with Parliament. Following the events of 1870, and the relatively simple derailing of the Irish Land Act's initial intentions, it was clear that Butt's view was naive. In 1874, when the members of the Home Rule League were elected to Parliament in such large numbers, they formed themselves into an identifiable group: the Irish Home Rule Party. Butt's leadership of this group was ineffectual, and Gladstone's enthusiasm for Irish reform dampened, in the face of the Lords' intransigence and a welter of other issues he had to deal with.

THE ADVENT OF CHARLES STEWART PARNELL

The big change in the fortunes of the Irish Home Rule Party came in April 1875, when Charles Stewart Parnell, a Protestant landowner from a distinguished Anglo-Irish family, was returned as MP for Meath. Parnell was a fervent Irish nationalist, who believed in the force of constitutional nationalism. His passion for the cause of Irish freedom was far removed, however, from that of Butt. While Butt seemingly waited politely to see what titbits were thrown from the parliamentary table, Parnell believed that home rule was there to be fought for and won. It was as if he wanted to bring the passionate struggle of the Irish nationalists that had taken up arms – Tone, Emmet and the Fenians – and translate their vehemence, and belief, into the parliamentary arena.

Parnell's aim was to make the British parliamentary system unworkable. By building on a tactic that had previously been used by the Irish Home Rule Party member J. C. Biggar, that of obstruction, Parnell believed that he and his fellow Irish MPs could bring parliamentary business to a grinding halt. If this could be achieved, an obvious sense of crisis would arise amongst the British political parties, and their minds would, by necessity, be concentrated on the Irish question. Throughout the second half of the 1870s, Irish Home Rule MPs made long speeches, introduced countless amendments to bills, and demanded votes and parliamentary divisions on minor issues, so that the business of government ground to halt. The government was so desperate that it turned to Butt for assistance, requesting that he check the activities of his party members. Butt duly admonished Parnell in public for his tactic of blocking parliamentary business. Butt's decision to act with the government, rather than standing by his own MP, was the death knell of his political career. The Irish who followed Parnell and the Home Rule Party did not wish to hear that their supposed leader had sided with the foreign government. Butt died in 1879, by which time Parnell was effectively the head of a vibrant, and for the government, highly problematic parliamentary party.

The second half of the 1870s, and the early years of the 1880s, signal a key period in attempting to understand the vibrancy of, and wide-scale support for, the campaign in support of home rule. In the 1870s, Irish agriculture, despite all the structural changes that had been brought about by the famine, was once more in a state of chaos. American agriculture emerged as a force within the European markets, and this affected crop and produce prices in both Britain and Ireland. An agricultural depression plagued most of the 1870s, and many tenants fell into arrears. As a result, the number of evictions from the land spiralled once more. For many of the Irish, those very people who had managed to survive the terrible devastation of the famine two decades earlier, poverty and hunger stalked the land once more. The situation was made far worse in 1877 and 1878, when the potato crop failed again. Despite the hardships caused by the famine, and all the lives that had been lost, over large tracts of Ireland the population still survived solely or predominantly on a home-produced potato crop. Only a quarter of the potato crop was saved in those two years, and the same cycle of devastation that had been such a feature of the famine re-emerged. Death, emigration and eviction became common features of the lives of many of the poorest Irish, especially those in Connacht.

In the face of such devastation, the parliamentary and political scene in Ireland was transformed and radicalised. Parnell forged alliances with the two most important populist and radical movements that existed at the time. The alliances were driven in part by mutual admiration, but also by practicality. Each of the forces needed the support, and either the respectability or radicalism, that each afforded the other. In the late 1870s, Parnell and the Fenians reached an accommodation. While Parnell was undoubtedly welded to the idea of constitutional, as opposed to violent, reform, he understood well the power and influence that the Fenian network possessed, particularly amongst Irish-Americans. The Fenians, impressed and partially won over by the effectiveness of Parnell's campaign of belligerence in parliament, agreed to give Parnell their financial and vocal support. Such an alliance gave Parnell a hard, and potentially threatening, edge. While it is clear that he was never won over to the idea of violent revolution, and the Fenians never jettisoned their belief in physical-force nationalism as part of their accommodation with Parnell, no one in British parliamentary and government circles could ever be sure of the exact nature of the Parnell–Fenian alliance.

The accommodation reached between Parnell and the Fenians, important though it was, does not compare to the importance and impact of the alliance between Parnell and Michael Davitt.

THE LAND LEAGUE AND THE LAND WAR

Michael Davitt was a committed Fenian. He had spent from 1870 until 1877, enduring a sentence of hard labour for possessing arms, after which he travelled to America. He returned to Ireland to observe the effects of the late 1870s potato failures, and the ensuing evictions. In the face of such evictions, Irish tenants were taking matters into their own hands. Large parts of the countryside, particularly in the west of Ireland, witnessed attacks on landlords and their property, and there was regular violence against the various middlemen and law enforcers who oversaw evictions.

Davitt drew on the chaos and violence, and brought the Irish tenantry together under the auspices of the Land League. The aim was to protect all tenants from the effects of sudden and dramatic increases in their rent, and the fear, or experience, of eviction. The Land War meant that there was a ready supply of disenchanted or fearful individuals who would follow Davitt in an attempt to protect themselves. The Land League's principal enemies were the landlords, who were held responsible for the spiralling number of evictions, and the constant transformation of land use from tillage to pasture. In the context of the time, the landlords came to symbolise more than agrarian hardship. Their very presence in Ireland, the abuse of their power and their flagrant disregard for Ireland and its people, meant that there was a ready link made between the land issue and that of home rule. The achievement of home rule would, by necessity it appeared, lead to the solution of the land problem. In June 1879, Davitt invited Parnell to appear in Westport, Co. Mayo, and address a meeting of the Land League. Parnell spoke openly against the landlords, and in doing so forged a clear link between the twin issues of the land and home rule. The parallel agendas of the two movements meant that in October 1879, Parnell was invited to become President of the Land League. The triple alliance that would mount the most sustained challenge to British control of Ireland to date was complete. It ranged from the secretive, yet extremist Fenians, through the populist and disruptive Land League, and was headed, publicly at least, by the respectable and efficient Parliamentarian Parnell. Such an alliance covered all shades of political and cultural opinion within nationalist Ireland, and presented a cohesiveness of belief that had never before existed. The question was, how would the British react?

Parnell's difficulty was that he had to walk a tightrope. He believed that he could only win home rule for Ireland constitu-tionally. If that was to be the case, the British electorate, and its MPs, had to be convinced that the Irish cause was a just and fair one. Most importantly, the British establishment had to be sure that the move towards home rule, and its eventual achievement, would not lead to a violent destruction of the values, local prop-erties and imperial politics that they held dear. Against such an awareness of the British perspective, Parnell had to also retain the support of his Irish followers. He needed their support, and their threatening presence was certainly a boon in winning over, indeed frightening, many British politicians and commentators to the cause of home rule. The spectre of an underground and tenant army, that he could only control if concessions were granted, was a useful tool for Parnell to have within the British context. In Ireland however, Parnell had to work with the Land League and the Fenians, and try to secure as many concessions as quickly as possible to assure them that their continued support was worthwhile.

Up until 1880, Parnell's biggest problem was that there was a Conservative government in office, which would have no truck with the idea of Irish home rule. In 1880, Gladstone was returned to office with a parliamentary majority. Gladstone still believed that the Irish situation was one that needed addressing urgently, but he did not want to rush at the issue at the start of his parliament, and risk losing legislation that was ill thought out. Parnell, however, demanded swift action. The Irish Home Rule Party had won sixty-one seats in Ireland. In doing so he had secured, with the exception of the Ulster constituencies, an overwhelming endorsement for his cause from Irish voters. As a consequence of the popular approval of his party's policies and activities, Parnell would not accept Gladstone's more thoughtful approach to Irish matters. Rather than delay, especially in light of the continuation of evictions across Ireland, Parnell introduced a private bill to protect Irish tenants. The bill was eventually incorporated into a larger piece of government legislation. If successful, it would have afforded all tenants faced with eviction, protection against their landlords, so long as the cause of eviction was non-payment of rent due to crop failure. As in 1870, the House of Lords refused to look favourably on such legislation, and the spirit of Parnell's bill was lost.

Despite Parnell's overwhelming endorsement by the electorate, the House of Lords, the apparent bastion of landlord interest, had prevented positive and pro-tenant legislation from being enacted. In response to such a rebuff, and in the face of continued evictions, membership of, and support for, the Land League continued to gather pace. The Land War grew in intensity. New tactics were developed by the League, such as boycotting those who had anything to do with the process of eviction, and the total social exclusion of any Irish who were prepared to take on land from which families had been evicted.

While Davitt and Parnell did not believe the that Land League should be a violent organisation, it was perhaps inevitable that the Land War would become inflamed, and that brutal acts would be conducted in the name of the League. To illustrate how extreme the situation became, one needs look no further than the experience of Captain Charles Boycott. He was a land agent who had carried out evictions, and was thus boycotted (hence the term) by local labourers when he needed his crops harvesting. The boycott was so complete that Boycott had to bring in a team of Protestants from Ulster to carry out the harvest. The rage in Mayo against Boycott was so great, and the threat to his Ulster workers so real, that 7000 troops were sent to maintain the peace during the harvest. While there was no violence in the face of such a large army presence, disturbances elsewhere were commonplace.

By the end of 1880, large parts of rural Ireland were becoming ungovernable. Gladstone, so often the friend of Ireland, had no choice but to introduce a series of Coercion Acts, which became law in February 1881. The problem for Gladstone, indeed for all involved, was how to move forward. While the Coercion Acts might have made Ireland easier to govern, they did nothing to prevent outbreaks of violence. Crimes against the person and property continued at high rates, as did the evictions. Gladstone could not hold a resolutely oppressive line in Ireland, even had he believed in such a stance, as Parnell, his party, the Land League and the Fenians were all still active and popularly supported. Gladstone's only option was to attempt further reform: to give the Land League what it demanded.

In the spring of 1881, Gladstone introduced a new land bill for Ireland. The bill gave the Land League most that it had campaigned for: fair rents that would be agreed by a Land Tribunal, security of tenure, acknowledgement of the tenants' right to sell their occupancy, and government loans so that tenants could purchase their land. Gladstone's bill had the potential, if it became law, to revolutionise the system of land ownership, particularly for tenants, across Ireland. Gladstone omitted one central tenent of the Land League and Home Rule Party's demands for land reform: secure tenure for tenants in arrears. Gladstone's view was that such an undertaking had resulted in the loss of the 1880 legislation, at the hands of the Lords, and that such a stipulation in the proposed 1881 Land Act would have the same effect.

What would the reaction of the different interested groups in Ireland be? The Land League was broadly welcoming of the proposed bill, as was Parnell. He was, however, concerned with his bigger goal, that of home rule. If the proposed 1881 Land Act was a success and the Irish tenantry was given most that they had long campaigned for, would they lose interest in home rule? Parnell began questioning the working of the Land Act, and urged tenants not to trust its spirit, but to put each aspect of the legislation to the test. Such an intervention from Parnell was unwelcome, and he was duly arrested as an agitator, and placed in Dublin's Kilmainham jail.

Following the arrest of Parnell, the Chief Secretary of Ireland, W. E. Forster, also used the Coercion Acts to arrest Davitt, and to suppress the Land League. Forster's actions, as ill-guided as they may seem, had the effect of quickly galvanising the situation. Parnell and Gladstone drew up the Kilmainham Treaty, which would ensure Irish co-operation over the passage of the Land Act in return for the insertion of tenant protection from eviction into the bill. With the exception of the murder of the newly installed Chief Secretary of Ireland, Lord Frederick Cavendish, and his assistant by a shadowy extremist group centred around the Irish Republican Brotherhood, all progressed smoothly. By the time of the 1885 election, the Land Act had become law; the Land League had been replaced by a body concerned expressly with home rule, the Irish National League; and a semblance of order had returned to Ireland.

THE HOME RULE BILL AND THE FALL OF PARNELL

At the 1885 election, the Home Rule Party swept the board in the Irish constituencies in Ireland, the only exceptions being seats in Ulster and those in Trinity College, Dublin. Such a powerful block of sitting MPs would have formed a formidable political force in any context. The Home Rule MPs were extremely effective. They sat as a single group, and were concerned essentially with a single issue: Home Rule. When it became clear that Gladstone, for all his support for the cause of Ireland, would not attempt to enact a home rule bill within the new parliamentary session, Parnell withdrew his backing for the Liberal administration. Gladstone was wearily left in a no-win situation. To lose the support of the Irish Home Rulers, was to relinquish power to the Conservatives. To try and force a home rule bill through parliament was potentially to destroy his own party.

Gladstone decided, whatever the risks, and with his hands tied by Parnell, to move with the latter choice. In the first weeks of 1886, he put forward a home rule bill for Ireland. The formula suggested within the bill was straightforward, and would have been familiar to campaigners of old, such as O'Connell or Butt. The suggested shape of home rule was a parliament and executive in Dublin, which would administer Ireland and its affairs, while the authority for matters of a global or imperial nature remained with Westminster. The backlash against his bill, and the concomitant collapse in party discipline that Gladstone had envisaged, came horribly true. In June 1886, the home rule bill failed and the Liberal Party was left in tatters. While some had followed Gladstone in his reforming zeal, a large number of Liberals had broken free of the party and stood in opposition to home rule, as the Liberal Unionists.

Gladstone's only choice in the face of such a total defeat, was to take the issue to the electorate, and hope that they would support him. The mood in the country, however, was equally opposed to, and unready for, the prospect of home rule. For many, the only result that they could foresee emerging from a successful home rule bill, was a belligerent and awkward neighbour, which would stand in constant opposition to Britain's interests. The election result decimated the Liberals, and returned the Conservatives to power. Parnell's support remained largely unchanged, but the size of the Conservative majority made the presence of the Home Rule Party at Westminster largely academic. The simple mathematics of the new parliament meant that Parnell and his followers could not affect the future direction of Ireland. That task lay firmly in the hands of the Conservative government.

The late 1880s led to the complete destruction of the political machine that Parnell had built. The first years of the Conservative government's administration shadowed a period of crop failure in Ireland. Rents remained unpaid, and violence between tenants, middlemen and landlords ensued. In response, the Conservative government enforced a whole scries of Coercion Acts on Ireland and utilised the forces of law and order to ensure that evictions were successfully completed. Although Parnell and the Home Rule Party had effectively become politically sterile, the ongoing unrest in Ireland ensured that support for the party remained high. In December 1889, however, Parnell's world, and the cohesion of Irish support for his party, came to a crushing and sudden end.

In December 1889, Parnell was cited in a divorce case that emerged as a result of a long-standing affair he had been conducting with Katherine O'Shea, wife of the Irish Home Rule MP William O'Shea. Mrs O'Shea had borne Parnell three children, and her husband appears to have accepted the complex personal situation that had evolved around him. The divorce proceedings were played out in the full glare of a hungry and, in the context of Victorian Britain, voyeuristic press, that reported every twist and turn in the court hearings. The name of Parnell, one of the most important politicians of the time, featured large in all the reporting.

Parnell was given the support of his own party in the initial stages of the scandal. It soon became clear, however, that the Liberals, those vital partners in the cause of home rule, could not square their Nonconformist religious beliefs with Parnell's decade-long adultery. Liberal members demanded that Gladstone force the Home Rule Party to jettison Parnell. Once it became clear to many Home Rule Party MPs that they could lose the all-important Liberal support, they decided to dismiss Parnell. The decision to remove Parnell from the party leadership, although supported by the Catholic hierarchy in Ireland, split the Home Rule Party down the middle. It was not until the early years of the twentieth century that political Home Rule at Westminster would reconfigure itself into a cohesive grouping that could once more exert pressure on the major British parties. Parnell attempted to battle on from a much-weakened position, but he could not engender the support necessary to win popular votes. In 1891, months after finally marrying Mrs O'Shea, Parnell died at his home in Brighton, at the age of forty-five.

The remainder of the nineteenth century was a period in the wilderness for the political cause of home rule. The Conservatives were in office from 1886 until 1905, apart from a brief Liberal interlude that lasted from 1892 to 1895. The Conservative ministries during that period had little interest in

Ireland, and none in the ideal of home rule. The Liberals, when briefly returned to office under the leadership of Gladstone, did present a home rule bill to parliament in 1893. While the Commons passed the bill, it was lost to an overwhelming majority in the Lords. Home rule it seemed, politically at least, was dead.

CULTURAL NATIONALISM

Running parallel with the successful emergence of an effective Home Rule Party under the leadership of Parnell, was the steady realisation amongst many within Irish life that independence was not solely a political goal. Alongside legislative freedom, there had to exist an independence of the mind, a freedom of expression. In common with many nationalist thinkers and activists across Europe, it was clear to many Irish nationalists, that the traditional forms of Irish cultural life had, at best, become marginalised, or else disappeared completely by the last decades of the nineteenth century.

The effects of the famine had been devastating on all aspects of Irish life. The total dislocation that it caused had a debilitating effect on Irish social life. In the context of death, disease, migration and emigration, traditional sites of social and cultural activity, such as the great fairs or religious holidays, had ceased to be common features of the calendar. Alongside the effects of the famine, were the actions of the Church and the presence of the British in Ireland. The Church, especially as it became an increasingly important, and ever-more-organised aspect of people's lives in the second half of the nineteenth century, frowned upon many traditional forms of social and cultural behaviour, as they were not seen as conducive to Catholic worship. The British presence in Ireland, especially in the years of union, had forced a degree of standardisation on Irish life. The Irish language disappeared from everyday use in many parts of the country; the language of work and business was English, and popular forms of entertainment, social behaviour and customs were increasingly drawn from the British experience. It was the loss of cultural difference that most concerned many Irish nationalists. If home rule were won from the Westminster parliament, what would remain of Ireland? Would it be a free nation that spoke English, and behaved in exactly the same fashion as the British?

The cultural nationalists began organising themselves in the 1880s, but their existence was of the greatest importance during the 1890s. In the political vacuum that had been left by the demise of Parnell and the divisions within the Home Rule Party, cultural nationalist organisations offered Irish men and women a cohesiveness of cultural experience, and most importantly, a clear sense of an Irish identity. The task facing the cultural nationalists was not an easy one. The late nineteenth century was a time of great imperial power for the British. Their forms of behaviour, social customs, educational systems, business methods and their language spread across the globe. If far-flung corners of the world were open to the effects of British imperialism, and the concomitant destruction or alteration of native habits, then how could the Irish, who were geographically so close to Britain, resist?

The method of resistance was culture. In 1884, Michael Cusack founded the Gaelic Athletic Association (GAA) in Thurles. The GAA aimed to halt the incursion of British sports and pastimes into Irish life. By promoting Irish forms of athletics, the sports of hurling and Gaelic football, and many other forms of distinctive Irish culture, the GAA aimed to reclaim the leisure time of the Irish man and woman for the cause of the nation. Rather than playing, as the GAA hierarchy saw them, the effeminate games of cricket and soccer, which reinforced norms of British behaviour and manners, the Irish would play their native sports and games, which would imbue the Irish athlete with traditional manly attributes, physical fitness and the fighting spirit necessary to free Ireland. The GAA was immensely popular from the start, and quickly won a huge following amongst the Catholic section of the population. As a vehicle for the preservation of Irish traditional pastimes, the GAA was undoubtedly successful, as the comparative failure of other team sports to dominate the twentieth-century scene clearly demonstrates. In the late nineteenth-century context, the GAA was an important conduit for the transference of nationalist ideology to a mass audience. In the 1890s, the GAA was infiltrated by sections of the radical Irish Republican Brotherhood, and would, in due course, become a centrally important force in the physical battle to free Ireland during the revolutionary period.

While the GAA managed the affairs, and primed the bodies, of the lower classes and those in rural areas, the Gaelic League functioned in the higher echelons of Irish society and worked relentlessly to preserve the native language. Founded in 1893, the Gaelic League aimed at saving what pockets of the Irish language remained, and promoting its use elsewhere. The first President of the Gaelic League was Douglas Hyde, who argued that the Irish language was far richer than the English, and that to use the native vernacular was an issue of patriotism, not one of expedience.

In promoting the Irish language, the Gaelic League turned its attention to selections from Ireland's ancient texts, traditions and history. In doing so the League promoted an ancient vision of an idyllic Ireland that existed in pre-famine and pre-union times. Here, in the ancient texts, there existed a far richer and purer Ireland that had been the sole concern of Irish people. In studying the language and literature of the ancient Irish land, the League encouraged the belief that the Irish nation could profitably exist, as it had done centuries before, free of British control and influence. To speak Irish, to study the literature of Ireland's past and to work within the various cultural festivals and literary events that the League organised, was to reject West Britonism, and to embrace the future Irish nation. While in no way as numerically strong as the GAA, the Gaelic League is always seen as having an instrumental aeffect on Irish life, and the future of the nation. While it is certain that its various events, dinners and readings were meeting places for those who would lead Ireland politically and militarily to its eventual independence, it is the legacy of certain key members that is most often remembered.

The Gaelic League attracted the leading individuals from the literary and dramatic world into its ranks in the 1890s. Alongside Douglas Hyde, was the poet William Butler Yeats. In addition to promoting the linguistic, cultural and political message of the Gaelic League, Hyde, Yeats and those who formed a group around them, became the patrons, advocates and adherents of the Irish Literary Renaissance and revival. This group of individuals produced some of the most important works of Irish, if not global, literature of the late nineteenth and early twentieth century. From one of its initial homes, at Lady Gregory's Coole Park, in Co. Galway, the group transferred its centre of activity to the Abbey Theatre in Dublin. The Abbey formed the focus for a centrally important literary group, which was supported by a network of journals and publications, and would promote a new vision of Irish identity through the use of language, literature and drama. Alongside Hyde and Yeats, men and women such as James Joyce, John Millington Synge and Maud Gonne involved themselves, at various times, with the activities of the Abbey group and the Gaelic League. In addition to the group of luminaries, who would find lasting fame in the world of literature while they promoted the cause of Ireland, were fellow travellers in the Gaelic League who became centrally important in the narrative of Ireland's history. The name of Patrick Pearse, who will be discussed in detail later, is key amongst such members of the Gaelic League: individuals who saw cultural nationalism as a key tool in the reawakening of the Irish nation, so that its freedom could be won through political, and if necessary, military means.

LAND REFORM

The passing of Parnell had not been mourned amongst the political elites of the Conservative and Unionist sections of the Westminster parliament. Equally, the existence of the forces of cultural nationalism, while a minor irritant at times, did little to move Parliament towards support for home rule. The Conservatives did decide, however, that the contemporary state of Ireland in the final decades of the nineteenth century could not be allowed to continue. There were still major problems around the broad issue of the land; and ownership was key amongst these. While not wishing to challenge the status quo in any way, the Conservatives did realise that simply to ignore Ireland as an issue would give rise to greater levels of violence, and potentially encourage violent populist demands for a change in the legal status of Ireland.

The Conservatives decided that their wisest course of action would be an attempt to remove any impetus that could lead to demands for home rule. A policy of 'killing home rule with kindness' emerged.

The biggest threat to the stability of Ireland was the land issue. All the major Irish political figures of the nineteenth century had used the issue of land and its ownership as a rallying call to mobilise people behind the larger banner of home rule and independence. In the vacuum left behind after the fall of Parnell, the Conservative government wanted to avoid the risk of another Davitt or O'Connell coming to the fore on the coat tails of a land reform agenda. The Conservatives concluded that a land reform programme would solve the Irish problem in a single sweep. They believed that if Ireland could be converted from its contemporary state of largely absentee land ownership, into a country of independent and content small holders, then the ideal of home rule would lose its allure. Many commentators believed, perhaps correctly, that the majority of small farmers and tenants in Ireland at that time had no real interest in national politics. All that they wanted was a patch of land to call their own, so that they could support their family. In the absence of such personal land ownership, opportunistic and personally motivated politicians had been able to convince such people that the real problem was the political status of Ireland.

Whatever the exact thinking behind the Conservative land reforms in Ireland during their time in office, they were certainly the most far-reaching and sustained attempt to alter the pattern of Irish land ownership ever undertaken. Such reforms changed the map of Ireland forever, and did meet the demands of many of those whose livelihood depended on the land. The bulk of land purchases were overseen and controlled by the Conservative Chief Secretary Arthur Balfour. Huge tracts of land across the length and breadth of Ireland were bought from the large landowners. Loans were then offered by central government to the local Irish, who had traditionally worked or else rented the land, so that they could purchase the land themselves. Balfour had begun a revolutionising process that was completed by his successor in office, George Wyndham, whose Land Purchase Act of 1903 was the culmination of all the different pieces of legislation, and ensured that even the most sceptical landlords were convinced that it was in their best financial interests to sell their land to the government. In the five years that followed,

Wyndham's legislation ensured that some 317,000 smallholdings were transferred into the hands of peasant proprietors.

The Conservative government, although not moving at all on the issue of Irish home rule, transformed Ireland. By the time of the First World War, Irish landlordism, with all the ills that had traditionally accompanied it, had become a thing of the past. One of the root causes of Irish demonstrations and grievance, that had been such a common feature of the nineteenth-century experience, and in part given rise to the famine, and which had assisted radical movements such as the Land League, was largely removed. Despite this, and although the Conservatives had hoped such a successful implementation of the land legislation would kill demands for home rule, the political dynamic did not disappear from Irish politics.

When Ireland achieved its freedom from Britain in the 1920s, the first governments of the new state did not have to deal with the issue of land ownership and the manner of its distribution. The Conservatives had already done that job for them. At the turn of the century however, despite the Land Acts and the demise of the political figurehead in the shape of Parnell, the spirit of home rule was still alive and well. Its home was primarily within the ranks of the cultural nationalist organisations, amongst the small extremes of the physical-force movements, and it was carried forward by the Irish Parliamentary Party at Westminster. The continued existence of a home rule ideology resulted, in part, in the sustained rise and increasing politicisation of Unionism.

THE MOBILISATION OF UNIONISM

Even after the Land Acts, which did so much to change the economic fortunes of the majority of the Irish, the bulk of wealth in Ireland was concentrated in Ulster. In the north-east corner of Ireland, the predominantly Protestant population had thrown themselves full square behind the nineteenth-century pursuit of Empire, and had benefited accordingly. Whereas the bulk of Ireland remained agricultural, Ulster was predominantly industrial. The urban centres of Belfast and Londonderry, as well as a host of other smaller towns, provided work and wealth for a steadily growing population. Institutions such as Queen's University Belfast had grown into respected centres of excellence and provided future political leaders, industrialists and the professional classes. The fact that Ulster was Protestant, and loyal to the institutions of state and crown, meant that it shared much in common with Britain. It had accordingly avoided the excesses of any of the nineteenth-century Coercion Acts. Since the advent of union, those pockets of Presbyterianism that had followed co-religious nationalists such as Wolfe Tone, had ceased to look to an Irish solution to any problems that they may have had. The experience of the nineteenth century had demonstrated to the Protestant and Presbyterian populations of Ulster (and also to those unionists elsewhere in Ireland) the importance of maintaining the link with Britain, which was where their wealth and their cultural heritage emanated from.

It is clear that in the second half of the nineteenth century, unionists across the country felt threatened by talk of home rule. Selfishly, and perhaps understandably, they thought that the advent of home rule, and thus a predominantly nationalist and Catholic Ireland, in severing the link with Britain and the Empire, would destroy their comparative economic wealth. In the demands for home rule, within the cultural nationalist movements and amidst the overriding power of the Catholic Church, unionists could see little that appealed to them. Their chosen path was one of resistance. They would use whatever means were possible to resist the moves towards home rule, so that they might protect their position and maintain their particular loyalties to what they considered their land, nation, crown and religion.

Resistance, or at least the organised form of such, had emerged with the likelihood of Gladstone choosing to back home rule. The long-existent Orange League was rejuvenated at the prospect of battle. In 1867, the Ulster Defence Association emerged as an elitist social organisation aimed at defending the union. The tabling of Gladstone's home rule bills had spurred an alliance between the forces of British Conservatism and that of Ulster unionism. In 1886, the Conservative Lord Randolph Churchill spoke in Belfast, and in uttering the phrase 'Ulster will fight, and Ulster will be right,' encapsulated the spirit of unionist resistance for the decades ahead, as the home rule ideal was fought over.

The putative resistance that emerged in Ulster against the force of home rule in the late nineteenth century was a precursor of what was to come. While the fortunes of Parnell rode high at times, it was always inconceivable that Westminster, especially in the form of the Lords, would ever countenance the idea of home rule legislation. As a result, the unionist opposition to Irish nationalism, while vociferous and well organised, never had its mettle truly tested. The onset of the twentieth century would change that situation, indeed the whole of Ireland, completely.

5

· · · · · · · ·

Founding the States

For many who have given a fleeting thought to Ireland, the twentieth century probably appears as the island's most problematic and bloody century. It began with a constitutional crisis over home rule that would, after the devastation of the First World War, give way to a period of revolution and civil war. The century has ended with three decades of paramilitary violence, and a peace process that is as complex as the Gordian knot that it is trying to unravel. While this most recent of centuries has seemingly involved the peoples of Ireland, especially, most recently, those in the north of the island, in constant problems and difficulties, one has to wonder whether these are profoundly different from the various dilemmas and disasters that have struck previously. One would suggest that the notoriety of twentieth-century Ireland is a product of its familiarity. This is meant not merely in the chronological sense, of being close to us in time, but also in the technological sense. While the various combatants of the revolutionary period can be viewed hurrying across the screen in that double-pace walk of all silent-film footage, the often bloody chaos of modern Northern Ireland has been transmitted direct into our homes in the form of vivid television pictures. We are all familiar with the varied symbolism of Northern Ireland, such as its marching season and gable-end murals, even if we do not fully understand it. By contrast, while we may read of the devastation of the famine or the intercommunal massacres of the seventeenth century, there exists no immediacy, no instantaneous images, no voices that we can hear, nor faces we can see. While it is imperative that a book such as this covers the twentieth century, as it is the story of our times, that is not to say this is any more important than any other time in the history of Ireland.

The Irish twentieth century began in relative peace. The Conservatives were in power in Westminster, where they would remain for a further six years. There was no portent of the upheavals of the First World War, which would blight Europe and radically affect Ireland. The Irish Parliamentary Party was steadily reforming and regrouping after its long post-Parnellite drift. The forces of cultural nationalism were popularly supported, while those of extremist physical-force nationalism, though always a minority, were constantly readied for the battle. The unionists were equally ready. They watched carefully the developments south of Ulster, for any sign of future mobilisation amongst the nationalists. Economically, Ireland moved ahead steadily. Land ownership was changing rapidly, and family incomes stabilised as a result. In the industrial areas there were slight downturns and small booms, but here also, there was predominantly stability. The real question for the first decades was how, if at all, the forces of unionism and nationalism could accommodate each other? If that could not be done, which way would the British jump? Would they enforce the will of one of the groups in Ireland, against the wishes of the other? Also, would there be factions within either unionism or nationalism which would be prepared to reach settlements unacceptable to their fellow travellers?

NATIONALISM RE-EMERGENT

Politically, the important developments in Ireland in the initial years of the twentieth century emerged from among the various followers of the nationalist cause. The developments demonstrated that while the nationalist movement had a single goal, that is, some form of home rule, there existed radically different interpretations of what form it should actually take, and how it should be achieved.

In 1900, Parnell's former party, which had remained divided between those who had supported him, and those who had not, finally re-emerged as a single political unit. John Redmond took the leadership of the Irish Parliamentary Party. The transition to being a single party once more, was a simple step that caused few ructions. The only real loss was the departure from the new party of William O'Brien. He had been the leader of the United Irish League, founded in the late 1880s expressly to celebrate the spirit of the men of 1798, during their centenary year. O'Brien was a brilliant organiser, who would have been invaluable to Redmond's party. He resigned from the party executive in 1903, as he found that there was no room for the ideal of inclusiveness, which had been at the heart of 1798.

It is imperative that those wishing to understand what was happening at the turn of the century recognise that, despite outward signs of tranquillity, the late nineteenth and early twentieth century had led to a profound shift in the ideal of what nationalism stood for. The spirit of 1798, that of a cross-religious impetus leading Ireland to a freer and better future, had been lost, in part, during the nineteenth century. Leaders of the nationalist movement in the nineteenth century, such as O'Connell and Parnell, although seeking a constitutional answer to Ireland's problems, primarily began seeing the national issue as one that was concomitant with a belief in Catholicism. While there was a respect for the concerns of the broad unionist population, there was no great attempt to carry them along. In the wake of cultural nationalism, the 1798 centenary, and the nationalist fervour that surrounded the Boer War (especially the defeats of the British), the political spirit of nationalism and the conception of the ideal nation took a step further towards the Gaelic perspective of what Ireland should be.

While Redmond brought Parnell's party back together, it was a party transformed, which had been ideologically influenced by the ideals of cultural nationalism, and possessed an altered perspective of what home rule was for. While Redmond, and many of his followers, believed wholeheartedly in the constitutional route to home rule, and supported the ideal that Ireland should have a place within the Empire, their future plan for the construction of an independent Ireland, carried with it a belief in a Gaelicised nation.

Alongside the arrival of Redmond, and the reconstruction of a single dominant nationalist or home rule party within Westminster, was the foundation of a political group that stressed a more fervent, and expressly Gaelic, vision of the nation. Arthur Griffith founded the Sinn Féin party in 1905. The aims of the party were wide, and all-encompassing: Sinn Féin aimed to secure independence for the whole of Ireland. The vision for the nation, once formed, was vague, but the party utilised the language of Gaelic Ireland, which was so popular amongst contemporary cultural nationalists. It was an Ireland that cared little for the unionist population, wanted no relationship with Britain or her Empire, and promised a broad socialist-minded and common prosperity for all. Arthur Griffith was a man of great organisational abilities, a journalist who had established his own paper, the *United Irishman*, and someone who, despite being non-violent in personal belief, was aware of the reality that Ireland might have to win its freedom through a campaign of violence. Sinn Féin was a minority party in the run up to the First World War, as Redmond's Irish Parliamentary Party dominated the political landscape. Across the country, small Sinn Féin clubs were set up to publicise the party message, and to bring people together. The party did not have mass popular support. The local clubs became vehicles for local campaigns, which dealt with issues such as land ownership, rather than being the launching pad for a movement of national action.

If the Irish Parliamentary Party and Sinn Féin were the most important manifestations of political nationalism, the forces of a more militant and violently minded nationalism shadowed them. The physical-force nationalists ranged within the Irish Republican Brotherhood (IRB) were the descendants of the Fenians. They were funded directly from Irish-America, and their basic aim was the complete expulsion of the British from Ireland, and the creation of an independent nation. The IRB had accepted, in the wake of the failure of the 1867 insurrection, that any future military action had to be conducted with the support of the mass of the people. It became a largely moribund organisation through the years of Parnell's successes, although it never disappeared. In the early twentieth century, the IRB was reinvigorated by its increased links with the broad nationalist movement. Men such as Arthur Griffith, Bulmer Hobson and Seán MacDermott, who would feature so centrally in the story of Sinn Féin, also assisted, at various times, in the reorganisation of the IRB. While remaining, as it always had been, a secret organisation, the IRB slowly and steadily recruited an increasing, though never huge, number of members in the run up to the outbreak of the First World War. The IRB's basic function was always to be ready, to be prepared for any situation that would leave Britain weak, and which might bring the majority of the people behind the idea of rebellion. The question for the IRB, indeed for the whole spectrum of nationalist groups, was: when would that time come? Would it be signalled by British repression, or was it dependent on the complete failure of constitutional means?

THE IMPACT OF BRITISH POLITICS

For all the changing currents in the broad sweep of nationalist movements, and any resistance that may have been considered by the unionists, the future of Irish politics was ultimately dependent on events at Westminster. It was clear from the rebellious interlude of 1867, that Britain was far stronger than any physical-force movement could ever be. While Britain, Liberal or Conservative, held its nerve and wished to remain in Ireland, an uprising was unlikely to be successful. The same was true for constitutional politics. Unless one of the British parties, usually the Liberals, were dependent on Irish support, as Gladstone had once been, the Irish in parliament were unlikely to achieve much by the way of constitutional reform.

The Conservatives had resigned from office in 1905, and been replaced by a Liberal administration which won a landslide victory in the election of 1906. The Irish Parliamentary Party, under Redmond, performed well at the election, but in the face of such a Liberal majority they were powerless. The Liberals offered the Irish an Irish Council as a way of returning some limited powers of debate to a specifically Irish chamber, but Redmond rejected such overtures.

The real sea change in the nature of Irish politics came in 1910. The Liberals fought an election in which they managed to win only two more seats than the Conservatives did. If the Liberals wished to stay in power and form a government, they had a simple choice: accept the support of the Irish in return for a home rule bill. The Liberal leader, Asquith, was well aware of political reality, and was prepared to accept overtures from

Redmond. However, what both of them understood was that while they could steer a home rule bill through the Commons, by virtue of their combined numerical superiority, they could never steer such legislation through the House of Lords because of its power of veto. For Asquith, this was as true for any Irish legislation he might wish to see passed, as it was for much of his own reform programme. Asquith decided, partially because of Irish concerns, to take a step that would forever change constitutional politics in Britain, and would bring the Irish one step closer to independence. Asquith decided to go to the country on the issue of the power of the House of Lords, and its ability to veto any legislation passed by the Commons.

The second election of 1910 was even less decisive than the first. The Liberals and Conservatives won exactly the same number of seats, and as a result, Asquith and his party remained reliant on the Irish to support their reform programme. In a period of intense negotiation, bluff and counter-bluff, Asquith finally threatened the House of Lords with the massive creation of loyal Liberal peers, unless they agreed to give up their right of veto. Rather than face a huge influx of such peers, the Lords acquiesced. The new constitutional arrangement between the Commons and the Lords meant that while the upper house could reject legislation, it could no longer kill it by veto. Any legislation that was passed in three successive years by the Commons would, even in the face of continued Lords' opposition, become law. The implications for British politics of such a change were enormous: for the Irish they were life- changing. In return for support on the Lords issue, Asquith now had to give Redmond his home rule bill. Such legislation, although undoubtedly bound to be rejected by the Lords, would become law in three years. Ireland, it appeared in 1910, was within touching distance of the freedom from Britain that so many of its citizens had long dreamed of.

THE THIRD HOME RULE BILL

What is surprising about the Third Home Rule Bill, is the almost cavalier manner in which the Liberals treated its passage. To them it was dealt with, in the early stages at least, as some kind of *fait accompli*, a piece of legislation they had agreed to, and had to see through to the end. They seemed blithely unaware of the storm clouds in Ulster, and the sustained resistance that any talk of home rule for Ireland would engender.

The bill itself was essentially an early twentieth-century inter-pretation of the old Gladstonian legislation. The bill would allow for the instigation of an Irish parliament to be based in Dublin. The parliament would consist of an elected Commons, and a nominated upper house, the Senate. The parliament would have free run of all sectors of the legislative process with the excep-tion of those pertaining to war and peace, foreign policy, the Crown and imperial affairs. Those would remain in the hands of Westminster. As the London parliament would continue to control certain aspects of Irish life, the Irish would still return 42 MPs to Westminster, to protect their interests there. The proposed legislation signalled the achievement of freedom for men like Redmond, and for many of the Irish population. Support for the home rule bill was not, however, universal.

It seemed as if the Liberals would simply be glad to see the legislation through the Commons, then wait three years until it could be guided past the Lords under the new constitutional arrangements, and then Ireland would be free. As a free nation, the Irish would no longer be a drain on British resources, and would no longer be a thorn in the side of any governmental party. The Liberals appear to have completely misjudged, or at least misunderstood, the depth of animosity and opposition that the proposed legislation would produce in Ireland amongst the unionist population.

UNIONIST OPPOSITION

The unionists had begun mobilising against the very ideal of home rule when it had become a potential legislative reality under Gladstone. In the 1880s and 1890s, such opposition grew increasingly vociferous and organised. The last two decades of the nineteenth century witnessed the establishment of a whole host of different organisations dedicated to defending the ideal of Ireland as part of the union. Such organisations included the Ulster Loyalist Anti-repeal Union, the Ulster Defence Union and the plethora of Unionist Clubs. To see the strong and resolute reaction of the unionist population as solely a product of the proposed 1910 legislation, is to misunderstand the nature of unionism itself. The battle lines had been drawn in the latter decades of the nineteenth century. Unionism was prepared to defend itself, its religion and its links with Britain, at all costs.

The already existing unionist organisations, which were assembled and ready to oppose any legislation that might alter their status, were fully mobilised in 1910, when it became clear that the Irish would hold the balance of power in the Commons. The unionists recognised that Asquith would do anything neces-sary to hold onto power, so that he could pursue the larger Liberal reform agenda. That such an agenda would lead to the destruction of the Lords' veto, and the presentation of an unstop-pable home rule bill, meant that the only real opposition to the end of union could come from the unionists themselves. The Lords had effectively been neutered, and the Conservative and Unionist MPs in parliament were in a minority position. Effective opposition could only come from within Ireland.

In 1910, the Irish Unionist Party elected Sir Edward Carson as their leader. Carson was a southern unionist and barrister. He held an absolute belief in the value of the union between Ireland and Britain, and argued that any breaking of that link would be a disaster. Carson would do anything to ensure that the union was maintained, and that home rule was stillborn. He successfully mobilised a mass movement that fed off a whole host of fears. Home rule, Carson argued, would destroy unionist businesses, would lead to a break with the Crown and the Empire, and worst of all (but best for its rabble-rousing potential), the end of union would result in the victorious ascent of Popery: the successful championing of Catholicism across the length and breadth of Ireland, and the total destruction of Protestantism and Presbyterianism. The nightmare scenario that Carson and his fellow campaigners sketched, for those who listened to their speeches and read their columns in various newspapers, mustered huge levels of support across the unionist population of Ireland.

The populism of unionism's anti-home rule campaign was underpinned by a hard paramilitary edge. Carson, and many of his followers, accepted that if home rule could not be derailed constitutionally, then the force of arms might be necessary. Despite being loyal servants of the Crown, the forces of unionism would not balk at taking up arms to prove their loyalty. The intransigence of unionism, especially in Ulster, would lead to a concerted challenge against the passage of home rule.

The monster meetings, organised by the unionists from 1910, demonstrated the paramilitary style that was so readily adopted in the defence of the union. In September 1911, over 50,000 members of the Orange Lodges and the Unionist Clubs marched from Belfast to Craigavon. At Easter 1912, double that number marched through the Agricultural Showgrounds in Belfast. They filed past Carson, who stood watching from a platform. The force of unionist commitment was summed up that day, when the massed ranks passed a resolution against home rule. The rising tumult came to its most impressive head on 28 September 1912. On that day, and across Ulster, thousands upon thousands of unionist supporters signed the Solemn League and Covenant against home rule. By the time that the Covenant was closed for signing, over 218,000 men and 228,000 women had added their signatures. That signing the Covenant was such a popular statement of opposition should have been worrying enough for the Liberal government and the Irish nationalists, but its very language held a chilling portent of the future. Those signing the Covenant, some of them in their own blood, promised to 'use all means necessary to defeat the present conspiracy to set up a Home Rule parliament in Ireland'. To reinforce the sense of threat contained in the Covenant, Ulster men paraded that night through Lisburn by torchlight and carrying dummy rifles. The question for the whole of Ireland in the autumn of 1912 was: How long would it be before the rifles would be real?

In January 1913, the unionists took their next step. The decision was made to form the Ulster Volunteer Force (UVF)· its aim, the defence of the union. The UVF was to gather together nearly 100,000 men, who were regularly drilled. In April and July 1914, the UVF finally armed itself. Major Fred Crawford landed 20,000 rifles and 3 million rounds of ammunition in Larne, which were rapidly distributed to the UVF across Ulster. The Liberal government was faced with a serious problem. For all its will to force through the home rule legislation, was it prepared to put down a rebellion of countless thousands of well armed and efficiently organised unionists, when the link between Ireland and the union was severed?

POLITICAL DYNAMICS

Politically, the debate over the home rule bill forced all the major figures into specific, and highly divided camps. Carson was supported in all his efforts by Sir James Craig, Unionist party MP, business millionaire, and a believer in Ulster's right to fight for the preservation of union. Andrew Bonar Law, who claimed Ulster descent, led the Conservative Party at this time. Bonar Law was a fervent supporter of Carson and Craig, and spoke out against the whole process of home rule as often as possible. There was, however, one important distinction between the attitude of Bonar Law, and that of Carson and Craig. In the early years of the whole home rule debate, Carson and Craig refused to countenance any talk of any form of independence for Ireland. For them, the preservation of all Ireland within the union was the goal. Although the mass of the unionist population lived in Ulster, they could not betray those segments of their society who lived in Ireland's three other provinces. Bonar Law was different. While he believed that maintenance of the union was the all-important goal, he accepted that preservation of the majority unionist population, that is, the area of Ulster, was of key concern. Bonar Law was prepared to accept the partition of Ireland between an Ulster in the union, and Connacht, Leinster and Munster under a Home Rule Ireland.

Bonar Law's belief that partition, while far from ideal, was workable, informed much of the debate that would swirl around the home rule issue in the years leading to 1914. By 1913, Carson had been won over to Bonar Law's thinking. In the Commons he proposed that all the nine counties of Ulster should be excluded from the terms of the Home Rule bill. Such an emasculation of the idea of Home Rule Ireland, based, as this idea was, on an organic and geographic notion of Ireland as a nation, was unacceptable to Redmond.

The nationalist groupings demonstrated a high degree of cohesion in the years that followed the presentation of the home rule bill to Parliament. While the groups outside Westminster, such as

Sinn Féin and the IRB, may not have agreed ideologically with the exact shape of the nation that Asquith had offered in the legislation, independence was achievable. All the minority groupings seemed content to accept that Redmond had majority support in the country, and that Home Rule would be enacted. The threat of losing nine counties from the home rule legislation, as Carson suggested in 1913, was doubly problematic for Redmond. First, it flew in the face of the bill that he had agreed with Asquith. Secondly, any weakening in the idea of what would physically comprise independent Ireland would offer succour to Redmond's nationalist opponents.

During the course of 1913, the resolve of Asquith, and as a result, that of Redmond, weakened. Carson was able to win the day over his amendment. It was announced that the counties of Ulster would be allowed to opt out of Home Rule, for three, and then six years. The amendment, although suggested by Carson, thrilled no one. Carson saw it as a stay of execution for Ulster, rather than a permanent freedom from Home Rule. Redmond, while understanding the practicalities of such a move in the context of Unionist concerns, felt that the essential unity of Ireland had been breached. Sinn Féin and the IRB felt betrayed, but such action by the Westminster parliament only served to illustrate what they had long believed: freedom would never be given by a foreign parliament, it had to be won.

NATIONALIST RESPONSES

In such a period of impasse, and in the face of the establishment of the UVF, Irish nationalism sought to mobilise itself. There was a feeling within nationalist circles that there had been too much trust placed in the integrity of Westminster, and that they had misread the strength of opposition to home rule within the unionist camps. In November 1913, two important essays were published in Dublin-based journals. The first, by the Gaelic Leaguer Eoin MacNeill, identified the UVF as an army formed to protect the union. The second, penned by a Gaelic Leaguer, language activist and educationalist, Patrick Pearse, looked to a future where the nation would be won or lost. Such victory or defeat would, in Pearse's mind, be dependent on whether the

Irish were prepared to use arms and fight to the death for the cause of the nation. While the ideas of MacNeill and Pearse may be seen as inflaming further an already flammable situation, they expressed a belief that lay at the heart of contemporary nationalism. If the Unionists could bully their way out of Home Rule by instigating the UVF threat, then what would the nationalist reaction be? Would they continue to rely on the British parliament, and the debating prowess of Redmond, or would they seek to fight for their own conception of the nation?

The momentum of argument and the climate of fear that was summed up in both essays led, in part, to the formation of the Irish Volunteers in November 1913. Within a matter of months, the membership of the Irish Volunteers had swelled to well in excess of 100,000. The Irish Volunteers were, in many ways, a carbon copy of the UVF. Its members paraded and drilled. It was not established as an illegal organisation aimed at the destruction of the state or of civil order. Its purpose, as with its Ulster counterpart, was gently to remind the government of its duty to the Irish. Whereas the UVF formed a potential threat to the government, aiming to drive them away from Home Rule, the Irish Volunteers served as a pressure group to keep the government on the Home Rule course.

Despite both organisations, stressing the democratic support for their respective functions, the existence of two private armies within the country was hugely problematic. The aim of both the UVF and the Irish Volunteers was to oppose the government through physical force if necessary, and if that happened, then they would certainly oppose each other. Civil war, and a protracted campaign by one of the parties against the force of government, in 1913 appeared a distinct possibility.

The situation was further exacerbated in 1914 by two events: the Curragh Mutiny, and the arming of the Irish Volunteers. In March 1914, the government, understandably concerned about the steady militarisation of civilian politics within Ireland, sought to tighten military security. One of the issues that emerged during the planning of future military policy at this time was the role, if any, of Ulster-based officers, should the army ever have to be used against the UVF or other forces within the province. Sir Arthur Paget, Commander-in-Chief in Ireland, won an agreement from the military command. The

agreement meant that any officers who had a home in Ulster
could, if they wished, refuse to take part in military action in
Ulster. Any other officers refusing to serve in Ulster would be
dismissed. When Paget put these choices to the officers of the
British Army based at the Curragh army camp, they intimated
that they would resign, rather than take up arms in Ulster. A
similar decision was forthcoming from officers based in
Aldershot. While not a mutiny in the true sense, the events at the
Curragh placed the government in an unenviable position. It
appeared, on the evidence of the mutiny, that if the UVF ever
took up arms against the state in the name of the union, the
British Army would have no officers willing to enter Ulster to
reinforce order. To make matters far worse for the government,
July 1914 witnessed the first shipment of arms into Ireland, via
Howth, for use by the Irish Volunteers. The Irish Volunteers,
formally unarmed until that date, brought barely 1000 rifles and
only 29,000 rounds of ammunition into the country, but paltry as
that sum was, by comparison with the UVF arsenal, the fact that
the Volunteers were able to march their weapons from Howth
into Dublin under the noses of the police and the army was an
illustration of how far any semblance of normality had disappeared from Irish life.

In the summer of 1914, it seemed that the government was
facing some form of disaster in Ireland. The Home Rule Bill was
due to become law, both nationalists and unionists were formed
into private armies, and the forces of the Crown, in the shape of
British Army officers, were refusing to take on a job that might
be demanded of them. Perversely, it seems as though the onset of
World War must have provided the Liberal government with a
sense of relief.

THE FIRST WORLD WAR

In the context of the momentous events that took place both in
Ireland and across Europe in the period of the First World War, it
is often forgotten that on 18 September 1914, the Home Rule
Bill actually became law. Despite the fact that it was automati-
cally suspended for one year or the duration of the war, the
passage of everything that nationalist Ireland had always aspired

to, was met with great celebration in Ireland. With the war under way against Germany and its allies, the various Irish groupings met to decide which way they would jump. Whatever they did decide, it has to be remembered that the common belief in the late summer of 1914 was that the war would be over by Christmas. The pursuit of adventure on the western front, and the accompanying illustration of trustworthy loyalty to the Crown, were seen as temporary diversions until the debate over Home Rule was once more entered into.

UNIONISTS AND THE WAR

The years of the First World War are most often remembered as the period that catapulted Sinn Féin into prominence, and led to the instability that would give rise to the War of Independence. As most of the attention of the First World War period is often focused on the south, the experience of those in Ulster, particularly the unionist population, has often been overlooked. As loyal servants of the Crown, it is perhaps unsurprising that unionists so readily volunteered for war. For them, the war in Europe was not solely a battle for the survival of small nations, as the British officially contended, but it was a war that swirled around the whole issue of Home Rule. The war gave the unionists an opportunity to position themselves as loyal to the Crown, Westminster and the whole conception of the British nation as encapsulated by the union.

Conscription was never applied by the British government to any part of Ireland, and thus any Irishmen or Ulstermen who went to war, went of their own free will. Certainly, many of those who travelled to Europe went for adventure, as part of a communal journey undertaken by a group of friends, or to earn vital shillings in the King's service. These are the common reasons why many men from Britain and Ireland went to war in 1914–18. There was also a hard political edge to the personal choices that were made, especially in Ulster. In August 1914, Lord Kitchener, the Minister of War, accepted that the existence of a well-organised and trained force in the form of the UVF was a boon in the initial days of the war. He agreed that the UVF should be reorganised within the British Army as the 36th Ulster

Division. The 36th would have its own insignia, and would select its own officers. To many within unionist circles, the freedom that the 36th was given was due reward and recognition for the essential loyalty of the anti-Home Rule movement.

The 36th Ulster Division was active across the western front throughout the war, and proudly carried with it the fortunes of Ulster unionism. During the 1914–18 war it was likely that many families in Ulster would receive bad news of sons or other family members who had been killed and injured. Such a sacrifice in the name of the union would have done much to reinforce the loyalty of Ulster to Britain anyway, but the events of 1 August 1916 proved to have far greater ramifications. During Easter 1916 many nationalists, as will be explained later, rebelled against British rule. In the face of such nationalist belligerence, and bearing in mind the number of Ulstermen serving in Europe, the 36th Ulster Division was a shining symbol of loyalty to the Crown and the union. On 1 August 1916, the British and Allied forces began a huge operation at the Somme, in an attempt to move the western front forward. The losses suffered on the first day of the Battle of the Somme are legendary. In the middle of the slaughter were the men of the 36th Ulster division. In one day, the 36th suffered 5104 casualties, over 2000 of whom died. The losses of the 36th Ulster Division were the fourth highest suffered by any division in the British Army that day. That the 36th had lost so many men in a single day would obviously have a penetrating effect on the memory of the First World War amongst the population of Ulster.

Such losses would come to form the cornerstone of a process of remembrance that is central to the unionist calendar to this day: 1 August is annually reserved for remembering the men of the 36th. The power of the memory of these men is reinforced by their obvious bravery, and because amidst the carnage of the first day of the Battle of the Somme, they were the most successful of all army divisions in attacking the German lines. They penetrated deeper than any other division, and took more than 500 German prisoners. Traditionally, the military success of the 36th has been contextualised as a memory imbued by the actions of men sharing a total belief in the cause for which they were fighting: the future of Ulster. Whatever the reasons for their success may have been, the memory of the 36th Ulster Division exerted a powerful pull on Ulster unionism. For the people of Ulster, the idea of Home Rule was abhorrent enough, but in light of Ulster's sacrifice at the Somme, anything but total opposition to Irish aspirations would be to belittle the memory of Ulster's dead.

REDMONDITE NATIONALISM AND THE WAR

For the Irish nationalist, the war posed real problems. To fight alongside the British would be to fight with the nation so long considered the oppressor. To stay at home, would allow the unionists to claim any potential glory, and prove the value of the union to the British. The Irish, faced with such a conundrum, split into two camps. The largest group followed Redmond to war, while a minority of committed physical-force nationalists stayed in Ireland.

Redmond's decision to commit the broad sweep of constitutional nationalists to the war, was publicly declared the day before Britain entered the fray. In a Commons speech, Redmond fully pledged Ireland to supporting Britain in a period of need and danger. He offered the Irish Volunteers as a force that could defend Ireland, so that any British troops stationed there could travel to fight in France. While Redmond was applauded for such an approach by many London commentators, he used his offer of support to ensure that the Home Rule Bill was made law, as it duly was on 18 September 1914. Redmond intimated privately to Asquith that if full passage of the bill was not to be forthcoming at the end of hostilities in Europe, then he could not guarantee the security or loyalty of Ireland in the war. Redmond's less than veiled threat regarding the safety of Ireland was successful, and Asquith assured him that the suspension of the Home Rule Bill for the duration of the war was only temporary.

Two days after the passage of the Home Rule Bill, Redmond made a speech in Woodenbridge, Co. Wicklow, in which he further emphasised the total support of the Irish for the British war effort. His basic argument was that as Home Rule had been secured, Ireland should play its full and proper role as a nation, alongside those Allies fighting in Europe. He changed the position of the Volunteers from a solely defensive force, into one that would fight 'wherever the firing line extends'. For Redmond, indeed for the whole constitutional nationalist movement, his offer to move the battle lines was a profound shift. It opened the way for mass recruitment of Irishmen into the British Army on the one hand, while it also brought about a damning critique from physical-force nationalists. While those in Sinn Féin and the IRB, amongst others, were prepared to go along with the passage of the Home Rule Bill, they were not prepared to let Irish lives be sacrificed in the name of the British Empire. Duly, in September 1914, the Irish Volunteers split: 150,000 followed Redmond and became the National Volunteers, 13,500 followed the Sinn Féin/IRB line, retained the name the Irish Volunteers, and stayed at home.

Redmond's enthusiasm for the war, and his belief that it would heal the rift that existed between unionists and nationalists over the issue of home rule, was highly popular during 1914, and in the first half of 1915. The thinking behind enrolment was simple: the war would be short and Ireland could gain the trust of Ulster and Britain for having taken part. By the end of 1915, 81,000 Irishmen had voluntarily enlisted in the British Army and travelled to fight on the western front.

The problem for Redmond was that the war dragged on. It was not a quick spat in the fields of Flanders, which was over by Christmas, but became a bloody morass in which Irish volunteers were poorly treated, injured, maimed and killed. The treatment meted out to the Irish volunteers during the war, especially in symbolic terms, was appalling. The Ulster volunteers were allowed divisional emblems (the red hand of Ulster), and fast-tracked into commissions. The Irish were refused the right to wear any form of national emblem (they wished to wear a harp on their uniforms), they were denied commissions unless they had undergone full training, and all of them were referred to as British, despite the passage of the Home Rule Bill and the achievement, legally at least, of nation status. The death toll was terrible across the western front. What should have been a war of months, dragged on into years. Men began travelling home with stories of what they had seen, or with injuries they had sustained, or else they never came home at all. For all Redmond's rational thinking as to what participation in the war meant in terms of Irish freedom, the actual experience of men who went to fight was far removed from the context of political expediency. So many Irishmen, as 1915 progressed into 1916, had to ask what they were fighting for.

Support for Redmond did appear, at least through 1915, to be holding up. Irish Parliamentary Party candidates won all the by-elections called during that year. By the end of 1915, however, the viability of Redmond's attitude to the war was clearly encountering serious difficulties.

In June 1915, Asquith formed a wartime coalition government. Both Bonar Law and Carson entered the cabinet. Asquith offered Redmond a place at the cabinet table, but he declined. While such a move was understandable, as Redmond did not wish to appear to be selling out any principles for a placement of power, it left Home Rule vulnerable. Asquith was surrounding himself with the forces of loyalty, the forces of unionism. The longer the war dragged on, the more he would be open to their arguments and their beliefs. Would Asquith lose sight of the nationalist perspective? As 1915 turned into 1916, support for Redmond, now so closely tied up with support for the war, began to fall away. Membership of his local party organisation started to diminish, as did the numbers of volunteers joining the British Army. Redmond was becoming unpopular in Ireland; he had excluded himself from government in Britain, and the war showed no signs of ending. Redmond's one achievement, Home Rule, seemed further away than ever.

PHYSICAL-FORCE NATIONALISM AND THE 1916 RISING

While support for Redmond fell away in Ireland, at least in the period to Easter 1916, there was no popular alternative to him. People may have been doubting the viability of participation in the war, and the rationale behind Redmond's policies, but there was no other course open to them. Constitutional nationalism was a one-party concern. The only alternative to the National Volunteers was to embrace the various physical-force nationalist movements; those who had stayed out of the war and were centred on the Irish Volunteers. For the vast majority of the Irish, support for the Irish Volunteers was not an option, a fact borne out by the relative strengths of the two organisations. To decide, in the context of late 1915 and early 1916, that Redmond had got it wrong, was not a decision that led directly to the door of the Irish Volunteers. Redmond may have made the wrong decision about participation in the war, but Home Rule was still on the statute book, and would be enacted at the end of the war. All the Irish had to do was sit tight and wait. Also, while many believed that Irish participation in the war was foolhardy, or maybe even wrong, such feelings were tempered by the fact that many people had fathers, brothers, uncles and cousins who were fighting in Europe. To support an organisation as radical as the Irish Volunteers was to be disloyal to relatives in the army.

While the Irish Volunteers did not have popular support, it did have a following. The support for the Irish Volunteers was predominantly drawn from the ranks of the extremist nationalists that had emerged from the broad Fenian grouping of the mid-nineteenth century. The Irish Volunteers were organised by a Provisional Committee that had steadily been infiltrated by members of the IRB, who believed fully in the ethos of physical-force nationalism. The Irish Volunteers contained two broad camps. The first, led by men such as Eoin MacNeill, believed that the Irish Volunteers were solely a defensive force. While opposing the policies of Redmond and involvement in the war, they argued that the Irish Volunteers should not be engaged unless Ireland was under a direct threat of attack or coercion. The other camp contained men such as Patrick Pearse, Tom Clarke and Bulmer Hobson. They too opposed Redmond, but held to the old Fenian notion that England's danger was Ireland's opportunity. For this group, the war offered the ideal opportunity for Ireland to strike for its freedom using physical force.

From as early as August 1914, the extremists began plotting a rebellion. At that time the American Irish group Clan na Gael arranged for Sir Roger Casement to travel to Germany to procure arms, and support for a rebellion in Ireland. Casement's trip was beset with difficulties, and the German attitude towards the plan for rebellion half-hearted. Eventually, however, the Germans chose to support the Irish, and dispatched 20,000 rifles on a ship, the *Aud*, to Ireland. The arms were to be landed on the Kerry

coast on 20 April 1916, where they would be met, first by
Casement, who would travel to Ireland by submarine, and
secondly by the Irish, who would be preparing to break into
open rebellion.

Casement had secured a good deal of military hardware that
could be used in any rebellion. Whether it could succeed against
the 6000 British troops in Ireland was another matter. Arms
would be nothing without a well planned and executed rebellion
that would engender public support.

It was in the planning and execution that the Easter Rising of
1916 would ultimately fail in the military sense. In January
1916, the secret Military Council of the IRB decided that the
time was ripe for rebellion. They sensed that Redmond, and the
war effort, were losing support, and they believed that the arms
from Germany would tip things in their favour militarily. At the
start of 1916, the Military Council of the IRB did not have the
support of the rump of the Irish Volunteers or of Eoin MacNeill.
Indeed, few people outside the IRB's inner sanctum knew of the
events planned for Easter Sunday. MacNeill and many others
were won over by the promise of the German arms, and the
secret Castle document. The Castle document, which it was
claimed was an order from Dublin Castle, the heart of the British
military and intelligence machine in Ireland, outlined a plan to
arrest all major leaders of the Irish Volunteers. For MacNeill and
others, the document demonstrated the British oppression that
was concomitant with their belief in the type of extreme situation that would allow them to rise. The fact that the Castle document was an IRB forgery, specifically designed to bring
MacNeill and other doubters on board, was irrelevant. The
momentum behind a rebellion was picking up.

Joseph Plunkett had drawn up the plans for the Easter Rising,
as far as they actually existed. The plan was for the forces of the
Irish Volunteers to take control, on Easter Sunday 1916, of all
the major strategic buildings in Dublin, and other main towns
and cities across the country. The German arms would be rapidly
distributed just prior to the time of rebellion, so that the British
did not detect any unusual activity in advance. Once the rebellion had begun, the Irish people would rise up, and the British
would be unable to suppress the country. Better plans than
Plunkett's have failed, so it was perhaps inevitable that such a

poorly thought out campaign of rebellion would not meet with success.

The *Aud* arrived off the Kerry coast, as arranged, on 20 April. The Military Council, concerned that such a large presence of arms, if landed in advance, would alert the British, had tried to delay the landing of the *Aud* until three days later. The *Aud* never received the message, and arrived in line with its original orders. No one was there to meet the shipment, and after two days of cruising up and down the coast, when a British warship intercepted the *Aud*, her captain scuttled the ship and its cargo. Roger Casement, aware of what had happened, attempted to land from the submarine that was carrying him, but was arrested before he could contact any of his fellow conspirators.

MacNeill, who had sanctioned the plan for the rising because of the promised weapons shipment, resolved that it could not go ahead. He placed a notice in the Sunday *Irish Independent*, on the day of the planned rising, stating that all Irish Volunteers parades for that day had been cancelled, a countermanding order that ensured the rising did not happen on Easter Sunday.

The Military Council did not agree with MacNeill's perspective, and decided to go ahead with the rising on Easter Monday, 24 April 1916. The men and women who gathered on the Monday morning were drawn from three main groups: some of the Irish Volunteers, the IRB and James Connolly's socialist movement, the Irish Citizen Army. Following MacNeill's countermanding order of the previous day, the numbers were thin on the ground, and apart from isolated outbreaks of violence in counties Meath, Galway and Wexford, the rising was restricted to the city of Dublin.

The total number of insurgents was no more than 1500. They were poorly armed, badly organised, and had no central plan of what was expected of them. Key buildings around Dublin were taken, such as the South Dublin Union, the Four Courts, and the rising's headquarters, the General Post Office (GPO) on Sackville (now O'Connell) Street. James Connolly said on the morning of the rising, 'We are going out to be slaughtered.' It was a fair assessment of the rebels' chances.

At noon on Easter Monday, one of the key events of the rising took place. The leaders, based in the GPO, marched onto its steps, and read the Proclamation of the Provisional Government of the Irish Republic. Thomas Clarke, Séan McDermott, Patrick Pearse, James Connolly, Thomas MacDonagh, Eamonn Ceannt and Joseph Plunkett signed the single-page document. The declaration of the Irish nation that was read out in 1916 would become the cornerstone of much nationalist and republican belief for the remainder of the twentieth century. Once the Proclamation had been read to an intrigued public, enjoying a walk through Dublin's main thoroughfare on a public holiday, the rebel leaders re-entered the GPO and awaited the British response.

The rising would last for a week, until Pearse surrendered the following Saturday. The rebels had failed to take either Dublin Castle or Trinity College, and had been left spread across Dublin, with little communication between them. There was some bloody fighting during the week, and much of Dublin was destroyed by British artillery attacks on the main rebel strongholds. In holding out for a week, the rebels had put up a credible performance against the might of the British Empire. The week left 450 dead, 2600 injured and large parts of Dublin destroyed.

The British response to such a rebellion, in what should have been a loyal part of its own kingdom, and in the middle of a major war, was swift and brutal. Martial law was declared across Ireland: all leading and known 'Sinn Féiners' were to be arrested, and the leaders of the rising, that is those who had signed the Proclamation, and all battalion commanders, were to be executed.

To unpack the British response is to understand the nature of Irish politics for the remainder of the war, and into the 1920s. Initially, when those who had taken part in the rising were marched to the Dublin quays for shipment to prison in Britain, they were spat at and roundly abused by the local population. The rebels had little public support. The Declaration, and enforcement of martial law, however, threw everyone in Ireland under suspicion, and made the general population suffer. The mass arrests, nearly 3500 people, more than had taken part in the rising, once more shifted the focus of the British away from the rebels, and onto the greater Irish population, causing understandable resentment. The decision to execute the leaders of the rising produced the most outrage. Between 3 and 12 May, the British executed fifteen of the rebels. Roger Casement would follow later, when tried and convicted in Britain for treason. Redmond and his deputy, James Dillon, warned the British that execution was the wrong path to take, but their pleas fell on deaf ears. The rising had posthumously lit the torchpaper that would, in part, lead to the destruction of constitutional nationalism, and the beginning of a sustained campaign of violence against British rule in Ireland.

THE RISE OF SINN FÉIN AND THE THREAT OF CONSCRIPTION

Two other great legacies of the rising that would exert their influence, in both the long and short term, were those quirky accidents of history that change the direction of a country's narrative. First was the apportioning of blame for the rising. It had been planned, and executed, by the Military Council of the IRB, and assisted during Easter Week by the Irish Citizen Army. The Dublin Castle authorities, ably assisted by the press, chose to apportion blame to the only public nationalist organisation that they were aware of: Sinn Féin. Although Arthur Griffith's party had played no part in the rising, they were held accountable, and many of their members targeted for arrest in the aftermath. In the long term, the labelling of Sinn Féin as the driving force behind the rising would result in the party emerging as the largest political force in Ireland. The second legacy of the rising was the sparing of one of the battalion commanders. Eamon de Valera had led operations at Boland's bakery during Easter Week, and had been the last commander to surrender to the British. He was spared execution, despite being a battalion commander, by virtue of having been born in the United States. At various times during the years following 1916, when he became the leader of Sinn Féin and a key figure in the Irish revolution, the British must have wished they had executed him when they had the opportunity. In being spared death in 1916, de Valera was able to go on to dominate Irish politics well into the 1960s.

Many of the prisoners that had been arrested as a result of Easter Week were released from their British prisons prior to Christmas 1916. While some of the leading figures in the nationalist movement, such as Arthur Griffith and Eamon de Valera, had been held separately, the majority had been placed in a temporary prison camp at Frongoch in North Wales. Frongoch has been dubbed 'the University of the Revolution'. Rather than quietly sitting and reflecting on their experience of Easter Week, those held in Frongoch were organised under the auspices of the Irish Republican Army (IRA), and spent their time studying Irish history, military techniques and the Irish language, and playing native sports. Rather than wallowing in their experience as a glorious failure, the men at Frongoch were preparing for their next attempt at national liberation. One of the key commanders in the camp was Michael Collins, a member of the IRB who had returned to Dublin from his job in London to take part in the Easter Rising. Collins, who would become a key figure in the military and political planning of the Irish revolution, was determined that a fiasco of the type that surrounded Easter Week would never happen again.

On their arrival in Ireland the former prisoners returned to their nationalist activities. Griffith began to organising a newly invigorated Sinn Féin and resumed publishing his newspaper. Support for Sinn Féin began to increase. In part this was driven by the mythology of selfless sacrifice that had grown up around the events of Easter Week, but it was also a response to the developing unpopularity of the war on the continent, and to rumours that the British were considering enforcing conscription in Ireland for the first time in the war. The changing nature of the political landscape was evidenced in 1917. A by-election was called in North Roscommon. Whereas Redmond's party had secured victory in every by-election so far during the course of the war, in North Roscommon they were defeated. The successful candidate was Count Plunkett, father of the executed signatory of the 1916 Proclamation of the Republic, Joseph Plunkett. Plunkett stood, as all Sinn Féin MPs would during this period, on an abstentionist platform. Once elected he would refuse to take his seat in the parliament at Westminster.

Support for Sinn Féin grew quickly through the course of 1917. The party, assisted by an efficient organisational machinery, won two further by-elections following the victory of Plunkett. Eamon de Valera won East Clare in July 1917, and in October secured his prominence within Sinn Féin, when he was voted in as president of the party.

The momentum behind Sinn Féin appeared unstoppable and, from the British perspective, uncontrollable. At the end of September 1917, Thomas Ashe, a survivor of the 1916 Rising, went on hunger strike in prison. He was force-fed by the prison authorities, but died. Whereas the authorities had been careful to deny those executed in 1916 a public funeral, which might become the focus for political demonstration, Ashe could not be denied his burial. His funeral turned into a huge exhibition of the force of, and support for, Sinn Féin and the Irish Volunteers. It is estimated that well over 30,000 people gathered to hear, a short speech by Michael Collins and a volley of shots over the graveside.

The difficulty for Sinn Féin was how to move forward. While they were undeniably gaining a mass of public support, many others still chose to support Redmond and his policy of backing the war effort. Continued support for Redmond was evidenced by the three by-elections that his party won in the first half of 1918. It appeared that the momentum behind Sinn Féin had reached its high-water mark.

In March 1918, the German Army scored a string of victories along the front at the Somme, and approximately 300,000 Allied troops lost their lives in a matter of weeks. The British Army was desperately short of troops. The threat of conscription that had hung over Ireland for the duration of the war, was finally enacted. The Military Service Bill was passed by Parliament on 10 April 1918. Although no Irishman was ever conscripted into the British Army, the passing of the legislation had a seismic effect. The Irish Parliamentary Party, depleted as they were by the death of John Redmond in March 1918, walked out of Westminster in protest at the Military Service Bill. In doing so, they effectively destroyed the *raison d'être* of constitutional home rule, and passed the baton of nationalist aspiration full square into the hands of Sinn Féin.

Sinn Féin began a nation-wide campaign against conscription. There was a one-day general strike in support of their campaign, and the Catholic hierarchy publicly stated that the Irish had the right to resist conscription. The government's response in the face of such widespread public outrage was regressive. It appointed Field Marshal Lord French as Viceroy to Ireland. This was read by nationalists as the appointment, not of a Viceroy, but of a military governor to control Ireland. French did not disappoint. In May 1918, French used rumours of German collusion with Sinn Féin to arrest leading nationalists. The fear of threatening consequences of a German–Sinn Féin relationship for British rule in Ireland was understandable, but an over-played card that emanated from Casement's dalliance with the Germans in 1916. While some Sinn Féin leaders, such as Griffith and de Valera, allowed themselves to be arrested so that they could acquire martyr status, the military and organisational wing of the party went to ground.

Michael Collins avoided arrest and continued to organise the IRB and the IRA, and other aspects of a counter-insurgency campaign which could be used at a future date. He was ably assisted by Harry Boland, who worked across the length and breadth of Ireland, organising local Sinn Féin clubs, which would form the bedrock of support for the party. Such clubs, which numbered over 110,000 by December 1918, gave the party a national network of volunteers and workers, and ensured a steady income from membership dues.

Although conscription was never enforced, the threat of it had changed the political landscape in Ireland completely. After the ending of the First World War in November 1918, a general election was called for December. Not only did the newly enfranchised voters, resulting from the Representation of the People Act, make a difference to traditional voting patterns, but the loss of Home Rule and the impotency of the Irish Parliamentary Party changed perspectives totally. Sinn Féin fought the election hard, utilised the organisational network of its clubs, and brilliantly capitalised on the continued imprisonment of many of its leading figures by placing posters across Ireland that read, 'Put Him In, To Get Him Out'.

The election result led to the near total defeat of the Irish Parliamentary Party, which managed to hold onto a mere 6 seats. The Unionist Party performed solidly in areas of traditional support and was able, in the face of the threat of Sinn Féin extremism, to raise their number of seats from 18 to 26. The most startling result was the number of MPs, all of whom would be abstentionist, returned by Sinn Féin. They entered the election holding 7 seats, and they left it with 73, a huge majority of the Irish seats. The question for Ireland at the end of 1918 was how such a changed political landscape would actually manifest itself in the coming years?

THE WAR OF INDEPENDENCE

The newly elected Sinn Féin MPs would not attend Westminster, so set about forming their own alternative parliament in Dublin. The Irish parliament, Dáil Éireann, was called together at the Mansion House on 21 January 1919. The Unionist and Irish Parliamentary MPs refused to attend, and only 27 Sinn Féiners were able to show up; 34 of them were still in prison!

The stated purposes of Dáil Éireann were very straightforward. It openly embraced the Proclamation of the Republic of 1916, and pledged to work for the creation of an Irish Republic by any means possible. In outlining such aims, it unilaterally declared Ireland as an independent nation. The social and political programme of the Dáil aimed at the creation of a classless and democratic country. Finally, it was resolved to send representatives to the post-war Peace Conference to argue for Ireland's freedom from Britain, in line with US President Wilson's belief in the rights of small nations. Underpinning, but not formally or publicly connected with, Dáil Éireann were the two military arms of the Republic: Michael Collins' IRB and, because of his position as Dáil Éireann's Minister for Defence, Cathal Brugha's IRA.

On the same day as the first meeting of the Dáil, the military wing of the IRA swung, perhaps mistakenly and prematurely, into action. At Soloheadbeg, in Co. Tipperary, two policemen who were escorting a supply of explosives to a local quarry were shot and killed by two IRA men seeking to steal the explosives. The War of Independence, although not reaching its bloody apotheosis until the late summer of 1920, had begun.

The second meeting of Dáil Éireann took place on 1 April 1919. By that time it was clear that the mission to the Paris Peace Conference was bound to failure. The British were not interested in hearing any claim for independence from the self-appointed members of the illegal Dáil Éireann, and British allies from the war, such as the Americans, were not prepared to upset imperial powers over the trifling issue of a small nation. At the second meeting of the Dáil, de Valera was appointed as President, Griffith as Minister for Home Affairs, and Collins as Finance Minister. Whereas men such as Collins and Brugha believed that some form of military campaign would be necessary to win the Republic, de Valera was far more reluctant to involve himself in such a struggle, and argued that he would be better utilised elsewhere.

Perhaps because of his American birth, or through his understanding of the Irish-American community, de Valera believed that the fate of the Republic lay in the hands of the US. Shortly after the second meeting of the Dáil, he left Ireland for America. His aim was to woo American politicians and business people, and win support and funding for the Irish Republican ideal. How useful de Valera's time in America actually was, is difficult to estimate. He undoubtedly raised funds and won over many contacts. In the context of the post-First World War isolationism of the US, however, he was unable to bring any American politicians onto the field of play, and into a position where they were prepared to try and influence British policy towards Ireland. One certain effect of de Valera's absence (his trip to the US lasted until December 1920) was to propel Michael Collins into a position of primacy.

Michael Collins used his post as Finance Minister to raise £317,000 for the Dáil, in the form of bond certificates that were repayable against the success of the future independent Irish state. As Director of Intelligence, he, and not Cathal Brugha, directed IRA actions during the war, and also retained a tight control of the IRB, which he utilised as an elite force in the shadowy war against British intelligence. It was Collins, and not de Valera, who became synonymous with the future of the Irish Republic.

The war itself was a vicious affair. It was not fought across open spaces, but from behind hedges and walls as a guerrilla campaign. The IRA and IRB were brutally effective at ambushing and assassinating their opponents. A largely supportive population, who ostracised police officers within their community and the forces of the British Army that visited their locality, assisted them. Any sections of the population who failed to show sufficient support for the forces of the Republic, who fraternised with the enemy or were suspected of working as informants, were harshly and violently treated. While such use of force against its own population may be an unpalatable memory for the sometimes mythologised heroism of the Irish victors of the War of Independence, such a war could never have been won without such a steely, and at times inhumane, attitude. The need to terrorise one's own community to such an extent, as well as fighting the enemy, was driven by the concomitant harshness of the British campaign in Ireland.

The British were beset with problems from the start. The war against the Irish was never a popular war within the British media or amongst the public. Those serving in Ireland in the army or the police, who were supposed to carry through the war, were often fighting amongst their own communities. In an attempt to circumvent such problems, and to bolster the war effort, the British recruited an auxiliary force that became known, because of its uniform, as the Black and Tans. The Black and Tans were ruthless and ill-disciplined. For every act of violence that the IRB or IRA committed, the Black and Tans would respond. Their target could not be their shadowy invisible enemy, but became, instead, the civilian population in Ireland. An ideal illustration of the course of the war, although there are many such examples, is the events of Sunday, 21 November 1920. On that morning, Michael Collins used an elite squad of men to kill eleven of the leading figures within British intelligence who were stationed in Dublin at that time. The effect on the British intelligence network would be devastating, but in the climate of the war, the Black and Tans wanted revenge for such a blatantly cold-blooded act by the IRA. That afternoon, a lorry-load of Black and Tans entered Croke Park where a crowd in excess of 10,000 was watching a game of Gaelic football. Firing randomly into the crowd, and at the players on the pitch, the Black and Tans killed twelve people.

Such events could not continue indefinitely, and the British Prime Minister, Lloyd George, would not be able to weather many more months of such excessive violence. On 9 July 1921, a truce was called between British and Irish forces, so that peace talks could begin.

THE TREATY

The question for the Irish, once they had fought the British to the negotiating table, was: What would they accept? During the War of Independence, Sinn Féin had functioned as a largely homogeneous ideological body. They uniformly supported the Proclamation of 1916 and the spirit of the 1919 Dáil Éireann, and were fighting for the cause of a 32-county Irish Republic. During the period of the war, Sinn Féin had increased its political power. It had won control of the urban councils of Ireland in January 1920, and the county councils in June the same year. In establishing the Dáil Land Commission, and evolving a system of arbitration courts (from 1920 these were formalised as Dáil courts), Sinn Féin successfully placed the legal control of the land in Ireland under its own jurisdiction. In doing so, it controlled, in part, the perennially thorny issue of land ownership from the outset, and brought about the adherence of the people to Sinn Féin through its constructive systems for settling land disputes.

In December 1920, Lloyd George's government introduced the Government of Ireland Act, in an attempt to restore peace to the country. Essentially the 1920 Act revisited Redmondite Home Rule. It proposed the setting up of two parliaments in Ireland; one in Belfast and one in Dublin. The Belfast parliament would oversee the affairs of the six Protestant-majority Ulster counties: Antrim, Armagh, Down, Fermanagh, Londonderry and Tyrone. The Dublin parliament would administer the remainder of the country. Both parliaments would only be responsible for their respective home affairs; foreign policy and defence would remain the preserve of Westminster. The Government of Ireland Act was an attempt to offer both the Ulster Unionists and Sinn Féin, as irreconcilable as their positions were, what Lloyd George believed they would each be prepared to settle for, while still preserving the essential unity of the UK.

The Unionists, while far from enamoured with the Act, tried to work within its terms. The 1920 legislation allowed them to establish their own devolved legislature, where they could be masters in their own house, while remaining wedded to the principle of union. King George V duly opened the Northern Ireland parliament in June 1921. Sinn Féin simply rejected the plan for a Dublin parliament. The party was still unified in its aims, and continued the fight for a Republic. As the end of 1920 passed, it was clear that Sinn Féin would not accept partition.

The truce between the two warring sides quickly ushered in a period of intense negotiation between the British and the Irish. Initially, it was de Valera, as President, who travelled to London to negotiate with Lloyd George. What was instantly clear was that Lloyd George was not prepared to compromise on the status of Northern Ireland. In the minds of the British, the status of the Province had been resolved under the 1920 legislation, and the future of the parliament that sat in Belfast was not up for debate. Such a clear statement of position by the British fractured the alliance that had existed within Sinn Féin since 1917. Rather than fighting for the ideal of a 32-county Irish Republic, the party now had to decide whether it would settle for less along the lines of British thinking.

De Valera argued that he had stated in 1917, in an address to his constituents, that if they were prepared to accept a lesser form of self-government, he would not continue to campaign for a Republic. Others in the cabinet, such as Cathal Brugha and Erskine Childers, held onto an uncompromising, doctrinaire Republican stance. Finally, there was a group led by Collins and Griffith that took a pragmatic line. They believed self-government was better than no government, and their choices were informed by Collins's belief that the IRA could not sustain any struggle against the British for much longer. The divisions in the Sinn Féin cabinet were replicated across the country.

The formal negotiations between the British and the Irish lasted from October until December 1921, and resulted in the Anglo-Irish Treaty. Collins and Griffith headed the Irish negotiating team in Downing Street, where the negotiations took place. Surprisingly, de Valera elected to remain at home in Dublin. The Treaty which emerged, gave Ireland dominion status within the Empire, a position similar to that of Canada. It allowed for a boundary commission to sit at a future date, which would assess the borders between Northern Ireland and the newly formed Irish Free State (but which could not challenge the sovereignty of the Northern Ireland parliament). Most contentiously for many, the Treaty outlined an oath to be taken by all members of the Dáil, pledging their primary allegiance to the King, rather than to the Free State. Other articles in the Treaty allowed for the presence of a British governor-general in Ireland, the retention by the British of certain key defensive naval ports around the Irish coast, and the continued repayment by the Irish to the British exchequer of annuities arising from turn of the century land-purchase schemes.

THE CIVIL WAR

The signing of the Anglo-Irish Treaty on 6 December 1921, led to an intense period of debate in the Dáil over whether to ratify or reject the article of Treaty. On 7 January 1922, a vote was taken and the Treaty was ratified by 64 votes to 57. The debate swirled around a series of key issues. Did those who signed the Treaty in London actually have the authority to do so, as they had failed to refer its contents back to the Dáil before they added their signatures? Did the Treaty give Ireland her freedom? Would the Treaty give Ireland peace? Did the oath of allegiance amount to a betrayal of the very ideal of an indepen-dent nation? The issue of the border was not of key concern in the debates, and occupied only a small amount of the Dáil's time. There was a common consensus, both amongst doctrinaire Republicans, and amongst those who were in favour of the Treaty, that the existence of the border was only a temporary inconvenience. Collins, who mounted the most passionate defence of the Treaty, argued famously that the agreement gave Ireland 'the freedom to achieve' the ultimate freedom desired by all nations.

In the wake of the ratification debate, Ireland split. On one side were the pro-treatyites, who would form the first govern-ment of the Irish Free State, led by Collins and Griffith. Opposing them were the anti-treatyites. Politically the leader of this group was de Valera, but behind him lay those who would take up arms to oppose the Treaty. This group was led by Cathal Brugha, Collins's former friend Harry Boland, Rory O'Connor and Liam Lynch.

Collins headed the new Free State Army, which retained the bulk of support from the old IRA. These former gunmen were now the army of the state. They were better armed, resourced and supported than their anti-treaty opponents. The Civil War began in earnest in April 1921, when the anti-treaty forces took over the Four Courts in Dublin. For weeks Collins stalled, rather than fight his former colleagues. By the end of June, the situation reached deadlock, and Collins finally led the attack on the Four Courts.

It was a short, but bloody war. The intercommunal cruelty that had marred the War of Independence continued through into the Civil War, but this time it set family against family, and friend against friend. It also cost Ireland dear in respect of a generation of potential political leaders and state builders. Cathal Brugha was killed when the anti-treaty headquarters were attacked in June 1921. Arthur Griffith died of a heart attack in August that year, to be followed weeks later by Michael Collins, who was shot in an ambush in west Cork. The anti-treatyites attempted in vain to hold a line that stretched from Waterford to Limerick, as they were strongest in the south and the west, but they could not match the strength of the new state. In September 1921, the pro-treatyites passed a Special Powers Resolution, which enabled them to treat all anti-treatyites who were captured in battle as rebels. In response, the leader of the anti-treaty forces, Liam Lynch, issued an order that any member of the government who had voted for the special powers should be shot. Anti-treaty forces killed two pro-treaty deputies, and in response Kevin O'Higgins, the Dáil's Minister for Home Affairs, ordered the execution of those anti-treatyites who had been captured when the Four Courts fell.

Before the end of the Civil War on 27 April 1923, the Free State government had executed 77 members of the anti-treatyite forces. It had interned over 10,000 of its opponents without trial, and had conducted the whole war with a ruthless efficiency. If the post-treaty split had not been damaging enough, the bitterness of the Civil War ensured that the divisions within Irish political life would disfigure Irish politics for decades. The Civil War itself cost more lives, and caused more destruction to the fabric of Ireland, than the whole period of violence and revolution that stretched from 1916 to 1921.

FROM PARTITION TO WORLD WAR

The two states in Ireland faced very different problems during the inter-war years. The status of Northern Ireland had changed in the sense that it now had a devolved parliament, but the basic foundation stones of the society had not shifted. Protestant and Unionist domination of the political and social systems continued in Ulster in the same fashion as it had done in the years before the First World War. Northern Ireland was still firmly wedded to the twin principles of Crown and state, and proudly retained its place within the mighty British Empire. Until the period of economic depression that swept across the industrialised world in the late 1920s and early 1930s, Northern Ireland remained a largely prosperous area of high employment rates (especially amongst the Protestant population), centred on a base of modernised agricultural production and a limited-scale, but highly developed, heavy industry. While having to make small adjustments that were a product of the partition of Ireland, the ruling Unionist group in Northern Ireland continued much as they had done before. Essentially the post-partition world offered the Unionist community a sense of continuity built around a set of core principles and beliefs, which could not be challenged by the new state to its south. Doubts did, however, remain. The Unionists of Northern Ireland were constantly alarmed by, and often exaggerated, the threat posed by the Catholic and nationalist community within the six counties. Intercommunal violence was a common feature of Northern Ireland's inter-war experience, especially in the early 1930s, and the perceived threat from IRA members within Ulster was always considered as high. To compound the sense of unease which internal considerations lent to the Unionist mind, external affairs also occasionally caused concern. Although the Irish Free State was largely inactive on the issue of partition from the mid-1920s, the issue was still a reality that existed. Northern Irish politicians always had to be on the lookout for signs of expansionist fervour amongst the former gunmen of the south. Equally problematic was the attitude of Britain; although supportive of Northern Ireland during its establishment, could the loyalty of the British state towards the Province always be assured? While many of these fears were never realised during the inter-war years, the existence of such concerns sheds much light on the nature of the politics of Northern Ireland during that period.

For the Irish Free State, life was completely different. The route that had been taken since the first moves towards home rule, under the direction of Redmond, through the chaos of 1916 and the revolutionary period, had resulted in independence. It was a freedom, however, that was contested from within, and one that brought division where there might have been consensus. The first elected Free State government that emerged from the post-Civil War election of summer 1923, Cumann na nGaedheal, had to build a new nation from division. The split was one that existed between the pro- and anti-treaty forces; it festered in the memory of those who had fought in the Civil War, and for many Irish nationalists it was symbolised geographically by the existence of the border between north and south. The Free State was a symbol of complete discontinuity, and representative of total upheaval. Where the Ulster Unionists could build their new state on long-held and deeply rooted certainties that revolved around a belief in Crown and state, the nationalists charged with constructing the Free State were no longer working from a commonly agreed blueprint. The uncertainties were exacerbated in that many of the inspirational and powerful leaders who should have been at the helm, lay dead as a result of the Civil War.

In Northern Ireland, the parliament that had been created in 1920 consisted of 52 MPs. The first Prime Minister of Northern Ireland was Sir James Craig, a stalwart of the anti-Home Rule campaign. The Northern Irish state was created in the self-interest of its majority population, the Protestants. As Sinn Féin had opted out of discussions surrounding the 1920 Government of Ireland Act, it had not been in a position to voice the need for measures aimed at protecting the rights of the minority Catholic population. As the status of Northern Ireland had not been a point of discussion during the Treaty negotiations, such safeguards had not been introduced then either. Effectively there was a Unionist and Protestant hegemony in Northern Ireland.

The first legislative instance of such hegemony occurred in 1923, with the passage of an Education Act for Northern Ireland. The Act aimed to create an inclusive and secular educational system. Within the school system there would be no set religious teaching. The Act flew in the face of religious division in Northern Ireland, offering a potentially secular footing for the education system. Both the Catholic clergy, and Protestant groups, campaigned against such secularisation and co-religious teaching. Few schools ever reached the promising haven of secularity, and instead the majority remained as either specifically Catholic or Protestant schools. The education issue was symptomatic of much that would hamper the development of Northern Ireland as a functioning and equitable state: the two groups had no wish to blur the distinctions between them. The need to maintain separate and insular ties that were clearly visible within the public sphere, could only lead to alienation in the long term.

Many of the problems in Northern Ireland stemmed directly from partition. Nationalists in the north felt betrayed, but believed it was only a matter of time before they would be assimilated into a larger Free State. Such a belief drove them to ignore many institutions that were constructed in Northern Ireland. They would not sit in Parliament, on school boards or in local government, or join any state institution. While such a rejection of the philosophy of a separate northern state was understandable, in the context of belief in a unified 32-county Ireland, it meant that Northern Ireland was fashioned according to the wishes of the Unionist majority. In abstaining from the construction of the northern state, the Catholics abrogated their responsibility, and failed to safeguard their own interests.

In response to the War of Independence and the Civil War, various special constabularies had been established to protect Northern Ireland. The A, B and C Specials were a totally Protestant force, and the majority was armed. Many of those who joined were fervent believers in the force of Unionism, and thus often connected with the Orange Order and other exclusively Protestant concerns. The Specials conducted a long-running war against the IRA, and the perceived threat of its wider organisation within nationalist communities, throughout the early 1920s. Inter-communal violence, conducted by both the Specials and the IRA, which resulted in many deaths and was utilised in the scare-mongering stories of both sides, did nothing to help the construction of an inclusive society in Northern Ireland in its first decade.

Politically, the Northern Ireland parliament and its government were dominated, throughout the inter-war years, by the force of the Ulster Unionist Party (UUP). Craig remained as Prime Minister until his death in 1940. At that time, five of his seven cabinet ministers had been in office continuously since 1921. Not only was the force of the UUP total, its personnel appeared largely unchanging. In the 1930s, Craig quite understandably stated that the Stormont parliament was 'a Protestant Parliament for a Protestant people'. The way that Northern Ireland politics functioned in the inter-war years clearly meant that there was little room for anyone else. The supremacy of the UUP within Northern Ireland politics was further secured in 1929. The scheme of proportional representation, which had originally been introduced for parliamentary elections, was abolished. A similar step had already been taken with respect of local government elections in 1922. The result of a return to a first-past-the-post system, was that Catholic votes often became impotent, as they were lost in constituencies that were dominated by a Protestant majority. The process of Catholic marginalisation was furthered at the local level as councils, most notoriously in Derry, redrew constituency boundaries and introduced a franchise system based on property ownership. This process, known as 'gerrymandering', effectively disenfranchised the Catholic voters of Northern Ireland, and led to their complete powerlessness – and, many have argued, their relegation, in all aspects of society, to the level of second-class citizens.

The marginalisation of Catholics in the political sphere was replicated in the world of employment. While Northern Ireland was badly affected by the 1930s depression, because of its dependence on heavy industry, it was Catholic workers who bore the brunt of the resultant unemployment. Official pronouncements by leading Northern Ireland politicians at the time did not help matters. Craig in particular encouraged employers to look to the ranks of the unemployed Protestant community to fill jobs, rather than to take on Catholics. During the 1920s and 1930s, indeed right through to the 1960s, the bulk of Catholics in work were to be found in the sphere of unskilled manual labour. Catholics dominated the unemployment statistics, and made up only one-third of the employed population. The process by which Catholics were excluded from the job market, were located in the worst sections of Northern Ireland's housing stock, and failed to enter public service, was, as one historian has commented, a system of 'consensual apartheid'.

Looking beyond the status of Catholics in inter-war Northern Ireland, a situation that would create problems for the future, one observes a Province that was, in certain areas, relatively affluent. For the majority of the Protestant population, who resided in a state that had been created as their own, Northern Ireland was a fruitful society within which to live. Despite the internal problems that emerged from intercommunal violence and the threat of IRA activity, the status of Northern Ireland remained unchallenged, and links with the union and the Crown were unchanged.

In the Irish Free State, the situation was somewhat more chaotic at times, but one that had, by the onset of the Second World War, produced a level of domestic contentment. The 1923 election that had followed the end of the Civil War produced a majority for the pro-treaty side, now organised under the party name, Cumann na nGaedheal. De Valera and his fellow anti-treatyite supporters, many of whom were languishing in prison, fought under the old name of Sinn Féin, and were easily the second largest party. Sinn Féin continued as an abstentionist party. They refused to accept the legitimacy of the Free State Dáil and did not take up their seats. As a result, Cumann na nGaedheal, led by W. T. Cosgrave, were a government without an effective opposition in the Dáil. The Labour Party, which had taken 14 seats against the government's 63, formed the small official opposition group.

Cumann na nGaedheal were, by their own admission, the most conservative revolutionaries in history. The government worked within the Anglo-Irish Treaty and did not attempt to challenge its terms. When Lloyd George's promised Boundary Commission sat in 1924, Craig refused to send a delegate. The year-long investigation, which reported back in 1925, suggested minimal changes. The Free State representative Eoin MacNeill resigned, claiming that the Commission had wrongly interpreted the relevant Treaty articles, and the border remained unchanged. Throughout the 1920s, Cumann na nGaedheal worked to establish a democratic society based around an agreed system of law and order. An unarmed police force, the Garda Síochána, was established; an incredible achievement considering the number of arms that were freely circulating in Ireland in the wake of the War of Independence and the Civil War. The governmental system of the Free State was, as with so many other aspects of the new nation, based solidly around the British model. The two Houses of the Irish legislature, the Dáil and the Senate, were based on the two British Houses of Parliament. The legal system equally reflected many of the established norms of British legal practice. The continuity between the systems of administration that had existed in the days of British rule and those in the new Irish Free State was informed, in part, by the continued employment of many key civil servants by the new government.

Economically, Cumann na nGaedheal was driven by the need to balance the budget, a policy in line with the overriding Western economic orthodoxy of the time. Although pursuing a long and detailed debate throughout the 1920s, over the merits and pitfalls of economic protectionism, the government followed a policy of free trade. The economy was firmly based around agriculture and its connected industries. In pursuing an 'agriculture for export' policy, Cumann na nGaedheal gave rise to a wealthy and powerful class of large landowners centred on the cattle industry. This group benefited most during the 1920s, while the lot of small farmers, and those in the cities, changed little. Free State government did not bring about growth, instead it ushered in a period of stagnation. The dream of independence did not bring about the wealth that many had envisaged.

Culturally, Cumann na nGaedheal failed to act on the issue of the language. Although the state became officially bilingual, the issue of language teaching was left in the hands of the schools. Although a majority did some teaching in Irish, the failure to impose the use of the language within the political or business spheres meant that English continued to predominate. In the moral sphere the government allowed the norms of Catholic teaching to take primacy, thereby reflecting the fact that the Free State was a denominational nation. Divorce was illegal, and many other beliefs that emanated from the religious sphere found a voice within either the legislature or the moral mood of the country. The central place of the Catholic Church within the new state was not simply a product of the overwhelming religious belief shared by the majority of the population, but a legacy of the Church's role within the long struggle for independence.

In 1927, the wounds of the Civil War brought about a sea change in Free State politics. In July 1927, IRA men loyal to the anti-treatyite side assassinated Kevin O'Higgins, the Cumann na nGaedheal Minister of Justice. In partial response to the spectre of having the forces of opposition outside the Dáil, Cumann na nGaedheal enacted an Electoral Amendment Act that effectively made abstentionism impossible. De Valera, now head of a new party named Fianna Fáil, which he had formed from the remnants of the anti-treatyite forces, had to choose between the political wilderness, or a seat in the Dáil.

Fianna Fáil, which had won 44 seats to the government's 47, in the June 1927 election, entered the Dáil in August that year in the wake of the O'Higgins assassination. To bypass the thorny issue of the oath of allegiance, such a sticking point in the debates that followed the signing of the Treaty, de Valera and those in his party signed their names in the Dáil register without reading the oath. The Free State was formally and functionally a multi-party democracy. The arrival of Fianna Fáil into the Dáil marked one of the Free State's greatest achievements. Within a few years of the ending of the Civil War, both sides that had taken part in such a bloody and divisive conflict were sitting in the same democratic chamber. While there were always elements within the Free State who looked to the use of violence as a means of advancing their political goals, 1927 was a watershed: the two largest groupings from the Civil War, while not forgetting their differences, began to work within that same democratic chamber.

In 1932, Cumann na nGaedheal's period of office came to a close with the formation of the first Fianna Fáil government (albeit dependent on the support of the Labour Party). Despite various rumours, circulating at the time, that old scores might be settled during the hand over of government, the transition of power from Civil War victor to Civil War loser was peaceful. For all the failures of the Cumann na nGaedheal government to deliver the supposed spirit of the revolutionary period, and the radical policies envisaged by Sinn Féin, 1932 serves as a testament to their success in government. Their construction of state services and institutions, and their establishment of a communal belief in parliamentary democracy, ensured that the anti-state gunmen of 1922–3 could peacefully take office a decade later.

At the time of its formation, Fianna Fáil had sketched an

image of an Ireland that would strive towards the status of a Republic, would aim at national self-sufficiency, and would attempt to restore Irish traditions, including the language, to common usage. It was a message that, especially in view of the moribund performance of Cumann na nGaedheal in the late 1920s, was highly popular. In 1932, Fianna Fáil called a snap election that gave them an overall majority. They would remain in office until 1948.

The period in government of Fianna Fáil, was one of rapid change for the Free State with relation to the Treaty of 1921. Although briefly challenged between 1933 and 1935 by the uniformed members of the Blueshirt movement, so often termed or regarded as Ireland's fascists, de Valera faced no serious or sustained opposition during his period in office. The effect of losing two elections back to back was so demoralising to Cumann na nGaedheal that they sought an alliance with the Blueshirt forces and the small Centre party. The resultant new party was called Fine Gael. They formed the Dáil opposition for the remainder of the 1930s, but could do little to stop the changes envisaged by de Valera.

Until the outbreak of the Second World War, de Valera's main targets in office were the terms of the Treaty. He abolished the oath of allegiance to the British Crown, and reduced the office of Governor-General to the point of irrelevance. Throughout the 1930s de Valera fought an 'economic war' with Britain because of his refusal to meet the annuities debts that were enshrined in the Treaty. Although the 'economic war' was costly to Irish agriculture, as Britain placed huge duties on imports, it was ended in 1938 with a one-off payment of £10 million to the British, which freed Ireland from any future financial obligation. The 1938 agreement also transferred the so-called 'Treaty ports', those ports that were retained as British naval bases as part of the 1921 agreement, to Irish control.

In 1937 de Valera reached, constitutionally at least, the pinnacle of his career. He put his new constitution for Ireland, *Bunreacht na hÉireann*, before the people in a referendum on 1 July 1937. With a majority of 160,000, the 1937 Constitution of Éire came into being. The constitution, although drawing in large part on the one that had been drafted in 1922, was largely the work of de Valera himself.

The constitution contained countless articles that outlined the legal scope of Ireland, the nature of the country and the structures of its power systems. Most important, within the context of the partition of Ireland, were articles 1, 2 and 3. Article 1 stressed the sovereign right of the Irish people to direct their own affairs. Article 2 made clear that the territorial jurisdiction of the Irish state spread across all 32 counties, though such jurisdiction would only be applied to the 26 counties until, as article 3 outlined, the 6 northern counties were reintegrated.

In dealing with how government would be run, the constitution abolished the post of the Governor-General, and introduced instead the post of President. The Presidency was a job that was similar, in many ways, to that of a constitutional monarch. Under the new constitution a Taoiseach (Prime Minister) and Tánaiste (deputy Prime Minister) would head the government. The 1922 Senate, which in de Valera's eyes had been modelled too closely on the British second House and possessed too much power, was replaced by a relatively powerless Senate, the members of which were selected by groups of vocational interest.

Other articles in the constitution made Irish the first language of the state. It placed the family unit at the heart of the nation's affairs as the natural unit within society, and imbued that grouping with inalienable moral rights. Alongside such protection of the family, which was in line with the conservative nature of Irish Catholic orthodoxy of the time, the constitution allied the state, although not exclusively, to the Catholic Church. It recognised the special position of the Church as it represented the faith of the majority of the people. The constitution, notwithstanding the primacy that was given to the Catholic faith, recognised and gave protection to the other religious beliefs that existed within the state. De Valera, while recognising the central place of Catholicism, did not wish to offend or alienate members of other religious groups within the state. Such an attitude of apparent compromise, indeed the whole constitution, reflected what one historian has termed, 'an uneasy accommodation between Catholicism and liberalism'.

The end of the 1930s would throw the whole world into a state of chaos as another global war began. What, though, had de Valera achieved during the 1930s? Indeed, what had the Free State achieved since its formation in 1921 and the bloody Civil

War that followed? The most impressive achievement of the Free State in the period to 1939 is that, despite the deep wounds, it avoided falling back into the inferno of renewed Civil War. On the back of such contentious disagreement, it serves as a remarkable testimony to the politicians of both sides of the Treaty split that they adhered to largely democratic and non-violent forms of political discourse. The Cosgrave years were a model in state-building. True, they were not the most exciting of political times, nor were they driven by a radical agenda, but they did introduce the main cornerstones of an electoral-based democratic state into the newly independent Ireland. That they gave up power in the face of an electoral defeat is proof, if such were needed, of their democratic beliefs. De Valera and Fianna Fáil, although pursuing a much more overtly political agenda, continued the process of state-building. In doing so, de Valera, through his battles with Britain over debt, and politically culminating in the 1937 constitution, acted as the standard bearer for one of the most oft-repeated ideals of Michael Collins. In the Treaty debates, Collins argued that Ireland had not won freedom, but the freedom to achieve it. Working within the democratic framework of the Free State, as established by Cumann na nGaedheal, de Valera was able to win many of the freedoms for Ireland that he, and many other anti-treatyites, argued had been lost in 1921. With the exception of the border issue and the lack of movement on the question of transforming that state into a formal Republic, de Valera's agenda of the 1930s freed Ireland from the terms of the 1921 Treaty. The test of such an assessment, and of the reality of Éire's freedom, is clearly evident in the choice of neutrality, which the country was able to make in 1939.

THE SECOND WORLD WAR

In 1939, with the onset of war, the two parts of Ireland had to make choices. The judgement was whether to commit themselves to participation in the war. In many ways the situation was similar to that of 1914. The decisions that were made demonstrated an allegiance to a self-perceived ideal of the nation in the case of Éire, and loyalty to Britain for Northern Ireland.

The decision in Northern Ireland was as straightforward as it had been in 1914. Northern Ireland, as a proud and integral part of both the British nation and its Empire, had to fight in the war. With the experience of the First World War, the British decided not to enforce conscription in Northern Ireland, for fear of alienating the nationalist population, but recruitment into the British Army, despite the absence of conscription, was steady throughout the duration of the war, and came from both sections of the community. The economy in Northern Ireland benefited, in part, from increased war production, and a switch from peacetime industry to some form of munitions output. The scale of such a switch, however, was in no way comparable to the experience of the rest of industrial Britain, and therefore the comparative effects on working practices, employment rates and incomes were much reduced. While the state of Northern Ireland was full square behind the war effort, the whole experience of the 1939–45 period appears to have been slightly unreal. Certainly Northern Ireland was at war, but in a sense it all seemed to be far away, and there was no general sense of the war ever exerting a compelling force on the Province. The main event to bring the war dramatically home to Northern Ireland was a bombing raid in April 1941, one of several in the course of the war, that destroyed hundreds of homes and businesses, and led to the deaths of over 700 people.

By the end of the Second World War, Northern Ireland had moved closer to Britain. Despite the different nature of the wartime experience in the Province from that of many industrial and urbanised regions in Britain, Northern Ireland remained loyal throughout, and made an important contribution to the war effort. In 1949, the link between Northern Ireland and Britain was further formalised and cemented with the passage of the Ireland Act. Put in place by Attlee's Labour government, the act ensured that Northern Ireland would remain part of the United Kingdom until such time as a devolved parliament stated otherwise. For many in Northern Ireland, such an undertaking by the British government was a just reward for loyalty in the war.

Éire took a completely different line on the whole idea of participation in the Second World War. Whereas Redmond had chosen participation in the 1914–18 conflict as a way of demonstrating loyalty to the Empire so that the promise of Home Rule might be honoured, de Valera and his government made their decisions from within an actual, rather than a promised, independent Ireland. The various factors that informed the Irish decision to choose neutrality in the conflict had been reinforced by the return in 1938 of the Treaty ports. It would have been impossible for Éire to remain neutral if the British were still stationed in six ports around the Irish coast. With the British gone, and the independent statement of the 1937 constitution public, Éire had no reason to enter the war. In choosing neutrality, de Valera, and the voices that supported him within the Dáil and across the country, made the most explicit statement of Irish independence. Of all the powers of decision-making that a state is supposed to possess, the right to make war or sue for peace is the most powerful. The decision of neutrality was driven, not by a moral choice between Nazism and Allied notions of democracy, but by a desire to demonstrate to the whole world that Éire was the master of its own destiny.

Much of the academic writing that has explored the 'Emergency', as the war was dubbed by the government, has examined how strictly neutral Éire actually was. In the context of its geographical location, next to Britain, and physically joined to a combatant piece of the United Kingdom in the form of Northern Ireland, total neutrality would have always been difficult. The best conclusion seems to be that Éire remained neutral throughout the war, but that such a policy worked in practice in favour of the Allies; 50,000 Irishmen travelled into Britain and joined up to fight in the Allied forces. Allied aircrews that crash landed in Éire were sent home, whereas Germans were interned. In 1941, when Belfast was bombed, fire engines travelled from Éire into Northern Ireland to assist in fighting the resultant inferno. Although there was a shortage of many goods across the country, and everyone had to endure rationing, the economy, especially the agricultural one, benefited as Britain was desperate for produce. The 1939–45 period repaired all the damage that had been done to trading relationships between the two countries during the economic war of the 1930s.

In a desperate attempt to bring Éire into the war in December 1941, Churchill had telegraphed de Valera, and offered him Irish unity in return for an end to neutrality. As appealing as Churchill's offer, 'a nation once again', may have been, de

Valera rejected it. How serious Churchill had been is question-
able, and how he ever intended to persuade the Northern Irish
Unionists that they would have to join the rest of Ireland, was
never explained. The choice of neutrality, and the decision not to
investigate Churchill's offer further, demonstrate de Valera's, and
many other Irish politicians, state of mind. While the unification
of Ireland, something that many of them had fought for two
decades earlier, was desirable and was enshrined in article 2 of
the 1937 constitution, most accepted, in their minds at least, that
such a goal was unfeasible in the context of the mid-twentieth
century.

In the wake of the Second World War, and the various forces
of post-industrial modernisation that would exert such a powerful force on the whole of Ireland, the situation would change
once more. Unfortunately for the people of Northern Ireland, the
twentieth century would end as it had begun its first two decades
across the whole island, in a state of violent disorder.

6

Post-War Ireland and the Modern Troubles

Éire and Northern Ireland emerged from their very different experiences of the Second World War further apart than ever. The war itself had contributed much to the sense of alienation that existed between the two parts of Ireland, as did their very different economic structures. Northern Ireland's involvement in the war had given a boost to its traditional heavy industries and these businesses would continue to dominate the immediate post-war period, and remain the largest employers of the Province's people. In Éire, the war had led to a reinvigoration of agriculture. The country profited greatly from supplying a British market that had been devastated by wartime shortages. If such elements created a sense of difference between north and south, the continued divisiveness of religious affiliation and the schism that existed, ideologically at least, over the border question, served to cement the separation.

FEELINGS OF SEPARATION

Two important statements of policy, one from Éire in 1943, and the other from the British government in 1949, officially sealed the sense of alienation between the two parts of Ireland. In 1943, de Valera made what was to become his most famous speech. He used the traditional St Patrick's Day radio address to outline his vision of what Éire might become. He argued, perhaps in acceptance of the contemporary immobility of the border issue, that national independence was about building a community with shared goals. He stated that the Irish should aim, not for material wealth, but for a life built around a satisfaction in 'frugal comfort' in a land

> whose countryside would be bright with cosy homesteads, whose fields and villages would be joyous with the sound of industry, with the romping of sturdy children, the contests of athletic youths and the laughter of comely maidens.[1]

There have been many interpretations of the 1943 speech, and debate surrounds whether de Valera was sketching an unobtainable and idealised vision of Ireland, or whether this was a statement of future policy. What is apparent, and is backed up in part by Éire's relative inability to industrialise and modernise, is that the speech was perceived by those opponents of Fianna Fáil, as a statement of anti-modernism; it demonstrated a backward-looking rural state, dominated by images of the family that were closely linked with an adherence to Catholic orthodoxy. By contrast to the speculative nature of de Valera's speech, the 1949 Ireland Act was a definite piece of legislation. It wedded Northern Ireland to the United Kingdom for as long as the majority of the people wanted the union to remain. As the majority of the people of Northern Ireland were Protestant, and many of them relied on the force of modernism in the shape of industry for their family income, membership of the UK was far preferable to the rural backwater of Éire.

The passage of the Ireland Act was driven by the passage, on 21 December 1948, of the Republic of Ireland Act. In a general election in February 1948, the Fianna Fáil party was finally voted from office, after sixteen years of continuous rule. Although Fianna Fáil was the largest party in the Dáil, they could not form a government. In the event a coalition was formed that consisted of Fine Gael, the Labour Party, the National Labour Group, Clann na Talmhan and Clann na Poblachta. It was an eclectic mix of parties from across the political spectrum, all driven by a desire to see de Valera removed

---

1. M. Moynihan (ed.), *Speeches and Statements of Eamon de Valera, 1917–73* (1980), pp. 466–9

from office. The Taoiseach, John A. Costello, was not the most heavyweight political figure within the coalition, but the only one that was acceptable to all involved, because of his lack of a civil war pedigree. The government quickly resolved that it had to clear up the whole issue of Éire's constitutional and legal position in the context of British and Commonwealth relations. Costello's argument in the Dáil debate on the issue was straightforward. All associations with Britain and her Commonwealth had to end, with Ireland established, unequivocally, as a Republic. When the bill was passed in December 1948, the 26 counties formally became the Republic of Ireland, and all remaining legal links with Britain and her Commonwealth were severed. Many opponents of the move towards the status of Republic argued that such a move would make the partition of Ireland permanent. The British response, the Ireland Act of 2 June 1949, while giving all citizens of the Irish Republic full rights whenever they travelled to Britain, effectively proved the opponents of the 1948 Act right. In the wake of the war years, in the face of the differences that existed between north and south and in the context of the Republic of Ireland Act and the Ireland Act, partition was copper-bottomed for the foreseeable future. The sense of separation between the two parts of Ireland appeared wider than ever before.

THE POST-WAR REPUBLIC OF IRELAND

In the wake of the establishment of the Republic of Ireland, the coalition government attempted to resolve some of the more pressing social issues that troubled the country. Noel Browne, at the Health Ministry, left the greatest legacy of the inter-party government. In the last years of the 1940s, he increased the number of hospital beds that were available. Previously, the number of beds had been insufficient to allow the country to tackle some of its most serious common ailments. By his actions, Browne enabled the Republic finally to defeat its long-standing tuberculosis problem. Browne also oversaw the establishment of a blood transfusion service across the country. In this, and other innovations, Browne established many of the tenets of a commonly shared and accessible health service. This ensured that the people of the Republic were in a far better state of general health than had ever been possible before. While such initiatives clearly lagged behind the concomitant developments elsewhere in Europe, most notably the British instigation of a National Health Service, they were centrally important in Ireland.

Browne took one step too far, however, and his time as a minister was curtailed. In attempting to further his reforms, he instigated a 'mother and child' scheme that aimed at the establishment of free ante-natal and post-natal care for all women, and free health care for all children to the age of 16. While such proposed legislation might now be viewed as the height of enlightenment, and was certainly in line with contemporary developments taking place within the British welfare state, Browne's ideas ran directly against the thinking of the Catholic hierarchy. The Irish Republic was still in a position, at the start of the 1950s, where all government legislation that the Church might have an interest in, was referred to the Bishops. The status that the Church had been given under the 1937 constitution meant that while the Catholic hierarchy had no formal powers, governments did well not to ignore their standpoint. This situation, which may appear to some as incongruous in a parliamentary democracy, was the product of the long historical partnership that existed between the politics of the nationalist struggle and the central place of the Catholic Church within Irish society.

Browne failed to understand this with the 'mother and child' scheme. The Church objected that such legislation would allow the state to interfere with that sacrosanct unit, the family. Also, the direct involvement of the state in matters of ante- and postnatal care signalled, in the eyes of the Church, the interference of the state in matters of divine creation, and bordered the shadowy line of clinical intervention and abortion. Costello was approached directly by the Catholic hierarchy, and Browne was left with no support for his proposals. The 'mother and child' scheme was lost, Browne jettisoned into the political wilderness, and the power of the Church in the Republic was demonstrated for all those, especially the anti-Papists of Northern Ireland, who would see its hand everywhere.

Faced with the loss of the 'mother and child' scheme, the work of the inter-party government ground to a halt. In May 1951, it lost power to a resurgent Fianna Fáil. The 1950s were not a good decade for the Republic. Neither Fianna Fáil, nor the second inter-party government (1954–7), could stamp their authority on the political situation, and the nation drifted into a moribund state. The Republic remained a country dominated by agriculture, in a world, and especially a Europe, that was becoming ever more industrialised and urban. The rate of growth in the Irish economy remained one of the lowest in Europe across the whole decade. By 1960, only 14.3 per cent of the workforce were employed in the industrial sector: agriculture remained supreme. The largest single problem for the Republic, for its economy and society, was the return, in its most excessive form, of a nineteenth-century problem.

Irish emigration had never ceased in the post-famine years, nor into the twentieth century. It had, however, reached levels that were considered acceptable. In the 1950s the sluggish nature of the Republic's economy, and its seeming inability to regenerate in any positive fashion, led to a huge upsurge in emigration. By 1961, the population of the Republic had fallen to 2.8 million. Most alarmingly for any country, its young people were leaving in their droves. The economy, as it stood in the 1950s, could not feed nor gainfully employ all of its people. Of all the children born in the 1930s, the very people who should have been changing and building up the Republic in the 1950s, when they were at their prime, 80 per cent would emigrate. The effect of such population loss was devastating for large areas of the country. Those areas traditionally reliant on family-based farming, such as the west of the country, were decimated. The problem for the people of the Republic was that their governments of the 1950s, of whatever party, could not envisage a solution. More fundamentally, they could not see beyond the economic ideal of Irish self-sufficiency.

The situation changed radically in the 1960s. In June 1959, de Valera finally released the reins of governmental and party power that he had held for over four decades, and allowed Seán Lemass to take over as Taoiseach. Lemass was, despite being firmly rooted within the history and ideals of Fianna Fáil, a moderniser. The solution that Lemass, supported by the work of T. K. Whitaker at the Department of Finance, offered to the

Republic's ills was rapid industrial modernisation and reintegration into the field of European economic activity. During the 1960s, Lemass oversaw a quite remarkable redevelopment of the Irish Republic. He was able to capitalise on a period of growth that was common across the developed world, and thus, to an extent, Lemass was merely part of a wider trend of modernisation and growth. It is clear that the Republic did not become the richest, or the most profitable country in Europe, and when judged by many comparative European economic indicators, actually under performed. The Lemass programme did, however, bring an end to the negative policies of the 1950s. Foreign companies began locating in the Republic during the 1960s and a growth rate of 4 per cent was achieved across the decade. Emigration did not stop, but the rates slowed considerably and returned to traditionally acceptable levels. By 1966, the Republic was recording population growth for the first time in its history. Most important in the long term was the slow shift of production and employment from agriculture to industry. While the various programmes introduced by Lemass were never aimed at relegating agriculture to a secondary position, it did not respond to the different reforms as rapidly as the industrial sector. By the end of the 1960s, those employed in industry (54 per cent of the total workforce) were in the majority for the first time ever. While such changes were important in the context of the 1960s, they also produced an unstoppable chain of events that affect the Republic to this day. The country became steadily more urbanised and fewer people worked the land.

Alongside the specific economic programmes introduced by Lemass, the 1960s witnessed a series of wider social and cultural changes that exerted an equally powerful effect on life in the Republic. The development of mass air travel, symbolised by the success of the national airline Aer Lingus, enabled the Republic to be opened to a huge flow of foreign tourists. The influx, driven by the work of the Irish Tourist Board, Bord Fáilte, enabled many Irish-Americans to return 'home' for the summer relatively cheaply and easily. The opening up of Ireland to tourists in the 1960s was replicated by changes in the role of the media. The social impact of the arrival of television in the Republic is something that still requires academic investigation. While excellent work has been conducted that examines the establishment of Radio Telefís Éireann (RTÉ) in 1960, the effects of people opening their homes to the TV set and the images beamed into it, have yet to be studied and understood. RTÉ broadcast a diet of news, Irish language and other programmes, with the aim of preserving and developing national culture. One thing about RTÉ is clear: its national broadcasting was watched on a wide basis. The screening, in 1966 (during the 50th anniversary celebrations of the Easter Rising), of the historical drama *Insurrection*, a reconstruction of the events of Easter Week, was the Irish televisual equivalent of the death of J. F. Kennedy in the psyche of the American nation; a television event that captivated everyone in the country. Along with the development of RTÉ, television also brought 'foreign' broadcasters, in the form of the BBC, into many people's homes. Television served to challenge and question the norms of authority, moral or political, in the Republic, in a way that had never been envisaged. Whereas the Church had been able to control the proposed 'mother and child' legislation of Browne in the 1950s, it had great difficulty in controlling what was broadcast and what was watched on television. The Republic was, throughout the 1960s – that legendary decade in many other western European countries – turning its eyes to a wider world. In doing so, the Irish were forced to question many of the central beliefs that they had held since the period of revolution.

In the 1970s and 1980s, the government of the Republic was shared between a series of Fianna Fáil and coalition Fine Gael governments. Many of the social changes that had begun in the 1960s were continued. The rate of consumption grew rapidly and the Republic's embrace of foreign culture, particularly American and British, continued unabated. In 1973, de Valera resigned as President of the Republic. Finally, 56 years after his election as an MP for East Clare, the leader, and self-appointed conscience of the nation, left the political scene. He died two years later. The departure of de Valera was a hugely symbolic moment. While the family names of those from the revolutionary period still featured in the Dáil, they belonged to the descendants of that generation. The Republic, in personnel terms at least, could finally move past the years of revolution, civil war and division.

In 1972, the Republic agreed to join the European Community, a step that was formally taken in January 1973, and it has remained a fervent supporter and active member ever since. In opening itself to, and embracing so fully, the other European states (and the many common laws that accompany membership of the EC), the Republic once more lost much of its insularity. In the late 1970s, the emergence of Charles Haughey as leader of Fianna Fáil and Garret FitzGerald as leader of Fine Gael, marked a move towards a competitive and exciting period of two-party personality politics in the Republic.

The process of secularisation continued. The position of the Catholic Church as the foremost religious faith was never challenged, but its right to interfere with politics and many aspects of daily life was curtailed. Throughout the 1980s, there was a constant debate in the Republic over the rights of the individual to be able to divorce, to have free access to contraception and to seek an abortion. In a referendum in November 1992, the vote was in favour of women having access to abortion advice, and the freedom to travel outside of the Republic to seek such a procedure. In a referendum of November 1995, the smallest of majorities ensured that couples who had lived separately for five years could seek a divorce. Although premises selling contraceptives still require a licence, the general availability of birth control has increased considerably. One of the changes that underpinned all the 'yes' votes in the different referendums, was the growth of Dublin as the largest concentration of inhabitants within the country. The city has undergone massive growth, and is inhabited by an increasingly young and economically active population. As a major metropolitan centre at the heart of Europe, however, Dublin is out of step with large parts of the Republic which have not developed with such speed. One of the problems that the country will have to tackle in the next decade is the sense of alienation that exists between the capital city (controlling as it does the national media, with the bulk of the nation's wealth and holding the majority of opinion formers), and the remainder of the Republic (seen by many in Dublin as a rural backwater, still clinging to the old certainties of the land and the Church).

In the 1990s two key events, which remain to be fully assessed, transformed the Republic. The first, in 1990, was the election of Mary Robinson as President. Robinson was a new phenomenon, as a woman, and as someone from outside the

Fianna Fáil-Fine Gael loop (she represented the Labour Party). She used the office of President to pursue her vision for Ireland. As a liberal moderniser, Robinson was a key force in the promotion of the right to abortion and divorce, and a supporter of women's rights across Ireland. It will be some years before her legacy is truly understood, but the fact that her successor, Mary McAleese, was elected from a group of four candidates, three of whom were women, demonstrates how the Republic has changed. The second event of the 1990s, still ongoing and set to continue into the twenty-first century, was the advent of huge economic growth within the Republic. In the mid-1990s the Republic recorded a growth rate of 7 per cent, and it was one of the fastest growing economies within Europe, of that decade. Such growth earned the Republic the label the 'Celtic Tiger'. The wealth that was created was a product of a boom in information technology, huge inward investment and the careful utilisation of European Union regional development money. While parts of the Republic benefited from the phenomenal growth within the economy, the feeling that Dublin and the remainder of the country are different, was reinforced in the minds of many as they believed that the capital was benefiting far more than anywhere else from the influx of wealth.

For many commentators in the Irish Republic, there is a feeling that the country has successfully negotiated its twentieth-century journey. It has achieved a level of wealth, modernity and secularisation which is on a par with its European neighbours. There is thus a feeling that they have lain to rest many of the shibboleths of the nation's violent past.

POST-WAR NORTHERN IRELAND.

The onset of the modern troubles in 1968 has meant, perhaps understandably, that within the popular mind at least, Northern Ireland is often, and simply, equated, with a violent battle over the partition of Ireland. The origins of the troubles, however, are far more complex than the question of whether a line on a map is permanent or temporary. Following the Second World War, Northern Ireland, no matter the assurances that were made territorially in the 1949 Ireland Act, was awash with long-standing social and political problems. These problems did not, for the most part, revolve around the question of the border. The main concerns for both the Protestant and Catholic sectors of the Province's population, was how they could ensure the future protection of their own cultural, religious and historic traditions, and secure the best representation for their communities.

In the initial post-war years, the Protestant community, represented by the force of unionism, was in a seemingly unassailable position. It controlled the Province politically, possessed the bulk of the wealth, held the best jobs and lived in the finest housing that was available in the context of each social grouping. The years after 1945, however, signalled a downturn in the dominance of the heavy industries which had always been the cornerstone of Northern Ireland's wealth. The traditional family firms that had owned factories in long-standing industries such as linen production, had failed to invest in new technology; their competitiveness fell rapidly and unemployment ensued. Businesses began to go under with alarming rapidity. Likewise, the industrial ship-building giant of Belfast, Harland and Wolff, an employer of over 20,000 in 1960, had cut its workforce in half by the end of 1962. Northern Ireland was in a state of industrial free-fall. The difficulties were compounded by the costs of applying the Labour government's welfare state reforms to Northern Ireland. As welcome as such initiatives were, they caused a huge drain on Stormont's finances, and necessitated the direct fiscal intervention of the British state into the affairs of the Province. Such intervention was symbolic of the partial loss of Stormont and Northern Ireland's sense of devolved independence. The economic uncertainties of the post-war decades, and the slow shifts in the British–Northern Ireland relationship, caused unease amongst the Protestant sections of the population. For many, especially those in working-class areas, their sense of grievance was focused on the Catholic population.

In the post-war years, the lot of Catholics steadily declined as competition for jobs and other resources increased in the wake of the Province's industrial decline. The number of Catholics in the unskilled sector of the economy grew, and discrimination in areas such as housing provision, in certain parts of the west of the Province, accelerated. One of the most profound difficulties in Northern Ireland was the commonly held belief amongst the

Catholic population that discrimination was an everyday, and permanent feature of their life.

In 1963, the Ulster Unionist Party elected a new leader, Terence O'Neill. Although O'Neill was as assured as his predecessors in his belief in the Protestant hegemony in Northern Ireland, he understood that to maintain the position of the unionists, reform was needed. To counter the widespread Catholic belief in, or experience of, discrimination, Stormont had to put its house in order. O'Neill's problem was that once he had embarked on a programme of reform, many unionists claimed he had gone too far, while many Catholic campaigners argued that he had not gone far enough. In drawing attention to the need to tackle the issue of discrimination and the inequities that existed in Northern Irish society, O'Neill let the genie out of the bottle.

O'Neill's reform package, as far as it existed, aimed at solving the problems of Northern Ireland through renewed economic growth that would be shared by all. That many foreign firms were attracted to Northern Ireland during the 1960s was a mark of O'Neill succeeding in his goals. However, for every job that was created from new inward investment, one continued to be lost in old forms of heavy industry.

Three groups carefully watched over O'Neill's moves towards reform. For the first time, almost, since 1921, the government in Britain, then a Labour administration under Harold Wilson, started paying attention to the internal workings of Stormont and the Province. Throughout his time in office, Wilson put constant pressure on O'Neill to keep up the pace of reform. To many unionists such encouragement smacked of political interference in the state of Northern Ireland; interference that specifically favoured the Catholic population. The second group watching over O'Neill was a rising Catholic middle, and university-educated, class. Building on internal demands for reform, and capturing the spirit of change that was sweeping through student bodies and workers' movements across the Western world, the Campaign for Social Justice (CSJ, 1964) and the Northern Ireland Civil Rights Association (NICRA, 1967) emerged. Both the CSJ and NICRA started life as non-denominational organisations aimed at the internal reform of Stormont. They did not begin life as expressly Catholic organisations, and neither did they look to the destruction of the border and the reunification of

Ireland as the solution to their problems. What is clear, is that the CSJ and NICRA constantly pressurised O'Neill to continue with the reforms. Such demands for change were countered by the third group observing O'Neill's progress: those from within the Unionist camp. The reforms that O'Neill attempted, and particularly his symbolic meeting with Seán Lemass in 1967 (the first ever official meeting of Stormont's Prime Minister and the Irish Taoiseach), were bitterly opposed by many within the Unionist Party. They were accompanied by an increasingly vociferous group that stood outside mainstream Unionism. Such people believed that the Stormont government should have no relationship with the forces of either Catholicism or nationalism. These groupings, led most notably by Ian Paisley, saw the civil rights movements of the CSJ and NICRA as fronts for the aspirations of republican Catholicism, which aimed at the destruction of Northern Ireland and the reunification of Ireland.

In the late 1960s the situation began to progress at an increasing pace. O'Neill steadily lost control. Both the civil rights movement and its Paisleyite opposition took to the streets. The ensuing violence ensured that Britain had to become directly involved in the whole Northern Ireland issue, and the modern troubles began.

THE TROUBLES

In August 1968, the civil rights movement, following a pattern that had been set by the black civil rights movement in the US, took to the streets. The first of Northern Ireland's civil rights marches took the route from Coalisland to Dungannon. It was organised under the auspices of the CSJ and NICRA, and aimed at highlighting the removal of a Catholic family from council housing, to make room for a single Protestant woman who was employed by a local Unionist councillor. Such blatant discrimination as had happened in Dungannon was exactly the type of case that the CSJ and NICRA wished to highlight and prevent from happening in the future. This first march was met by a unionist counter-demonstration. Although the ending of that march was peaceful, it set the pattern for all such marches in the future. Any marches or meetings by the civil rights movement would be met with open hostility by many of the followers of unionism. Despite the true purpose of the civil rights campaign, to challenge injustices within the social sphere in Northern Ireland, the whole nature of protest quickly unravelled and became a battle in which forces that were perceived as representative of Catholicism and nationalism, were fighting against those from the Protestant and unionist population. While such labelling hides many of the complexities of the Northern Ireland situation, and in no way accounts for the motivations of all those who took to the streets in the late 1960s and 1970s, the situation did descend, at many levels, into a hopelessly sectarian 'them against us' situation.

In early October 1968, the second march planned by the CSJ and NICRA was banned by the Stormont government. Although the march never went ahead, such a blatantly political ban was vehemently opposed by many in the nationalist community, who saw Stormont as blocking any attempt to bring about further reform. In response to the ban there was rioting in nationalist areas for two days; a pattern that would become all too familiar in the years and decades to come. In January 1969, a new group in the civil rights mould, People's Democracy (PD), marched from Belfast to Derry. PD was a far more radical grouping than any that had previously been established, and was expressly organised and mobilised to keep the pressure on O'Neill. PD aimed at radicalising the whole political landscape, and transforming the political battle away from an internalised, Stormont-led reform of Northern Ireland, and to a wide-ranging questioning of the legitimacy of the state. Shortly before its entry into Derry, the PD march passed over Burntollet bridge, and was attacked by a force of loyalists. That the attack damaged any lingering faith that the Catholic population may have had in the intentions of many of the loyalist population in Northern Ireland was bad enough. However, the attack at Burntollet was filmed and screened on television across the Province and beyond, a fact which only served to fan the flames. For many of the marchers, the worst aspect of the attack was that among those throwing stones and wielding batons, were off duty members of the police force. It was also clear to many of the marchers who were attacked, that those police officers who were on duty, and charged with protecting the march, did little to help.

Burntollet became symbolic of the loss of faith in Stormont amongst the Catholic population, and the transformation of the Northern Ireland situation into one where the battle lines were drawn along the lines envisaged by PD. After Burntollet, there was a feeling that if the police force could not be trusted, then who would defend the Catholic population?

In April 1969, O'Neill finally gave up. After winning a less than convincing election victory in February (anti-O'Neill Unionists gained 17 per cent of the vote), his period in office was doomed. Throughout the summer of 1969, levels of disorder on the streets grew, and intercommunal violence escalated. In Derry particularly, the situation swept out of control, and it became clear that the police forces of Northern Ireland could not contain the rapidly escalating situation. Attacks on houses that were deemed to belong to those of the 'wrong' religion became a common feature throughout many areas of Northern Irish society during the summer of 1969. Large sections of the population were forced to flee their homes because the followers of their faith did not form a majority in their locality. Many took new addresses within areas inhabited by 'their own kind'; many Catholics fled south to the Republic, while others of both religious persuasions chose to leave Ireland altogether.

The breakdown in community relations had two profound effects on the future of Northern Ireland. First, the demography of the Province's housing changed dramatically, especially amongst the working classes. Where there had often previously been a mixing of religions in many housing estates and local areas, the troubles forced a realignment of many into religion-specific areas. How could Northern Ireland find any cross-community resolution to its difficulties when the majority lived their lives apart? The second consequence was the security response to the situation. In an attempt to calm the situation, restore order and reassure the Catholic population, the British Army was sent to Northern Ireland on 15 August 1969. While such an action was entirely understandable in the context of such chaos, the remit of the troops was never clearly defined. Uncertain of their role, and identified by many within the Catholic population as another force of control, the army in effect quickly became part of the problem, and three decades later, British troops are still stationed in Northern Ireland.

Despite the introduction of British troops to Northern Ireland in August 1969, British government thinking was not based on a long-term entanglement. They believed that the use of troops would be a short-term measure to restore order, and that once a semblance of calm had returned, Stormont would push on with reform. By putting its own house in order, Stormont would allow for the withdrawal of British forces, and the return, although in a modified fashion, of a traditional Northern Irish–British relationship. The almost ceaseless findings of various government-ordered commissions into events in Northern Ireland during 1968 and 1969, constantly showed the existing system to be wanting. Lord Scarman concluded in 1972 that the Province's police force, the Royal Ulster Constabulary (RUC), had totally lost the support of the Catholic population. Rather than diminishing, the problems appeared to be escalating.

In the midst of the chaos of the late 1960s and early 1970s, the political scene fractured. The forces of unionism, in the shape of James Chichester-Clark and Brian Faulkner, the last two Prime Ministers of Northern Ireland, attempted to hold their party together as a coherent unit. In practice this meant that despite any reforms that were forthcoming, few of the politically active groups in Northern Ireland appeared content. The stance of the Unionist Party, which aimed at the preservation of internal unity, ran directly against the advice of the British government, which was rapidly losing patience. To reform would placate the British, and go some way in meeting the demands of the Catholics and the broad civil rights movement. However, as the whole problem had become so wrapped up in issues of competing identities, any reform would be judged by many unionists as placating the demands of Catholicism and nationalism. In the face of any reform, there was only one winner: the increasingly belligerent face of unionism and loyalism, centred politically around Ian Paisley, and militarily a resurgent UVF. Against the potential and actual fracturing of unionism, the forces that had emerged under the flag of civil rights came together as a single political party: the Social Democratic and Labour Party (SDLP). The SDLP looked for reform of the political and social system in Northern Ireland along broadly socialist lines, and sought to resolve the nationality and border issues within the context of majority consent.

Alongside the political changes of the early 1970s a steady resurgence of paramilitarism was taking place. Certain groups were becoming disenchanted with the attempts at, or lack of, reform, and were being mobilised, instead, around the constant upsurges in rioting, intercommunal violence and attacks on opposition meetings. Loyalist paramilitary groups emerged in the late 1960s whose aim was to protect the union. The two most enduring from this early period of the troubles were the UVF, and the newly formed Ulster Defence Association (UDA). On the Catholic side, the only existing paramilitary group at the start of the troubles was the Irish Republican Army (IRA). Predominantly Dublin-based, and looking towards a policy of constitutional political involvement, the IRA was seen as woefully out of touch with the situation in the north when it sprang to life in the late 1960s. In the midst of attacks on Catholics and Catholic houses by loyalist paramilitaries, the response of some within the Catholic community was to establish its own force aimed at defending local areas against attack. The IRA split in January 1970. The northern IRA, known as the Provisional IRA (PIRA), was primarily concerned with the situation in Northern Ireland, while the Dublin-based Official IRA was seen as distant and ineffective. Increasingly the PIRA took the view that the only way to resolve the problems of Northern Ireland was to end the existence of that state, and to reunify Ireland. What had begun as a force for the self-protection of the Catholic population transformed itself into a force promoting Irish nationalism.

In protecting their own communities and political meetings, both loyalist and nationalist paramilitaries resorted to terrible acts of violence. From communal rioting, more sustained and planned acts of violence became a feature of the troubles, and the death toll rose accordingly. In the face of increasingly systematic violence the Stormont government had to act. After a period of intense rioting in Derry in July 1971, the SDLP demanded an inquiry, especially concerning the shooting dead of two rioters by the British Army. Faulkner refused to consider such an inquiry, and decided instead to act against the PIRA. The PIRA was becoming increasingly effective and its maintenance of no-go areas in Belfast and Derry exacerbated the sense of lawlessness, and further compromised Stormont's ability to rule the Province. Faulkner elected to restore order by arresting as many of the ringleaders as possible. Internment was to enter the language of Northern Ireland.

On 9 August 1971, British troops were sent out at dawn to arrest those who were supposed to be the leading figures behind the disturbances in nationalist areas. In total, 342 were arrested, many of them wrongly, and many on the basis of outdated intelligence. Internment did little to prevent the incidences of violence in Catholic areas, and contributed nothing to reducing the rise of the PIRA. In fact the reverse was true; the membership of the PIRA grew rapidly.

In the wake of internment, rioting ensued across Northern Ireland. In 72 hours, 22 people were killed, and thousands driven from their homes as a result of intercommunal violence. For the remainder of 1971, Northern Ireland teetered on the brink of outright civil war while the Stormont government struggled to maintain order. At the start of 1972, NICRA announced that it would hold a massive march and rally in Derry on Sunday, 30 January, in protest against internment. The event started peacefully, and many thousands marched through Derry. The job of policing the march fell to members of the Parachute Regiment, who were specifically brought from Belfast to Derry. At some point in the afternoon firing started. The Parachute Regiment, although excused in the official report that followed, have commonly been held responsible for the carnage that ensued. Over a hundred rounds of ammunition were fired into the huge crowd, and within minutes, thirteen lay dead and scores of others injured. As with so many other events in the early years of the troubles, the television pictures of 'Bloody Sunday' were broadcast from Derry around the world.

The outrage within the nationalist community was absolute. In the Irish Republic, a crowd burnt down the British Embassy, and elsewhere in the world Britain was condemned for allowing such a barbarity to happen within a supposedly modern Western democracy. The Conservative Prime Minister in Britain, Edward Heath, demanded that Stormont relinquish all its security powers. Faulkner refused, and Stormont was suspended on 24 March 1972. The era of the direct rule of Northern Ireland from Britain began. By the end of 1972, the cost of intercommunal violence, the presence of increasingly armed and organised paramilitary groups, and the failure of the British Army to control the situation and gain the respect of both communities, had led to over 10,000 shooting incidents in that one year alone, and a death toll of 467. From 1972 onwards, the search for a solution to the Northern Ireland troubles was on. The longer the search took, the higher the death toll rose.

Following the collapse of Stormont and the introduction of direct rule, the British looked for a solution which would allow the return of Northern Ireland to its devolved status. They did not wish to see direct rule on any permanent basis. The solution which the British proposed in October 1972 was contained in *The Future of Northern Ireland*, a document that would form the basis of the Sunningdale Agreement in November 1973. The October 1972 proposal was that while Britain would continue to stand by the 1949 Ireland Act, and not alter the sovereignty status of Northern Ireland until the majority of the people wanted such a change, any future devolved government would have to encompass, respect and share power with the minority in the Province. The legislation that evolved from the 1972 proposals allowed for the creation of a new Assembly for Northern Ireland, which would be voted for on the basis of proportional representation within multi-member constituencies. The principle was that while allowing for the end of direct rule, such a plan would enable the minority population to play a full role in the Northern Ireland political arena on a fairer footing. If that was accomplished, many of the demands that had been made by the civil rights movement would be permanently enshrined within the political structures of the Province.

In March 1973 a poll was held across the Province, which asked voters if they wished Northern Ireland to remain part of the UK. Essentially this was a test case for the 1949 Ireland Act. In the event, 57 per cent of the population of Northern Ireland voted to remain in the UK, and the border question was shelved. Two months later the elections were held for the new Assembly. The factions that had emerged within unionism were fully illustrated by the election results: the Official Unionists won 23 seats, the SDLP 19, the Alliance Party 8, the Vanguard Party 6, and the Democratic Unionist Party (DUP) 9. The leader of the Official Unionists was the former Prime Minister Brian Faulkner. He endorsed only those candidates who were prepared to work within the new Assembly. The seats he lost were to the Vanguard Party, that campaigned for an independent Ulster, and the DUP, which stood for the full integration of Northern Ireland within the UK. The DUP was led by Ian Paisley.

In November 1973, the various Northern Irish parties (but not Vanguard or the DUP, who boycotted), joined the British and Irish governments to decide on the format of the Council of Ireland, which would sit alongside the new Assembly. The Council of Ireland idea was straightforward. It allowed for the ministers of the Assembly to sit in Council with the representatives of the Irish government, as a way of safeguarding the rights of the Catholic population in Northern Ireland. As desirable as such a Council may have been in the context of the chaos of the early 1970s, for many unionists its existence embodied the development of the dreaded Irish dimension within their affairs, and challenged the integrity of Northern Ireland as part of the UK.

The Assembly sat for the first time on 1 January 1974, but was dead and buried by the end of May that year. Four days after the first meeting of the Assembly, Faulkner resigned as a result of a vote by the Ulster Unionist Council, which rejected Sunningdale and the whole idea of a Council of Ireland. The February 1974 general election became a plebiscite on the Sunningdale Agreement, and all but one of the twelve MPs returned to Westminster were members of the United Ulster Unionist Council (UUUC), which rejected the agreement. In May 1974, two weeks of general strike and civil disorder amongst the unionist population destroyed the Agreement and killed the Assembly. The strike was led by the Ulster Workers' Council and brought together an alliance of loyalist paramilitary groups and anti-Agreement Unionist politicians. The strike was so successful because it was supported by the bulk of the Protestant population, and brought the Province to a complete standstill: public services were halted, factories closed and the supply of petrol, gas and electricity reduced or stopped. The British Army reported to the government that it could not maintain essential services. For many nationalists, the strike symbolised their total alienation from the Northern Ireland political process. It appeared that the sheer weight of unionist and loyalist activism would always control the political will of the Province. The

Wilson government at Westminster folded in the face of the strike, and lost the Assembly that they had worked so hard to create. On the ground the strike showed that the loyalist paramilitaries had the strength to bring the country to a standstill, and that the forces of law and order could do nothing to stop them. In many areas, Catholics and nationalists turned once more to the Provisional IRA for protection and reassurance. Within unionist circles, the strike was a moment of great victory, a sign that not even the British government could force an agreement on the loyal people of Ulster if they did not want it. The language and actions of resistance, that were such a feature of unionism in 1912–14, appeared alive and well in Northern Ireland sixty years later.

The fall of the Assembly, and the victory of anti-power-sharing unionism, marked a stagnation of policy initiatives that would last into the next decade. The Labour government, which would remain in office until 1979, was wracked with domestic difficulties, and Northern Ireland slipped down the list of priorities. The IRA launched a sustained bombing campaign in 'mainland' Britain during the second half of the 1970s in an attempt to convince, the British public that its government should not be involved in Northern Ireland. The IRA also continued its campaign against the security forces in Northern Ireland, and played its role in the intercommunal violence of the Province. The Labour government sought to contain the situation. In 1974, it introduced the Prevention of Terrorism Act, which allowed for longer periods of arrest without charge, and exclusion from Britain, and gave the security forces far more legal freedom in their pursuit of suspected terrorist offenders. In 1977, the government introduced the army's notorious SAS into the Province, to undertake covert operations aimed at reducing the paramilitary menace.

In 1976, the government ended the whole process of internment. As a partial response to the ending of internment, but also in an attempt to criminalise those convicted paramilitary inmates that remained in prisons such as Long Kesh, the government altered the prisoners' status so that they were no longer seen as political. The removal of such status was bitterly opposed by republican prisoners. A period of prison protest began that would last from 1977 to 1981. The protests, although so clearly focused on issues within the prison, exerted a powerful effect on the politics of Northern Ireland.

The prison protests had three main stages. In the first instance, the prisoners refused to wear the prison-issue uniforms and would only clothe themselves in their blankets. In the face of intimidation from prison warders, the protest was stepped up, and prisoners refused to leave their cells. The 'dirty' protest gained the prisoners a great deal of publicity. The image of young men lying naked in their cells, their beards uncut and the walls covered in excrement, made for poignant viewing. Despite a popular outcry, and growing support for the prisoners' cause, the government, headed from 1979 by the Conservative Margaret Thatcher, was unmoved. In a final effort to shake the government, the prisoners began a series of hunger strikes in 1980. When it appeared that the government might make concessions, the strike was called off; but no changes in status were forthcoming, and the prisoners returned to their hunger strike in 1981.

Bobby Sands led the strikes inside the prison. Outside the prison, former internees and prisoners orchestrated a political campaign aimed at raising public awareness of the hunger strikers' cause. As Bobby Sands's hunger strike progressed, and the numbers of prisoners refusing food grew, Frank Maguire, MP for Fermanagh-South, died. Sands was nominated as a candidate in the ensuing by-election, and the SDLP stood aside so that the poll became a straight race between Sands and the Unionist, Harry West. On the fortieth day of his fast, Sands was elected as the MP for Fermanagh-South, having beaten West by 1446 votes in a huge turnout. The election engendered intense media coverage and led to a further escalation in support for the hunger strikers amongst the nationalist community. The question politically, was: would Thatcher allow a sitting MP, no matter how much she despised what he stood for, to die on hunger strike?

Sands, and the political machinery outside the prison, had carefully constructed a link between the campaign against prison conditions, and the demands for the reunification of Ireland as a solution to the problems of Northern Ireland. Amidst all the iconography of self-sacrifice, and under the glare of the global media, it was a powerful message. On 5 May 1981, Bobby Sands died. While Thatcher dismissed Sands as 'a convicted criminal' who had chosen to take his own life, 100,000 people attended his funeral. Between his death and 20 August 1981, nine further hunger strikers fasted to their deaths.

Throughout 1981, the hunger strikes exerted a powerful pull on life in Northern Ireland. It was a year of heightened violence, as each hunger striker's death led to a bout of rioting and increased paramilitary activity. By the end of 1981, the year had witnessed 101 people killed, 1142 shootings and 529 bombings. Electorally, the political grouping that formed around the hunger strike cause seemed unstoppable. Standing as H-block candidates (the name of the prison blocks where the hunger strikes were taking place), the supporters of the prisoners won 36 seats in the May 1981 district council elections in Northern Ireland. In the 1981 Irish Republic general election, H-block candidates polled 40,000 votes across the country and two were elected to the Dáil. In the by-election that followed the death of Sands, his electoral agent, Owen Carron, defeated the Unionist candidate Ken Maginnis by 2230 votes.

The hunger strikes deeply affected the nationalist population. While the ending of the strikes in the late summer of 1981 did not directly result in the prisoners' winning their demands for changes within the prison, they galvanised political support for the nationalist cause. The emergence of Sinn Féin in the wake of the 1916 Rising, has parallels with the situation in 1981. The mobilisation of support behind the hunger strikers' cause was the work of members and supporters of the Republican movement in Northern Ireland. The machinery that they built up around the prison protests would evolve to become organised as a political party: Sinn Féin. The party emerged in the wake of 1981 as a powerful force, with the potential ability to transform the political landscape. Sinn Féin's traditional policy had taken abstentionism to its extreme by refusing to recognise any elected body, and thus refusing to contest any elections. The success of the H-Block candidates convinced a new leadership that was emerging within the broader Republican movement, that electoral victories were the key to mobilising the people.

In 1981 the rising stars of the Republican movement, those who would redirect the party, began their take-over. This group included men such as Gerry Adams, Martin McGuinness and

Danny Morrison. It was Morrison, at the 1981 Sinn Féin Ard Fheis, who outlined a profound shift in the direction of the Republican movement. He famously asked the gathered delegates whether anyone would object if power in Ireland was won with 'a ballot paper in one hand and the Armalite in the other'.

From the political stagnation of the 1970s, and the apparent deadlock in the war between the paramilitaries and the forces of the state, Sinn Féin emerged as a galvanising force. The Republican movement would continue its armed struggle, but would seek the approval of the nationalist community through the ballot box. The success, and the force, of the twin strategy was demonstrated between 1982 and 1984. James Prior, Secretary of State for Northern Ireland, attempted to reintroduce a form of self-rule to Northern Ireland in 1982 in the form of his programme of 'rolling devolution'. In the October 1982 elections for Prior's new Assembly, Sinn Féin won 10 per cent of the vote, only 9 per cent behind the traditional nationalist party, the SDLP. In 1983, at the British general election, Gerry Adams won the parliamentary seat of West Belfast by beating the SDLP candidate into second place. While such popular success for Sinn Féin was vital in demonstrating their levels of support, the armed struggle continued. In 1984, the sophistication of the IRA as a paramilitary force was brutally demonstrated. It was able to bomb the hotel where the entire Conservative cabinet was accommodated during the Party Conference, and narrowly missed killing Margaret Thatcher. The journey from the Assembly elections of 1982 to the bombing of Brighton in 1984, demonstrated how powerful, and for those who opposed Republicanism, how problematic, the 'armalite and ballot box' strategy could be. While Sinn Féin fought, and performed well in, elections, an IRA statement was also warning the government after Brighton, 'We only have to be lucky once, you have to be lucky all the time.' The question for the government, indeed all politicians, was how to deal with the new challenge that Sinn Féin had brought to the troubles. Was it possible to embrace and work with a political party that was capable of winning votes and parliamentary seats, but which also appeared to be closely connected with acts of terrorism?

In 1983, the initiative to find some kind of solution to the problems of Northern Ireland, and to temper the effectiveness of

Sinn Féin, came from the government of the Republic. The New Ireland Forum was the product of meetings between the government of Garret FitzGerald, the SDLP and the Alliance Party. The Forum resolved that there were three potential solutions to the Northern Ireland problem: a united Ireland, a federal settlement, or joint Irish–British authority. Margaret Thatcher rejected all three options, as did the Unionist parties. What is important about the Forum is that it was a public attempt at addressing the whole Northern Ireland question from the perspective of constitutional nationalism. It was also driven by a concern, which existed within the Republic and the SDLP, that the rise of Sinn Féin was deeply problematic. Sinn Féin signalled a move towards violent republicanism, and a potential rejection of constitutional nationalism. Since 1981, the party had been taking seats from the SDLP and had also been polling well in elections in the Republic. The clear links that existed between Sinn Féin and the IRA, and its potential for violence, made it an unpalatable political force for many of the leading politicians in Dublin. The New Ireland Forum was an attempt by Garret FitzGerald to produce a model of joint authority between Britain and Ireland which would oversee Northern Ireland and ensure the primacy of constitutional politics. FitzGerald's rationale was carried forward to 1985, and resulted, in part, in a joint British–Irish governmental meeting at ministerial level.

On 15 November 1985, the Anglo-Irish Agreement was signed between the Dublin and London governments. Driven by the security concerns of both governments, the growth of Sinn Féin and the apparent immobility of the whole Northern Ireland situation, the two governments signed up to work closely together. The level of co-operation was not the close-working joint authority favoured by FitzGerald, but was a formalisation of a policy of inter-governmental co-operation. Alongside regular ministerial and prime ministerial contacts, the 1985 Agreement established a permanent joint Anglo-Irish secretariat in County Down. For the two governments, the 1985 Agreement signalled a new spirit in attitudes towards the troubles. The Agreement was supposed to bolster constitutional politics in Northern Ireland and draw nationalist support away from Sinn Féin. Both in the short term with respect of unionist opposition, and in the long term in the context of continued support for Sinn

Féin, the Agreement failed to achieve the envisaged goals. While the SDLP warmly embraced the Agreement, Sinn Féin was far from impressed, and the Unionist parties were horrified. To the forces of unionism, the 1985 Agreement appeared as Sunningdale revisited and the initial reaction was much the same.

On 23 November 1985, over 100,000 unionists marched on Belfast City Hall to protest against the Agreement. Later that day, all fifteen Unionist MPs resigned their seats at Westminster, and forced by-elections that would effectively be fought as a referendum on the deal. Fourteen of the MPs won their seats back (the marginal Newry and Armagh seat was lost to the SDLP's Séamus Mallon), and the overall Unionist vote rose to 418,230. On 3 March 1986, a Unionist Day of Action was held that took the shape of a general strike, and culminated in rioting across Protestant areas. The 1985 Agreement, despite the many difficulties that dogged its early months, was a watershed in Northern Ireland's history of crisis resolution. Despite the very effective and populist support for the unionist campaign against the Agreement, it was not to be the 1974 strike revisited. Northern Ireland was not brought to a standstill, essential services were maintained and the government never buckled. While 1985 in no way signalled the death of unionism as a polit-ical force, it demonstrated that the gut reaction of 'Ulster Says No!' to any initiative that included an Irish dimension, did not have the political force it once had. In view of the survival of the Agreement in the wake of unionist protest, it is evident that new realities were in place, and the unionists, along with all other groups would have to adjust.

The 1985 Agreement weathered the brief storm that erupted around its signing, and functioned as a consultative body, to the broad satisfaction of both governments. In 1988, talks began between Sinn Féin and the SDLP which signalled the beginning of sustained attempts to bring a peaceful solution to Northern Ireland. While the violence in no way abated, as the murders of eleven Protestants at the Enniskillen Remembrance Day service in 1987, and the acceleration in the level of blatantly sectarian murders by loyalist paramilitaries, demonstrate, the political desire in London and Dublin to resolve the conflict became the guiding light of the 1990s.

PEACE PROCESS

The Sinn Féin–SDLP talks in the late 1980s were an attempt by
John Hume to persuade Gerry Adams that the British no longer
had any strategic interests in maintaining the union between the
Province and the UK. Hume argued that it was the job of the
SDLP and Sinn Féin to persuade the British government and the
unionists that the best interests of all were served by a new
Ireland. While the talks never produced a concrete and
commonly agreed way forward, they demonstrated a willingness
to discuss the problems of a shared approach from within the
nationalist community. In response, the British government
began a series of inter-party talks in the period from 1990 until
1992. The talks involved the London and Dublin governments,
the Ulster Unionist Party, Ian Paisley's DUP, the SDLP and the
Alliance Party. Sinn Féin was not invited to participate because
of its links with the IRA, and their unacceptability to the
Unionist parties. The aim of the talks was to explore how a new
agreement could be made that would replace and improve on the
1985 Anglo-Irish Agreement. Strand one of the talks involved all
parties explaining their vision of Northern Ireland in the future.
All the parties, with the exception of the SDLP, envisaged some
form of Northern Ireland assembly that would administer its own
affairs. The SDLP argued that the Province should be administered by six commissioners, backed by an elected assembly.
Three of the commissioners would be appointed by the people of
Northern Ireland, while another three would be appointed by the
Irish and British governments, and the European Community. It
was a radical plan that gained little support from the other
parties, but introduced the idea of involving a third party in any
future resolution of the Northern Ireland situation. Strands two
and three of the talks process envisaged discussions between the
representatives of Northern Ireland and the Republic, and finally
issues pertaining to London and Dublin. Strand two was beset
with difficulties, and the whole process stalled. The unionists
could not find any common ground with the Republic's government, and the process was consigned to the list of failed initiatives.

During 1992 and 1993, the peace process was reinvigorated by
movements between the British government and the nationalists.

Despite the failure of the three-strand talks, the British government admitted that it had been in close contact with representatives of the IRA, in an attempt to find an acceptable method of moving from a position of paramilitary violence in Northern Ireland to one of peaceful conflict resolution and reconciliation. In 1992, the Sinn Féin document *Towards a Lasting Peace in Ireland*, demanded that the London and Dublin governments play a key role in any moves towards peace. The central point was that they should become 'persuaders' of the unionist community, so that they might jettison their belief in the permanence of the Northern Ireland–UK link. In 1993, a joint statement was made by John Hume and Gerry Adams which made clear that the nationalists, while accepting the desire for a resolution of the various issues within the context of Northern Ireland and its relationship with Britain, envisaged an Irish dimension within any future agreement.

Although the various statements and gestures were broadly welcomed within nationalist circles, they produced a familiar response from loyalist paramilitaries, who feared the emergence of a nationalist-driven settlement. In October 1993 alone, 27 people were killed as a result of paramilitary violence. Although this was initially driven by loyalist hostility to the political situation, reciprocal killings by the IRA heightened tension. The governmental response to all the political movement, and to the upsurge in violence of 1993, came in December that year, with a British–Irish initiative, the Downing Street Declaration. Both governments reiterated the spirit of the 1949 Ireland Act, in declaring that any future plan for the status of Northern Ireland would have to be given with the consent of the people. Such reassurances were designed to placate the unionist population. The British declaration, that it had no 'selfish strategic or economic interest in Northern Ireland', was aimed at convincing the nationalists that the British were not remaining in the Province for any reason other than as security for the majority population. The hope was that the Downing Street Declaration would produce the right climate for a cease-fire by all the different paramilitary groups. If that could be achieved, then full negotiations between all those with a stake in Northern Ireland could begin, and a lasting peace could be found.

On 31 August 1994, the IRA declared a cessation of violence

in order to 'enhance the democratic peace process'. On 13 October 1994, the Combined Loyalist Military Command, which spoke for the major loyalist paramilitary groups, announced that they too would declare a cease-fire so that negotiations might happen. While the declaration of a paramilitary cease-fire was welcomed by everyone, difficulties remained. The two groups declared their respective cease-fires with one eye on the prize of peace, but also to ensure that their own agendas could be achieved. The IRA cease-fire was underpinned by an expectation that the negotiations would lead to an end of British and unionist intransigence, and that an Irish solution to the troubles would result. The loyalist paramilitary cease-fire was underwritten by a demand that there would be no end to the Northern Ireland–UK relationship. The road to peace was littered with difficulties. One of the biggest stumbling blocks was whether or not the cease-fires, especially that of the IRA, were permanent. Until that question was cleared up, and there was no sign during 1995 that either the Unionist parties or the British government could be convinced, there was no place for Sinn Féin at any negotiating table.

In an attempt to revitalise the process, *Frameworks for the Future* was published by the British and Irish governments in February 1995. The two parts of the document envisaged the setting up of a Northern Ireland Assembly, and the establishment of various North–South institutions to bring about reconciliation. The Unionist parties were uncomfortable with the document, as it seemed, yet again, to be a reinvention of Sunningdale.

Against the backdrop of an ongoing peace process, and the delicate negotiations this entailed, a flash point with a long-standing heritage emerged as a major cause of concern. A focus for unionist and loyalist protest was the traditional summer marching season, usually those marches centred around 12 July and the celebrations of King William's victory at the Battle of the Boyne, and in particular the contentious march in Portadown. The route along which the local Orange Order marched in Portadown, took them down the nationalist Garvaghy Road. In July 1995, the Orange Order was allowed to march along the Garvaghy Road in the face of nationalist opposition, and following a standoff when security forces had initially decided that they could not march. In marching their traditional route, the

Orange Order specifically, and the unionist population generally, felt that they had won an important victory, when so many of the key issues within the peace process of the 1990s had appeared to be flowing against them.

In January 1996, US Senator George Mitchell, who had been appointed to report on the prospects of decommissioning paramilitary weapons, delivered his verdict. In the arguments that had surrounded the permanence or otherwise of the paramilitary cease-fires, decommissioning had become a central issue. Many argued that if the paramilitaries gave up their weapons, their commitment to the peace process would be unequivocally clear. When decommissioning took place, it was argued, those political groups that were considered to have close connections with paramilitary organisations would be free to enter any talks process. Mitchell's report, delivered on 24 January 1996, concluded that the paramilitaries would not disarm before all-party talks. He suggested that the way forward would be to start the talks, at which time decommissioning could begin. The British Prime Minister, John Major, while accepting the Mitchell report, proposed an alternative way forward. He wanted to hold elections for the Assembly, envisaged by the February 1995 plan, as a way of securing a democratic mandate for all involved, and still insisted, as did the Unionist parties, on prior decommissioning.

The IRA's response to Major's handling of the peace process was swift and brutal. On 9 February 1996, they exploded a huge bomb at Canary Wharf in London and the cease-fire ended. From that point, the whole peace process went into a period of drift. Major's parliamentary majority was at a bare minimum, and the support of the Ulster Unionists, although not vital, was becoming increasingly important. A general election was looming, which all pundits suggested Major would lose to Tony Blair's Labour Party. The IRA campaign continued through the first half of 1996, and violence flared again at the Portadown Orange March in July that year.

In May 1997, Blair, as predicted, won the British general election. Working in tandem with his Secretary of State for Northern Ireland, Mo Mowlam, Blair enlisted the full co-operation of US President Bill Clinton, and the Irish Taoiseach Bertie Ahern, in an attempt to breathe new life into the whole peace process. By the end of 1997, a new IRA cease-fire was in place, and all-party talks had restarted. After a series of intensive negotiations, threats of walk-outs, the spectre of renewed paramilitary violence and the emergence of anti-Agreement factions within both the nationalist and unionist camps, the main parties and the two governments signed up to the Good Friday Agreement on 10 April 1998.

The Good Friday Agreement was widely seen as the most important document ever signed in Northern Ireland, was fully embraced by the media, and appeared to offer a real chance of peace. It allowed for the creation of a devolved Northern Ireland Assembly, which would be based on principles of power sharing and representation for all the main parties. Participation in the Assembly was conditional on all parties signing up to the principles of democracy and a rejection of the use of violence. All paramilitary groups were expected to make their cease-fires permanent, and to decommission their weapons. The Agreement also allowed for various committees to be set up to investigate issues of contention such as traditional marching routes and the policing of the Province by the RUC. In May 1998, a plebiscite was held on the Agreement in Northern Ireland, while the Republic held a referendum on whether or not to jettison articles 2 and 3 of their constitution (those that claimed jurisdiction over Northern Ireland). The votes in Northern Ireland and the Republic both produced huge 'yes' votes in favour of the Agreement, and of the alteration of the constitution, respectively. The belief of the London and Dublin governments was that the referendum on the Agreement would place the force of the people behind moves to peace. In light of such a huge vote in favour of the Agreement, it was hoped that all parties would work for peace in line with the wishes of the majority of Northern Ireland's population. The referendum on the constitution in the Republic was designed to reassure the unionist population that their links with the UK were safe.

In June 1998, two months after the Good Friday Agreement was signed, elections for the Assembly were held. The Agreement weathered the difficulties caused by the banning that year of the Orange Order March through Portadown, and the more serious risks posed by the bombing of Omagh in August 1998, by the Real IRA (a splinter group that had split from the

IRA in opposition to the terms of the Good Friday Agreement), which led to the deaths of 29 people. In 1999, however, the Agreement struck difficulties. The issue of prior decommissioning once more raised its head. The Unionists argued that while they accepted that Sinn Féin had a right to sit in the Assembly, they hadn't the right to join its executive until decommissioning had begun. In July 1999, Blair and Ahern spent a week in intensive negotiations with the parties of Northern Ireland in an attempt to make the Agreement work. They set a timetable that would bring the Northern Ireland Assembly into being, and set firm deadlines for the completion of decommissioning. If the various steps of the timetable were not adhered to, the Agreement would fail. The first key date in the series of deadlines was 15 July 1999. On that day, the parties were to attend the Assembly at Stormont and appoint ministers. In doing so the Assembly would become 'live', and would have legally taken charge of its devolved powers. The Ulster Unionist Party, led by David Trimble, refused to attend the Assembly session. As a result, ministers were not formally appointed, and the Assembly failed to take control of its devolved powers.

Blair announced a major review of the Good Friday Agreement in the wake of the apparent failure of the Assembly. The review body, once more led by George Mitchell, sat in the autumn of 1999. Blair insisted that the Good Friday Agreement, indeed the whole peace process, was merely 'parked', and had not 'crashed'. The period of review of the Good Friday Agreement coincided with the publication of the Patten Commission report on the future of the RUC, and the replacement of Mowlam as Secretary of State for Northern Ireland with Peter Mandleson. The Patten report, which included proposals for the renaming of the RUC and the recruitment of more officers from the Catholic community, was broadly welcomed, as was the appointment of Mandleson. It was felt that Mandleson could reinvigorate the peace process by virtue of his close connections with Prime Minister Blair, and his central role in the modernisation of the British Labour Party.

The aim of the Mitchell review, which took over ten weeks to complete, was to ensure that the Northern Ireland Executive was granted devolved power, and that the decommissioning of all paramilitary arms could be achieved by May 2000. On 16

November 1999, the Mitchell review was concluded. On the basis of information that was given to the head of the decommissioning body, General de Chastelain, it was announced that all paramilitary groups had signalled their willingness to disarm by May 2000, and that they would appoint a facilitator so that this could be achieved. In the light of the apparent success of the Mitchell review, and the belief that decommissioning would happen, the formal process of devolution began. On 29 November, the Ministers of the Northern Ireland Assembly were appointed, and the Devolution Order was laid before Westminster on 30 November. On 2 December, amidst much celebration and media attention, the Northern Ireland Assembly took control of its devolved powers, and a cabinet of Ministers, which included members of the Unionist Party, the Democratic Unionist Party, the SDLP and Sinn Féin, sat around the same table. Despite the hopeful beginnings for devolved power, there were no moves on the issue of paramilitary decommissioning by the end of January 2000. The Unionist Party signalled that it would not remain in the Executive without decommissioning, and on 3 February 2000 the British government suspended the Executive. Although only temporarily (it is hoped), devolution was at an end, and Northern Ireland once more under direct rule from Westminster.

At the time of writing, it is impossible to say if the devolved Northern Ireland Assembly will be reformed. Whether or not decommissioning will take place is equally difficult to predict, and it is certain that issues such as paramilitary weapons, the reform of the RUC and the future of contentious parades during the marching season, will test the resolve of all those involved. Northern Ireland is, however, at the start of the twenty-first century, in a profoundly different position from where it was at the start of the 1990s. There appears to be a real sense that the foundation stones of a lasting peace have been laid despite only temporary difficulties. Cardinal Cahal Daly, Roman Catholic Archbishop of Armagh, summed up the change in atmosphere when he said: 'I believe Ireland's hour may have come. I have never lost hope through these terrible days and now I can say it is being accompanied by optimism' (*Daily Telegraph*, 23 December 1999).

The long history of Ireland that has been offered in this book has covered a wide variety of themes and issues. Many of these have been present throughout the history of Ireland since the twelfth century. Ireland has continuously been shaped and affected by its relationship with the small, but far more powerful island on its eastern side. The Anglo-Irish interaction, while a source of continual disruption, has brought to life some of the key issues in Irish history. While the Catholic religion has to be seen as important in history because of its influence on a devotional Irish population, the creation of an oppositional element through the Reformation and the presence of a Protestant population, in part a result of the plantations, are direct results of the Anglo-Irish relationship. Equally, the contentious issue of land ownership, from absentee landlords through to the chaos of the mid-nineteenth-century famine, was a powerful continuity in Irish life and politics that emerged from the relationship that spanned the Irish Sea. Such concluding points do not serve to offer a linear, nationalist history of Ireland. They simply recognise that the history of Ireland has been profoundly shaped by many centuries of Anglo-Irish interaction.

External forces are extremely important in all history. The 1990s peace process in Northern Ireland was often sustained and invigorated by the involvement of the US generally, and of President Clinton and George Mitchell in particular. Since the 1960s, and, it can be argued, into the future, the overriding dominance of one external influence on Irish history – that of Britain – has been reduced, and will be steadily replaced by the force of a common European political mechanism. The Anglo-Irish relationship shaped the development of Ireland's religion, profoundly affected its economic development, and exerted a powerful pull on its society and culture. As the Irish Republic and Northern Ireland enter the twenty-first century, their cultures, political lives and economies will be affected by a host of new or emerging external forces. As in the previous millennium, people across the island of Ireland will manage or adapt to those forces, and create a whole new set of internalised and domestic changes and continuities for their history.

Chronology

c. 10,000 BC	Approximate date of the arrival of the earliest settlers in Ireland during the Mesolithic or Middle Stone Age period.
c. 3000 BC	Ireland inhabited during the Neolithic, or New Stone Age period. The important megalithic tomb at Newgrange in County Meath is built.
c. 2000 BC	Irish bronze age, relics of which are housed in the National Museum, Dublin.
c. 700 BC	The arrival of the Gaels in Ireland.
c. 200 BC	Early evidence of structured kingdoms in Ireland emerges. The country was divided into about 150 miniature kingdoms, each called a 'tuath'. A minor king ruled a 'tuath', subject to a more powerful king who ruled a group of 'tuath', who was in turn subject to one of the five provincial kings. Society is regulated by the brehon laws.
AD 77–84	Romans consider the annexation of Ireland.
431	Pope Celestine I sends Palladius to the Irish, as their first Christian Bishop.
432	St Patrick arrives in Ireland.
465	Death of St Patrick.
550–650	Height of monasticism in Ireland.
563	Columba founds Iona, and the Christian mission from Ireland begins.
615	Death of Columbanus at Bobbio.
795	First Viking incursions.
836	Viking attacks on Ireland spread beyond the coast.
837	Viking forces on the rivers Liffey and Boyne.
914	Vikings establish a settlement in Waterford.
916	Vikings establish a settlement in Dublin.
975–1014	Brian Boru is king of Munster, and later of Ireland.
999	Brian Boru is victorious at the Battle of Glen Máma.
1014	Battle of Clontarf, Brian Boru is killed.
1106–56	O'Connor, king of Connacht claims the High Kingship.
1166	Defeat of Dermot MacMurrough.
1169	Arrival of English forces in Ireland to assist MacMurrough.
1170	Marriage of Strongbow to MacMurrough's daughter Aoife.

1171	Death of MacMurrough. Henry II arrives in Ireland.
1176	Death of Strongbow.
1185	Prince John's first visit to Ireland.
1210	King John's second visit to Ireland; submission of the Irish kings.
1235	Richard de Burgh conquers Connacht.
1258	Arrival of gallowglasses from Scotland.
1315	Edward Bruce invades Ireland.
1316	Battle of Athenry.
1318	Defeat of Edward Bruce.
1333	Crown loses control of Connacht and Ulster.
1361	Clarence arrives in Ireland and attempts to restore order.
1366	Statutes of Kilkenny and an attempt to halt the Gaelicisation of the colonists.
1394–5	Richard II lands at Waterford, defeats the Leinster Irish, and gains the submission of the majority of chieftains.
1399	Richard II's second visit to Ireland.
1449–50	Irish chieftains and rebellious colonists submit to Richard, duke of York, as the King's lieutenant.
1459–60	Parliament at Drogheda supports Richard in the Yorkist–Lancastrian struggle.
1468	Rebellion in Munster.
1477	Gearóid Mór as justiciar and deputy.
1478–9	Opposition to the Crown when Edward IV seeks to replace Gearóid Mór as deputy.
1494	Gearóid Mór is replaced by Sir Edward Poynings; Poynings' laws are introduced.
1496	The Pale limited to an area around Dublin stretching only as far as Clongowes.
1509	Accession of Henry VIII.
1513	Death of Gearóid Mór; succeeded by Gearóid Óg.
1520	Earl of Surrey sent to Ireland to restore order.
1533	Gearóid Óg imprisoned; replaced as deputy by Silken Thomas.
1534–6	Rebellion in Ireland.
1536–7	Execution of Silken Thomas; meeting of the Irish Reformation Parliament in response to Henry VIII's policies in England.
1541 3	Irish parliament declares Henry VIII as King of Ireland. Redistribution of land under surrender and re-grant programme.
1547	Death of Henry VIII; succeeded by Edward VI.
1553	Death of Edward VI; succeeded by Mary I and the period of the counter-reformation.
1558	Death of Mary I; succeeded by Elizabeth I.
1560	Second Reformation parliament approves Elizabethan plans for the future of the Church.
1561–4	Periodic battles between Sussex and Shane O'Neill.

1580–3	Rebellion in Munster and Leinster.
1585–7	Plantation of Munster.
1592–1601	Period of rebellion in Ireland led, at various times, by the forces of Hugh O'Neill and Red Hugh O'Donnell. Rebellion ends with victory for the government forces at the Battle of Kinsale in 1601, despite the arrival of the Spanish to assist the rebels.
1603	Death of Elizabeth I; succeeded by James I.
1607	Flight of the Earls.
1608	Plantation of Ulster begins.
1621	Plantation of the Midlands agreed to.
1625	Death of James I; succeeded by Charles I.
1626	Charles I makes an offer of the Graces to the Irish, which offers succour to Catholics.
1634–5	Irish parliament meets and disregards the Graces. Plantation of Connacht is announced.
1641	Rebellion in Ulster. Chaos heightened by the start of the English Civil War in 1642.
1642	Confederation of Kilkenny.
1642–9	Ireland in a state of chaos as the Civil War rages.
1649	Arrival of Cromwell in Ireland; sieges of Drogheda and Wexford.
1652	Completion of Cromwellian conquest of Ireland.
1654–5	Cromwellian plantations begin.
1658	Death of Cromwell.
1660	Charles II is restored to the throne.
1661–5	Review of land ownership in Ireland in the wake of Cromwellian settlements.
1685	Death of Charles II; succeeded by James II.
1688	English Revolution; William of Orange is invited to accept the English throne.
1689	Siege of Derry.
1690	Arrival of William III in Ireland; defeat of James at the Boyne.
1691	Final defeat of the Jacobite army; Treaty of Limerick and Flight of the Wild Geese.
1695	Legislation against Catholics is introduced.
1699	Irish woollen trade restricted.
1720	Westminster parliament gains the right to legislate for Ireland.
1740	Famine in Ireland.
1775	Henry Grattan becomes leader of the Patriots.
1782	Dungannon convention calls for legislative independence (February); Irish 'Grattan's' parliament comes into existence (June).
1791	Foundation of the Society of United Irishmen.
1795	Orange Order founded.

1798	United Irishmen's rebellion in Ireland; French forces land in Ireland; Wolfe Tone is arrested and executed.
1800	Act of Union.
1803	Robert Emmet leads a rising.
1823	Daniel O'Connell founds the Catholic Association.
1828	O'Connell is elected as MP for Clare.
1829	Catholic Emancipation Act.
1840	Foundation of O'Connell's Repeal Association.
1842	*The Nation* is founded.
1843	O'Connell's Clontarf meeting is banned.
1845	First cases of potato blight are reported.
1845–51	Irish famine leads to mass emigration and over a million deaths.
1846	Repeal of the Corn Laws.
1848	Failed rising by Young Ireland.
1858	Irish Republican Brotherhood (IRB) is founded.
1859	Fenian Brotherhood is founded in the USA.
1867	Failed Fenian rising.
1870	Gladstone's first Land Act; Foundation of the Home Government Association by Issac Butt.
1873	Foundation of the Home Rule League.
1875	Charles Stewart Parnell is elected as MP for Meath.
1879	Irish National Land League is founded.
1879–82	Land War.
1882	Irish National League is formed.
1884	Gaelic Athletic Association is founded.
1886	First Home Rule Bill is introduced.
1889	Parnell is named in O'Shea divorce.
1890	Parnell is removed from being head of the party; ensuing split in home rule politics.
1893	Gaelic League is founded; Second Home Rule Bill is introduced.
1900	Redmond takes control of the Irish Parliamentary Party.
1903	Wyndham's Land Acts.
1906	Liberals win a general election.
1909	Land Purchase Act.
1912	Introduction of the Third Home Rule Bill; opposition from unionists to impending home rule; Ulster Covenant signed on 28 September.
1913	Foundation of the Ulster Volunteer Force, Irish Citizens' Army and Irish Volunteers.
1914	Importation of arms into Ireland by various private armies; outbreak of the First World War; passage and suspension of Home Rule; split in the Irish Volunteers between those supporting and opposing participation in the war.
1916	Easter Rising and ensuing execution of leaders.
1917	De Valera wins East Clare election; rise of Sinn Féin.

1918	Threat of conscription in Ireland; end of the First World War; Sinn Féin victories across Ireland in the 1918 general election; opening of Dáil Éireann.
1919–21	War of Independence.
1920	Government of Ireland Act.
1921	Truce in the War of Independence; Treaty negotiations followed by Treaty debates in Dáil Éireann.
1922	Ratification of the Treaty by Dáil Éireann; outbreak of Civil War.
1923	Ending of Civil War; Cumann na nGaedheal form a government; Ireland is admitted to the League of Nations.
1925	Boundary Commission sits.
1926	Foundation of Fianna Fáil.
1927	Kevin O'Higgins is assassinated; entry of Fianna Fáil into the Dáil.
1932	Fianna Fáil win victory in the election; constitutional dismantlement of the Treaty is begun.
1932–6	Blueshirts are active in Ireland; merger of the Blueshirts, Cumann na nGaedheal and the Centre Party produces Fine Gael.
1937	Constitution of Éire is introduced by de Valera.
1939	Outbreak of the Second World War; Éire chooses neutrality; Northern Ireland plays a full part in the war.
1941	German bombing of Belfast is at its height.
1946	Northern Ireland fully enters the British welfare state system.
1948	Legislation to create the Republic of Ireland is introduced (formalised in April 1949).
1949	Ireland Act gives assurance that union is secure.
1956–62	IRA border campaign.
1964	First meeting of an Irish Taoiseach, Lemass, and a Northern Ireland Prime Minister, O'Neill.
1967	Foundation of the Northern Ireland Civil Rights Association; and the first civil rights march.
1968	Clashes in Derry following civil rights marches.
1969	First deaths in the 'modern' troubles; British Army is sent to Northern Ireland; regular rioting across the Province.
1970	Social and Democratic Labour Party is formed; split in the IRA between Officials and Provisionals.
1971	Decision to reintroduce internment; widespread rioting ensues.
1972	Bloody Sunday in Derry; Direct Rule from Westminster is imposed on Northern Ireland; IRA campaign of violence is stepped up; bloodiest ever year in the troubles.
1973	Irish Republic and UK both join the EEC; Sunningdale conference creates the Council of Ireland as a way of underpinning Northern Ireland Assembly.

1974	Ulster Workers' Council strike brings down the Northern Ireland Assembly; Loyalist bombs kill 30 in Dublin and Monaghan.
1975–9	Labour Party follows a policy of containment in Northern Ireland.
1977	Beginning of prison protests.
1981	Hunger strikes lead to the deaths of 10 Republican prisoners; Bobby Sands is elected as an MP.
1983	Garret FitzGerald calls together the New Ireland Forum.
1985	Anglo-Irish Agreement is signed; opposed by Ulster Unionists.
1993	Downing Street Declaration is signed; British government stresses that it has no strategic interest in Northern Ireland; all-party talks on the future of Northern Ireland begin.
1994	IRA and loyalist paramilitaries declare cease-fires.
1996	Cease-fire breaks down in the face of slow progress in all-party talks.
1997	Labour Party wins the British general election; peace process reinvigorated and a cease-fire restored.
1998	Good Friday Agreement is signed by all the major parties in Northern Ireland; a Real IRA bomb in Omagh kills 28 people.
1999	Peace process stalls over the issue of decommissioning paramilitary weapons; Northern Ireland is granted devolved powers and a government is formed (December).
2000	Devolved Executive suspended and direct rule re-introduced (February).

Glossary

For fuller details of the terms listed below and many others, and for the biographical details of the main figures in Irish history, see, for example: S. J. Connolly (ed.), *The Oxford Companion to Irish History* (Oxford: Oxford University Press, 1998), and D. J. Hickey and J. E. Doherty, *A Dictionary of Irish History* (Dublin: Gill and Macmillan, 1980).

absentee landlords   Those landlords who have, throughout Irish history, taken ownership of land in Ireland, yet have failed to reside in the country. Noted as a problem as early as 1360, but especially important in the post-famine years, and during the land war.

agrarian protest   A regular feature of Irish rural life, and organised by various secret societies through the eighteenth and nineteenth centuries. Most prominent were the Whiteboys in Tipperary in 1761, the Oakboys in Armagh, Tyrone and Monaghan in 1763, the Hearts of Steel in Antrim, Down, Londonderry and Armagh from 1770 to 1772, and the Rightboys in Cork, Kerry, Limerick, Tipperary, Kilkenny and Waterford from 1775 to 1778. The secret societies sprang into life to protest against the process of enclosure, agricultural depression and the perceived injustices of land ownership and rent collection. While often seen as a predominantly rural Catholic phenomenon, many secret societies, such as the Hearts of Steel and the Peep O'Day Boys, were exclusively Protestant in composition, and are seen as the precursors of the United Irishmen and the Orange Order.

ascendancy   A term used to describe the Protestant landed elite that dominated politics in Ireland during the time of the penal laws. The term was coined by Sir Boyle Roche, MP, in 1782, and has generally been seen as an expression of Protestant desire to ensure and perpetuate the domination, or ascendancy, of Protestants over Catholics. In the eighteenth century, the Protestant ascendancy included the Protestant middle class, yet excluded Presbyterians and those who dissented from the Anglican Church.

Catholicism   Since the advent of Christianity in Ireland, Catholicism has been the faith of the majority. Despite the efforts of the Protestant religion, especially through the Reformation, the Cromwellian invasion

258

and the plantations, Catholicism has always remained the dominant religion. Through legislation such as the penal laws, and through the nineteenth and twentieth centuries, Catholicism has often been seen as oppositional to Protestantism. In the post-famine period and during the nationalist reawakening of Ireland from the 1870s, Catholicism has played an important role in underpinning the forces of nationalism.

Church of Ireland   The Church which has the largest following of any Protestant church in Ireland, the Church of Ireland was the official Church of State from 1537 to 1870, until its disestablishment. The Church of Ireland currently has a presence in both the Republic of Ireland and Northern Ireland, although the bulk, 75 per cent, of its 368,000 members live in Northern Ireland.

Coercion Acts   Laws used by the government to restore order in disturbed parts of Ireland. The Acts allowed for the declaration of a curfew, and the arrest and detention, without trial, of suspected unruly individuals. The Acts were a regular feature of British policy in Ireland during the nineteenth century.

Dáil Éireann   The Irish parliament, first established in January 1919 following Sinn Féin's victories in the 1918 British general election. Subsequently formalised as the parliament of the state under the constitution of the 1922 Irish Free State. Voting for the Dáil is by proportional representation, and elected members are called teachtaí dála (TD). The two major parties are Fianna Fáil (formed in 1926) and Fine Gael (formed in 1933). Fianna Fáil has dominated government in the twentieth century.

direct rule   A term used to signify the period from 1972 when the devolved government of Northern Ireland at Stormont was suspended, and the Province was ruled directly from Westminster. In December 1999, the governance of Northern Ireland was once more placed in the hands of Stormont as part of the peace process.

home rule   The predominant nationalist political philosophy from the 1870s until the close of the First World War. Home rule was championed by politicians such as Issac Butt, Charles Stewart Parnell and John Redmond, and was successfully legislated for by the Asquith-led Liberal government in 1914. Home rule aimed for the creation of a separate parliament or assembly for all 32 counties in Ireland, which would control domestic affairs, while Westminster would retain control of international relations.

Irish Republican Army (IRA)   The IRA has its origins in the period following the 1916 Rising, and came to prominence in the War of Independence. Officially swearing allegiance to the 1919 Dáil Éireann, the IRA was, in practice, a loose alliance of local units, which explains, in part, its fracturing during the Civil War in the wake of the Anglo-Irish

Treaty. The IRA has always had the foundation of a 32-county Republic as its ideological *raison d'être*, and this explains why the IRA fought against the Free State Army during the Civil War. The IRA mounted a bombing campaign against Britain during the Second World War, and a border campaign in 1956. The IRA was reinvigorated by the outbreak of the troubles in the late 1960s, and this led to the split between the Dublin-based Official IRA and the Northern Ireland-based Provisional IRA. The Provisional IRA waged an intensive campaign of violence during the troubles, although it called a cease-fire in 1994. In response to the IRA's involvement in the peace process, various Republican splinter groups formed, which do not believe that the political initiatives of the 1990s will ever produce a Republic. These organisations, such as the Real IRA, were responsible for much of the paramilitary violence of the latter half of the 1990s.

justiciar   Title of the governor of Ireland from the late twelfth to the mid-fourteenth centuries. The aim of the justiciar was to represent royal rule during the absence of the monarch. In Ireland the justiciar was responsible for administration, the military, and law and order.

nationalist   The ideal of a single and unified Irish people, with a common language and culture, is evident in Ireland in the period of the high kingships, but such an ideal at that time was, by its nature, weak. The vestiges of a nationalist ideology can be found during the counter-reformation and amongst the Jacobites. The first major vocalisation of a nationalist agenda came from the United Irishmen during the events surrounding the 1798 rebellion. The modern roots of Irish nationalist thinking, that is, legislative independence from Britain, appear during the latter half of the nineteenth century and are formalised in the campaign for home rule. In the twentieth century, nationalist thinking has been closely entwined with the struggle for independence and the achievement of a Republic. In Northern Ireland since the outbreak of the troubles, the nationalist community has often been viewed as synonymous with Catholicism and opposed to the maintenance of the union.

Orange Order   The Orange Order was founded in 1795 to commemorate the victory of William of Orange at the Battle of the Boyne. While its eighteenth-century history was loyalist, and often violent, the Order declined in importance in the first half of the nineteenth century. It was reinvigorated in opposition to the Land War, and became a central force in opposing home rule. It has remained an important organisation in the politics of Northern Ireland, and has close historic links with the politics of the Ulster Unionist Party and defence of the union. There is a small breakaway faction, the Independent Orange Order, founded in 1903, and currently associated with Ian Paisley.

Pale   A term that emerged during the fifteenth century to denote the defensive region of the English crown, and the product of the work of the deputy, Sir Edward Poynings. The Pale remained in place until the Tudor period.

Presbyterianism This has its roots in Ireland from the seventeenth century, and is a product of the migration of Presbyterian ministers from Scotland to Ulster. The efforts of the Presbyterian population in resisting Catholicism were rewarded by both Cromwell and William of Orange. The freedom of worship for Presbyterians was established by the Toleration Act of 1719. Presbyterians played an important role in the United Irishmen, but have, since 1800, been supportive of the Act of Union. While a branch of Protestantism, Presbyterianism in Ireland has to be seen as distinct. In Northern Ireland, Presbyterians form the largest denominational group. It remains a fiercely independent church having left the World Council of Churches in 1980. In 1951, Ian Paisley founded the Free Presbyterian Church of Ulster in protest against the growing ecumenism of the established Presbyterian church.

plantation A process begun under the Tudors, but most prominently under James I. The plantations took place mainly in Ulster and Munster, and led to the introduction of nearly 40,000 settlers by 1641. The idea behind plantation was that new settlers from England and Scotland would introduce Protestantism to Ireland, would stimulate the economy and regulate the behaviour of the native population.

Protestantism The religion of the state following the Reformation, and promoted by the Church of Ireland. The religion was largely introduced to Ireland by settlers and planters, and became dominant in Ulster. Protestantism has underpinned the continuance of the relationship between Britain and Ireland, and was a central political force in the main-tenance of union in the nineteenth century. In the twentieth century, Protestantism played a key role in the fight against home rule, and in the political force of Ulster unionism. It is not, however, as dynamic a force as Presbyterianism, and its political highpoint was in the centuries prior to the mid-nineteenth century.

republicanism Republicanism came to the fore as part of the later thinking of the United Irishmen, who were heavily influenced by the republicanism advanced by those pursuing revolutions in France and the USA. The core philosophy of republicanism was that Ireland should seek its independence completely separately from Britain, as opposed to keeping the linkages that remain within the home rule philosophy. In the nineteenth century, republicanism was promoted by the Fenians, and became a central belief of the Irish Republican Brotherhood. It was enshrined as a key Irish political philosophy during the 1916 Rising, and most visibly through the Proclamation of the Republic. The republican ideal was pursued by those who opposed the Treaty in the Civil War, and has been championed by Sinn Féin and the IRA during the Northern Ireland troubles.

unionism   Unionism has its origins in the late seventeenth century, but is primarily attached to the Act of Union in 1800. Unionism as an active political force came to the fore in the latter half of the nineteenth century when the Act of Union was perceived as being under threat from the movement for home rule. Unionism, although an important force in the south in the 1880s and 1890s, has predominantly been a philosophy attached to Northern Ireland. Unionism encompassed the philosophies of Protestantism and Presbyterianism, as well as that of the Orange Order, to become a powerful political force in British politics in the period from 1900 until 1920. Since 1920 and the passage of the Government of Ireland Act, unionism functioned as the dominant political force within the devolved Stormont government. In the late 1960s, unionism fractured, in part in response to the outbreak of the troubles. It has continued to represent the thinking of those who believe in the importance of the UK–Northern Ireland relationship, but is politically divided between the Ulster Unionist Party and the Democratic Unionist Party. The former, led most recently by David Trimble, entered into the peace talks of the 1990s, whereas the latter, led by Ian Paisley, has always stood outside a process that includes Sinn Féin.

Further Reading

The aim of this brief bibliography is to direct the reader to a variety of texts that are available which will expand upon the various events covered here. The bibliography is divided into sections that broadly correspond with the chapters in the book.

GENERAL SURVEY TEXTS

The two biggest series histories of Ireland are those published by Oxford University Press in its *New History of Ireland* series (9 volumes, published at various dates 1976–96), and by Gill and Macmillan in its *History of Ireland* series. The most recent major general histories published are Alvin Jackson, *Ireland, 1798–1998: Politics and War* (Oxford: Blackwell, 1999), and James Lydon, *The Making of Ireland: From Ancient Times to the Present* (London: Routledge, 1998). Other useful general histories that can be found are J. C. Beckett, *Making of Modern Ireland, 1603–1923* (London: Faber and Faber, 1981), T. W. Moody and F. X. Martin (eds), *The Course of Irish History* (Cork: Mercier Press, 1994), R. F. Foster's masterful *Modern Ireland 1600–1972* (London: Penguin, 1990) and his edited *Oxford Illustrated History of Ireland* (Oxford: Oxford University Press, 1991). For those wanting a pictorial and cartographic depiction of Ireland's history, the best recent text is Sean Duffy, Gabriel Doherty, Raymond Gillespie and James Kelly, *Atlas of Irish History* (London: Macmillan, 1997). The three most useful texts that cover aspects of Ireland's economic history are Mary Daly, *Social and Economic History of Ireland* (Dublin: Edco, 1981), L. M. Cullen, *An Economic History of Ireland since 1660* (London: Batsford, 1978), and Cormac O'Grada, *Ireland: A New Economic History, 1780–1939* (Oxford: Clarendon, 1995). For the ever-increasing debate that swirls around the nature of Irish historiography, see either Cieran Brady (ed.), *Interpreting Irish History: The Debate on Historical Revisionism* (Dublin: Irish Academic Press, 1995), or Alan O'Day and D. G. Boyce (eds), *Modern Irish History: Revisionism and the Revisionist Controversy* (London: Routledge, 1996). For an interesting perspective on the whole area of Anglo-Irish relations, see the fascinating Roy Douglas, Liam Harte and Jim O'Hara, *Drawing Conclusions:*

A Cartoon History of Anglo-Irish Relations, 1798–1998 (Belfast: Blackstaff Press, 1998).

THE 12TH – 16TH CENTURIES

For the earliest periods covered here, see Dáibhí Ó Cróinín, *Early Medieval Ireland, 400–1200* (London: Longman, 1995). For the initial period of English involvement in Ireland, a detailed text is Marie Therese Flannagan, *Irish Society, Anglo-Norman Settlers, Angevin Kingship: Interactions in Ireland in the Late Twelfth Century* (Oxford: Oxford University Press, 1989). For the period of lordship and colonisation, see Robert Frame, *English Lordship in Ireland, 1318–61* (Oxford: Clarendon, 1981), and Brendan Smith, *Colonisation and Conquest in Medieval Ireland* (Cambridge: Cambridge University Press, 1999). The best available general texts that cover the ground clearly are Art Cosgrove, *Late Medieval Ireland, 1370–1541* (Dublin: Edco, 1996), Seán Duffy, *Ireland in the Middle Ages* (London: Macmillan, 1997), Steven Ellis, *Reform and Revival: English Government in Ireland, 1470–1534* (London: Royal Historical Society, 1986), and Colm Lennon, *Sixteenth-Century Ireland* (Dublin: Gill and Macmillan, 1994).

THE 17TH AND 18TH CENTURIES

For an overview of the period, refer to T. C. Bernard, *Cromwellian Ireland: English Government in Ireland, 1649–60* (Oxford: Oxford University Press, 1975), Brendan Fitzpatrick, *Seventeenth-Century Ireland* (Dublin: Gill and Macmillan, 1998), Edith Mary Johnstone, *Eighteenth-Century Ireland: The Long Peace* (Dublin: Gill and Macmillan, 1994), and R. B. McDowell, *Ireland in the Age of Imperialism and Revolution, 1760–1800* (Oxford: Oxford University Press, 1979). For coverage of the economic potential of Ireland, see L. M. Cullen, *The Emergence of Modern Ireland, 1600–1900* (London: Holmes and Meier, 1981). For coverage of specific issues and events, see Thomas Bartlett, *The Fall and Rise of the Irish Nation: The Catholic Question, 1690–1830* (Dublin: Gill and Macmillan, 1992), Nancy Curtin, *The United Irishmen* (Oxford: Clarendon, 1998), and Marianne Elliott, *Wolfe Tone: Prophet of Irish Independence* (London: Yale University Press, 1989).

THE 19TH CENTURY

There is a wealth of material that covers the nineteenth century. For a solid introduction, see D. George Boyce, *Nineteenth-Century Ireland*

(Dublin: Gill and Macmillan, 1990). For the pre-famine period, refer to G. Ó Tuathaigh, *Ireland before the Famine, 1798–1848* (Dublin: Gill and Macmillan, 1990). By way of an excellent introduction to the condition of Ireland in the first half of the nineteenth century, and for an incisive study of the nature of emigration, see Kerby A. Miller, *Emigrants and Exiles: Ireland and the Irish Exodus to North America* (New York: Oxford University Press, 1985). Two of the finest works which chart the nineteenth-century upheavals and progress into the early twentieth century are F. S. L. Lyons, *Ireland since the Famine* (London: Fontana, 1985), and K. T. Hoppen, *Ireland since 1800: Conflict and Conformity* (London: Longman, 1998). For an excellent general introduction to the famine and for access to reproductions of original documents, see Peter Gray, *The Irish Famine* (London: Thames and Hudson, 1987), and in greater detail his *Famine, Land and Politics* (Dublin: Irish Academic Press, 1998). Of the many books that were published to mark the 150th anniversary of the famine, see Cormac Ó Gráda, *The Great Irish Famine* (Cambridge: Cambridge University Press, 1995), Frank Neal, *Black '47: Britain and the Famine Irish* (London: Macmillan, 1997) and Christine Kinealy, *This Great Calamity* (Dublin: Gill and Macmillan, 1994). On the land issue, see Paul Bew, *Land and the National Question in Ireland, 1858–82* (Dublin: Gill and Macmillan, 1978). For events and political movements in Ulster, see J. Bardon, *A History of Ulster* (Belfast: Blackstaff, 1992), and A. T. Q. Stewart, *The Narrow Ground: Aspects of Ulster, 1609–1969* (Belfast: Blackstaff, 1997).

THE 20TH CENTURY

Charles Townshend's excellent *Ireland: The 20th Century* (London: Arnold, 1999) is the perfect introductory text for the whole century. In more detail, and specifically concentrating on Northern Ireland, is Thomas Hennessey, *A History of Northern Ireland, 1920–1996* (London: Macmillan, 1997). Two specific texts that are based around research work and cover the whole century, are J. J. Lee, *Ireland 1912–85: Politics and Society* (Cambridge: Cambridge University Press, 1990), and Dermot Keogh, *Twentieth-Century Ireland: Nation and State* (Dublin: Gill and Macmillan, 1993). For the revolutionary period, key texts include: Joost Augustejn, *From Public Defiance to Guerrilla Warfare* (Dublin: Irish Academic Press, 1996), David Fitzpatrick, *Politics and Irish Life 1913–21: Provincial Experience of War and Revolution* (Cork: Cork University Press, 1997), Tom Garvin, *The Evolution of Irish Nationalist Politics* (Dublin: Gill and Macmillan, 1981), Michael Hopkinson, *Green Against Green: The Irish Civil War* (Dublin: Gill and Macmillan, 1988), A. Mitchell, *Revolutionary Government in Ireland: Dáil Éireann 1919–22* (Dublin: Gill and Macmillan, 1994), and E. O'Halpin, *The Decline of the Union: British Government in Ireland, 1892–1920* (Dublin: Gill and Macmillan, 1987). For the period of state-building, refer to: Richard

Dunphy, *The Making of Fianna Fáil in Power, 1923–48* (Oxford: Clarendon, 1995), Ronan Fanning, *Independent Ireland* (Dublin: Edco, 1983), Tom Garvin, *1922: The Birth of Irish Democracy* (Dublin: Gill and Macmillan, 1996), D. MacMahon, *Republicans and Imperialists: Anglo-Irish Relations in the 1930s* (New Haven: Yale University Press, 1984), J. Prager, *Building Democracy in Ireland* (Cambridge: Cambridge University Press, 1986), and John M. Regan's excellent *The Irish Counter-Revolution, 1921–1936* (Dublin: Gill and Macmillan, 1999). For the period of the modern troubles in Northern Ireland there are countless texts available, which cover every particular aspect of the conflict. The best general texts of recent times include: James Bowyer-Bell, *The Irish Troubles: A Generation of Violence, 1967–1992* (Dublin: Gill and Macmillan, 1993), Tim Pat Coogan, *The Troubles* (London: Arrow, 1996), Caroline Kennedy-Pipe, *Origins of the Northern Ireland Troubles* (London: Longman, 1997), and Sabine Wichert, *Northern Ireland since 1945* (London: Longman, 1999). For an indispensable chronological understanding of the modern troubles, see Paul Bew and Gordon Gillespie, *Northern Ireland: A Chronology of the Troubles, 1968–1993* (Dublin: Gill and Macmillan, 1993), and their *The Northern Ireland Peace Process, 1993–1996* (London: Serif, 1996).

Index

INDEX **269**

Faulkner, Brian, 233, 234, 235, 236
Fenians, 150, 151–3, 154, 158
Fianna Fáil, 212, 220, 223, 225
Fine Gael, 220, 225
First World War, 185–91
FitzGerald, Garret, 226, 242
FitzGerald, Gerald, 53, 54
FitzGerald, Lord Edward, 110
Fitzmaurice, Sir James, 13–14
Fitzstephen, Robert, 11
Flight of the Earls, 64–5
Flight of the Wild Geese, 78–80, 81, 84
Flood, Henry, 101
French Revolution, 104–5, 122
Frongoch, 196

Gaelic Athletic Association, 166–7
gaelic culture, 2–3, 6, 15, 28–9, 30, 62, 165–8, 225
Gaelic League, 30, 167, 183
gallowglasses, 24
Garda Síochána, 210
Garvaghy Road, 246–7
Gearóid Mór, 35–8
Gearóid Óg, 37–8, 39
Gender, 227
George III, 104
Gladstone, William Ewart, 153–4, 155, 160, 162–3, 177
Glendalough, 7
Gonne, Maude, 160
Good Friday Agreement, 248, 249
Government of Ireland Act, 202
Graces, 70–2
Grattan, Henry, 97, 99, 100–5, 109, 115, 123, 125, 128
Griffith, Arthur, 176, 195, 198, 200, 205

Hamilton, Sir James, 67
Harland and Wolff, 228
Haughey, Charles, 226
health, 221–2
Hearts of Oak, 106
Heath, Edward, 235
Henry II, 11, 12, 14, 17–19
Henry III, 22

Henry VI, 33
Henry VII, 37–8, 39, 42–4, 51
Henry VIII, xii, 16
High King,
and Vikings, 7–9
battle for, 10–14, 16–17, 25
origins, 3
Hobson, Bulmer, 176, 191
Hobson, Douglas, 167
Hoche, General, 110
Home Government Association, 154
Home Rule Bill,
1886, 163
1893, 165
1912, 178–9, 182–3, 185–6, 188
Home Rule League, 154, 156
Home Rule Party, 160, 164
Howth gun running, 185
Hume, John, 244
Hyde, Douglas, 167

internment, 235
Ireland Act, 220–1, 227, 236
Ireton, Henry, 74
Irish Citizen Army, 193, 195
Irish Council, 39–40, 60
Irish Land Act, 155
Irish Parliamentary Party, 174, 177, 190, 197
and Liberal Alliance, 177–8
Irish Republican Army, 196, 208, 212, 234, 235, 238, 247
Irish Republican Brotherhood, 162, 166–7, 176, 183, 191, 195, 199
and Easter Rising, 176–7
and Sinn Féin, 176–7
Irish Tenant Land League, 149
Irish Volunteers, 102–3, 184–5, 188, 190

Jackson, William, 107–8
James I, 65, 67, 69–70
James II, 75–80
Jesuits, 55
John I, 19, 20, 23
Joyce, James, 168

14 DAYS